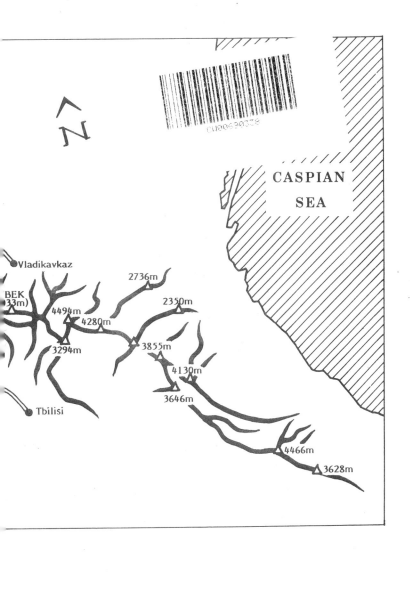

TREKKING IN THE CAUCASUS

Mount Ushba from helicopter

TREKKING IN THE CAUCASUS

by

Yury Kolomiets & Aleksey Solovyev

CICERONE PRESS
MILNTHORPE, CUMBRIA, U.K.

ISBN 1 85284 129 X
British Library Cataloguing-in-Publication Data. A catalogue record for
this book is available from the British Library.

ACKNOWLEDGEMENTS

Thanks to Michael Almond of Dundee University for the larger part of the
chapter on Caucasian flora and fauna. We are also most grateful to Alan
Chow, without whom the book simply could not appear and to Brian
Taylor, without whom the work could hardly be completed.

ADVICE TO READERS

Readers are advised that whilst every effort is taken by the author to ensure
the accuracy of this guidebook, changes can occur which may affect the
contents. It is advisable to check locally on transport, accommodation,
shops etc but even rights-of-way can be altered and, more especially
overseas, paths can be eradicated by landslip, forest fires or changes of
ownership.

The publisher would welcome notes of any such changes.

Front Cover: A lake. Looking up the Donguzorun valley

CONTENTS

Introduction 8

How to get there 10
Grading System 12
Fitness, Experience, Equipment and Maps 14
Food and Porters 15
Rescue Service 16
How to do it 17
Some useful phrases 18
Geography, Geology, Ethnography 19
Flora and Fauna 21
Weather 25
History, Culture and Religion 26
Georgia 31
Upper Svanetia 32

ROUTES 35
(The grades of the passes involved are given in brackets)

Baksan Valley 36

1. From Baksan Valley via Kilar Pass to Bashil (1B) 42
2. From Adyrsu Valley via Mestiysky Pass to Mestia (2A) 43
3. From Djantugan via Koyavganaush Pass to Adyrsu Valley (1A) 48
4. From Baksan Valley via Becho Pass to Mestia (1B) and return
   by Ushbinsky Pass (3A) 51
5. From Dolra Valley via Akhsu Pass to Baksan (2A) 57
6. Circuit from Baksan Valley via Donguzorun (1A), Bassa (1A),
   Chiperkarachai (1A) and Khotyutau (1B) Passes. 59
7. From Mestia via Donguzorun Pass to Baksan Valley (1A) 62
8. From Nakra Valley via Ledesht Pass to Dolra Valley (2A) 65
9. From Baksan Valley via Donguzorum West Pass to Nenskra
   Valley (1B) 67
10. From Baksan Valley via Chiperazau Pass to Nenskra Valley (1A) 69
11. From Baksan Valley via Azau Pass to Ullukam Valley (1A) 71
12. From Sandy Hotel via Ekho Voyny Pass to Khotyutau
    Snowfield (1A) 72
13. From Baksan via Syltran (1A), Kyrtykaush (1A) and N. Karakaya
    (zero) Passes to Malka Valley 73

14. From Malka Valley via Irikchat Pass to Baksan (1B) 75
15. From Baksan through Kyrtyk Valley 78
16. From Malka Valley via Balkbashi Pass to Khurzuk (1A) 78
17. From Khurzuk via Khotyutau Pass to Baksan (1B) 80
18. From Baksan via Djikaughenkez Pass to Malka (1B) 82

Chegem & Bezengi Valleys 84

19. From Bashil via Bashilauz Pass to Lekzyr Glacier (2A) 86
20. From Lekzyr Glacier via Bashil Pass to Tviber Glacier (1B) 88
21. From Bashil via Lychat Pass to Lychatsky campsite (2A) 89
22. From Chegem via Tviber Pass to Mestia (1B) 90
23. From Chegem via Koru (1A) and Rakit (1B) Passes to
    Bezengi base 93
24. Circuit from Chegem via Zeleniy Pass (1A) 94
25. From Mestia via Semi (2A) and Upper Tsanner (2A) Passes to
    Bezengi base 96
26. The Bezymyanny and Sella Peaks 99

West Caucasus: Gvandra 101

27. From Chiryukol Valley via Talychkhan Pass to Nenskra
    Valley (1B) 103
28. From Uzunkol base via Myrdy-Dalar Pass to Nenskra
    Valley (1B) 104
29. From Uzunkol base via Myrdy-Saken Pass to Saken
    Valley (1B) 106
30. From Uchkulan via Gondaray Pass to Omarishara (1A) 107
31. From Gondaray Valley via Klych Pass to Klych Valley (1B) ... 108
32. From Uchkulan via Nakhar Pass to Klych Valley (1A) 109
33. From Uzunkol base via South Dolomity Pass to Chiryukol
    Valley (1A) 110
34. From Uchkulan via Ak-Tyube Pass to Uzunkol base (1B) 112
35. From Uchkulan to Ullukel Lake 114

West Caucasus: Teberda-Dombay 115

36. From Gonachkhir Valley via Klukhor Pass to Klych Valley (zero) .. 118
37. From Dombay Glade via Ptysh Pass to Chkhalta Valley (1B) .. 119
38. From Dombay Glade via Chuchkhur Pass to Gonachkhir
    Valley (zero) 121
39. From Dombay Glade via Alibek Pass to Aksaut Valley (1A) ... 122

40. From Aksaut Valley via Aksaut West Pass to Chkhalta
    Valley (1B) 123
41. From Aksaut Valley via Khalega (zero) and Marukh (1A)
    Passes to Chkhalta Valley 125
42. From Aksaut Valley via Karakaya-Marukh Pass to Marukh
    Valley (1B) 127
43. From Aksaut Valley via Khamurza Pass to Chkhalta
    Valley (2A) 128
44. From Chkhalta Valley via Adanghe Pass to Bzyb
    Valley (zero) 130
45. From Gonachkir Valley via Kitche-Murudju Pass to Nakhar
    Valley (1A) 132
46. From Daut Valley via Uzlovoy Pass to Nakhar Valley (1B) 133
47. From Teberda via Epchik (zero) and Karachaiaush (zero)
    Passes to Uchkulan 134
48. From Teberda via Kyshkadjer Pass to Daut Valley (1A) 135
49. From Teberda via Nazly-Ryndjy Pass to Daut Valley (1B) 136
50. From Teberda via Baduk (zero) and Aruchat (1A) Passes to
    Aksaut Valley 138
51. From Teberda via Mukhu (zero), Kyzylaush (zero) and Ozerny
    (zero) Passes to Arkhyz 140
52. Circuit from Teberda via Azghek Pass (1A/B) 142

West Caucasus: Arkhyz 144

53. From Arkhyz via Bugoychat Pass to Marukh Valley (zero) 146
54. From Kizgych Valley via 810th Regiment Pass to Chkhalta
    Valley (1B) 147
55. From Arkhyz via Kongur Pass to Bzyb Valley (1B) 148
56. From Kizgych Valley via Kizgych Pass to Shkhabztsa
    Valley (1B) 150
57. From Arkhyz via Naur Pass to Bzyb Valley (1A) 151
58. Circuit from Arkhyz via Dukka (zero) and Brakonyerov
    (1A) Passes 153
59. Circuit from Arkhyz via Ayulyu Pass (1A) 155
60. Circuit from Arkhyz via Chuchkhur Pass (1A/B) 156
61. Circuit from Arkhyz via Sofiyskoye Sedlo Pass (zero) 158
62. Circuit from Arkhyz via Chilik (1A), Semnadtsati (1A), Mylgval (1A),
    Agur (1A) and Fedoseeva (1A) Passes 159

Mt Elbrus 161

Introduction

Compared with the walking and trekking traffic seen in many mountain areas nowadays, only a handful of western walkers can boast of having visited the Caucasus, the highest and largest mountain region in Europe. Thanks to the recent political changes in the late USSR, curious foreigners recruited by some daring western travel companies have begun to trickle through the geographical and bureacratic borders into the parts of Russia that are more wild and remote, than the Moscow Kremlin or the string of cathedrals along the Golden Ring.

Until the publication of some recent guides not much was known in Britain about climbing in the Caucasus, with the exception of Mt Elbrus. Even less information is available about trekking and walking, yet it is obvious that such a huge mountain barrier, about 1,500km long, can offer quite a choice of routes in all grades of difficulty. The trouble is that the routes are not distributed evenly along the grade scales. The needs of the modest walker were the last thing Nature was preoccupied with when creating those high and jagged ranges. What man has done to improve the similar situation in the Alps does not exist in the Caucasus. No paths hacked in steep rocks with hand-rails for safety and comfort, no long rope ladders, no huts with a door handle as a last handhold of a rock pitch, no cable ways over most walking impasses. Luckily for the lovers of wild nature and unfortunately for those who think of mountain walking only in terms of low graded trails, 90% of the Alpine Caucasus looks very much the same as it did at the end of the last century, when the indefatigable Freshfield was picking the plums, leaving for the Russians only minor, though numerous, firsts. The great explorer found the Caucasus much more appealing to his sense of beauty and majesty than the Alps and expressed this in many admiring words.

There are some very easy routes across the Main Range, following good, wide paths, but the fact is that the central part from the Klu'hor to Mamisonsky passes cannot offer such a boon. It does not mean you have to climb to get over the Range, but you should not expect a comfortable path up to the saddle and you have to be ready for scree, grass and snow slopes of up to 20-25° (30-35° on some passes). Not a big hardship, considering the reward in calm and seclusion, so rare nowadays.

By some political or bureaucratic whim mountaineering activity in the USSR was sharply and irreversibly divided into two parallel and never crossing branches: climbing and high mountain walking. The former was strictly (even severely if safety was in question) organized, channelled into a network of State supported and controlled mountaineering camps, now called "bases". A funny and not unusual product of the system was a climber, who, year after year, came to camps belonging to a certain sport society and had no notion of the parts of the Caucasus beyond the normal climbing routes of these particular camps. The other branch was a small army of high mountain walkers, much less disciplined, poorly trained and equipped (no control, no support!), crossing the Caucasus in all directions and visiting its remotest corners. These vigorous and ambitious lads, having missed by some chance the first branch and not satisfied with walking along the beaten tracks, invented a singular kind of mountain sport: the crossing of high and difficult passes with heavy packs, in many cases using the tactics of fixed ropes. It should be noted here, that in the Caucasus, with its almost total lack of wardened huts, cableways and good roads, any long distance walk has to be a small expedition with all the food and camping equipment carried on man's back.

The decades of this activity resulted in the closely woven net of passes on every range, ridge and even spur, with the exception of some north walls and sheer rock faces. In fact most of them are not passes, but just a playground for this strange game - that is, if you stick to the dictionary description: "a pass is the shortest and easiest way between two valleys, across the ridge". This is what the word means in this guidebook. All the walks described here are travels on foot from one valley to another via passes. In some cases there are several of them in a ridge, separating the valleys. If so, the shortest and easiest one is always chosen for the walk. More often than not the nature of the mountains, high and steep, cannot offer a wide choice, and usually there is just one pass feasible for walkers. For example, to get from the Baksan Valley to the Lekzyr glacier you can use seven passes, but all except one are pure climbing affairs, with steep (up to 55°) and long ice, snow or rock slopes. And the remaining one, Mestiysky, even if "the shortest and easiest", is not, maybe, all that short and easy as some walkers would prefer! Nevertheless in July 1991, a group of trekkers from Britain, most of them without any climbing background whatever, crossed the pass safely. They were guided through.

What is the Caucasus like in terms of walking? Again, one is inclined to compare the range with the Alps. Technically there can be no great difference in climbing or walking in these geologically similar ranges, even though the Caucasus is considerably higher. The main distinction for today's walker is the historical, ethnographical and cultural backgrounds, against which walking in the Alps and in the Caucasus will look strikingly different. In some respects the difference is even more pronounced than that between the Alps and, say, Nepal or Patagonia. Because of scarce and unreliable information, the Caucasus is bound to have the aura of a terra incognita for the British climbing and walking public. This book is the first attempt to fill up the gap and give an idea, even if general, of the Caucasus and its possibilities as a vast and interesting playground.

No guide can possibly cover all the Caucasus, nearly 1,500km of the Main Range with the numerous ridges, to the north and south. Nonetheless, the areas covered are the main scene of climbing and walking activity; the highest, heavily glaciated and most scenic parts.

The principle chosen for describing the walks is as follows: first the area as a whole and its valleys, where the routes' start and end are described briefly. The shortest and easiest ways connecting them are mentioned and details about transport and accommodation are given. In case some especially picturesque landscape, natural phenomena or historical relics are to be found on some more difficult (reasonably!) route between the same valleys, then it too is included in the walks. Each technical description of a walk is preceded by a short introduction, containing all the useful or interesting information about those particular areas which are crossed. The walks are described by day stages with an average walking time of 6 hours. No long distance walks are given, except for some combinative samples and useful tips, thus leaving the creative and exciting task of working them out to a would-be traveller.

HOW TO GET THERE

The usual way followed by all the western visitors to the Caucasus known to the authors is by air: to Sheremetyevo International Airport in Moscow and from there to Mineralny Vody or Nalchik airports (several flights a day to the former and one flight every other day to the latter. The duration is 100-110 minutes). Direct flights from Britain to Mineralny Vody would be convenient for those interested only in the mountains, not in Moscow sights, but the international status for this airport does not seem to be of paramount importance for the government. The prospects of such flights to the airports on the southern side Tbilisi, Sukhuimi and Adler, look even more vague, and Georgian independence, together with the armed conflict in Abkhazia (of which Sukhumi is the capital) does not simplify the

Mestia

situation. Adler Airport is on Russian territory but does not have international status either and, besides, to fly there means an additional 150km along the coast of the Black Sea from Adler to Sukhumi. Although more scenic, the southern approaches are much more complicated, may be even adventurous, than those from the north. You can count on good regular bus services connecting the Elbrus and Teberday-Dombay areas with all the northern airports and major railway stations.

There are no such recreation centres on the south and buses running to the uppermost villages were always unpredictable, the more so nowadays. The key villages are: Kvemo-Ajara, at the head of the Kodori River (90km from Sukhumi, 4-5 hours drive), for the Arkhyz, Teberda-Dombay and Gvandra (partly) areas; Khaishi, in the Ingury Valley (76km from Zugdidi, 3-4 hours), for the eastern part of the Gvandra and the westernmost fraction of the Elbrus area. The town of Mestia (144km from Zugdidi, 6-7 hours, 30-40 minutes by small plane or helicopter) is the starting point for the Central Caucasus. There are bus and railway services (every hour or so) between Sukhumi and Zugdidi (90km) and between Zugdidi and Tbilisi (340km, several runs a day).

If railway approaches are considered, then the key stations on the north are Nalchik and Mineralny Vody for the Central and Nevinnomyssk for the West Caucasus. On the south it is Sukhumi and Zugdidi. It takes 30-36 hours to get from Moscow to the northern stations and about 40 to Sukhumi. Going by train from London and opting for the shortest way, make a change at the border town Brest, take a train to Kiev and from there to Rostov-na-Donu. Several trains a day going to the south via the latter stop at Mineralny Vody, Nevinnomyssk, Sukhumi and Zugdidi and there is only one direct train to Nalchik. The route looks simple and cheap but at each changing point you will have to queue up for your tickets (if you do not have anyone to help you). It is bearable in June but July-August the situation worsens dramatically. Note that Byelorussia and the Ukraine, as well as Georgia, are independent states now, so make inquiries at the Russian Consulate in London about transit visas.

Going by car you can follow nearly the same line: Brest-Rovno-Kiev-Poltava- Kharkov-Shakhty-Rostov-Tikhorestsk-Nevinnomyssk, 1,900km and another 119km to Mineralny Vody. The way from Rostov-na-Donu to Sukhumi is via Novorossiysk and Sochi - 2,350km. Three points to remember. First, you will not be able to do 80-100 miles an hour on Ukrainian and Russian roads, 50-60 are a reasonable limit. Second, in this country there are no guarded car parks for travellers at airports and railway stations where you could leave your car for a couple of weeks. In the mountains some arrangements are possible, presumably with the staff of a hotel or base you stay at, and this seems to be the only way out. In Georgia quite a practicable thing, especially in villages, is to ask one of the locals if you can leave your car in his yard. It is very likely they will not take any money for this, then a present will do. And third, be ready to rough it because in the former USSR a motel and a road cafe are exceptions, not the rule. So use your stove, for making tea at least.

It goes without saying, no visits to Abkhazia can be planned until the region calms down.

GRADING SYSTEM

There are two grading systems in Soviet mountain walking, one for passes, the other for long distance walks. In strictly organized and controlled Soviet mountaineering the main purpose of the latter was to provide "the ladder of experience" of which no mountain walker, however fit and quick in learning, could miss a single step. So, both the systems can only give a very rough idea of what to expect on the route. The pass system is more technical and therefore useful. There are 3 grades in it, with two subgrades each, A and B, plus "the zero grade", that is below the lowest, easiest one. The highest grade, 3B, may mean a long (up to 3-4 days) and technical climbing route over a pass with difficult ice-falls, steep snow and rock slopes. This guidebook comprises only the passes of the first three subgrades (with the zero grade included of course) and these are explained here.

Grade 1A. Does not present any technical difficulties. Usually there are paths on both sides of the pass, except for its upper part, which is grass and scree of 15-25°. There may be a small inoffensive glacier and patches of snow. Early in the season snow may change the scene, turning some steepish but easy screes into snow slopes rather awkward for a nonclimber. It takes 5-8 hours to cross such a pass between normal comfortable grassy campsites in two valleys.

Grade 1B. May involve some glacier travelling with roping up, some easy rock scrambling but the average steepness is 20-30°, and no climbing skills are needed.

Grade 2A. Glacier travelling may be rather long but without heavily crevassed parts and some sections of snow up to 35-40° are quite likely. To cross some of these passes may take more than a day (eg. the Mestiysky pass).

The heights of the passes do not necessarily correlate with the grades, even through some of them, over 4,000m (eg. the Ushbinsky pass, 4,100m) are a little overgraded, owing just to their height. In describing the routes, the grade of each pass will be given first, with all the necessary details for the readers to get a clear idea of the difficulties to be expected.

Bearing in mind snow conditions, choose carefully the right time for your walk. Snow, having disappeared from grass and scree or from ice, can change the route dramatically. A high pass, free of glaciers is much easier in the second half of the season - July, August, September, when it is dry. A glaciated one, especially with steep ascents, turning to ice in August, is more practicable in June and July.

The stages of all the walks are timed so that the passes are crossed in the morning, after camping at their foot - even though fit walkers could do it in one day and a pass is free of glaciers with soft afternoon snow. This is based on the general principle that a very sensible approach to any high pass crossing is to camp as close to the saddle as possible. It gives you a large safety margin of day time to get out of any unexpected trouble and increases immensely your chances to have good clear morning views from vantage points.

Distance does not mean much in the mountains, with the exception of low graded valley-walks. It is *time* that high level walks are measured in. But, of course, the figures given in the descriptions are approximate. On the whole they are much closer to leisurely trekking than to fell-running!

Note that everywhere in the text "left" and "right" have always the absolute, orographic meaning when linked with "bank", "side", "mountainside", "tributary" and "valley". The same is true of "from the right/left" when a side-stream, flowing into a river is meant. In all the other cases it is relative, determined by the walker's position.

The authors would be glad to help anyone in need of further information about the Caucasus. The address to write to: RUSSIA, MOSCOW 103009, KOLOMIETS YURY VLADIMIROVICH. Fax number: 010-7-095-292 65 11- Cecna-5941.

FITNESS, EXPERIENCE, EQUIPMENT AND MAPS

All four are tied together and equally important for safe travelling in the mountains. Even though good experience and fitness can make up, to some extent, for the lack of good equipment, the latter can never substitute for the former. Owing to the nature of the Caucasus, high, wild and remote, and to the nature of the political system, under which all normal topographic maps had the title "secret" (and even deliberate mistakes were inserted in some officially published sketch-maps of certain "sensitive" areas), the level of fitness and experience required from self-reliant walkers in this region is considerably higher than that for any European mountains. Nine out of ten Caucasian valleys do not have any permanent population except for summer shepherds' dwellings and that means no accommodation, food supplies or fast help are available in case of an accident. Camping is unavoidable in mountains lacking mountain huts (with the derisive exception of three for the whole Central Caucasus!). And that will add the weight of camping equipment to your pack. If you are not lucky with porters that may mean a pack of 15-20kg, which makes even higher demands of your fitness.

All the maps you will have are sketch-maps, made and checked by mountaineers, who had spent many years walking and climbing in the Caucasus. Nonetheless they are not topographic ones, these still wait to be published commercially. So, to be able to connect the lines of the sketch-maps in this guidebook with the real ridges and glaciers you are expected to have some mountaineering experience. The author would never recommend total novices to embark on a high level walk in the Caucasus without an experienced leader or some local support, except, maybe, for two or three "caravan ways" at the peak of the season, when fellow walkers will just point to the right direction.

On no route in the guidebook will you need any other climbing gear than a rope, harness, karabiner with a screw gate, pair of crampons and walking ice-axe (see below for the full set of equipment). On many you will do even without this. On some routes with rather steep snow slopes (40-

45°) the use of an ice-axe and crampons is indispensable but most of them can be done with a pair of collapsible ski poles. An ice-axe, not used properly during a fall and flailing on the wristloop can be more dangerous than the fall itself. If you are not trained to do self-arrest, there is no point in carrying the superfluous 700-800gm of an ice-axe, dangerous on snow and useless on trail. Soft snow of 25-30° can be tackled easily with ski poles and the toes of your boots, kicking steps in it, but morning frost can turn the slope into one demanding crampons. Late August can do even more to turn it into ice. So, a pair of light walking crampons is highly advisable on all the routes with glacier travelling and snow slopes, even if they are just 20-25° steep. A rope, 9mm x 40m (one for 3 or 4 walkers), is a must when crossing any snow covered glacier, except in two or three special cases, noted in the route descriptions. Always take a rope if a serious wade is anticipated. As for camping equipment it can be of the same type as used elsewhere in Europe. For camping above 3,000m, where night temperatures can drop to -5-10°C, you will need a four seasons sleeping bag. For camping on snow a karrimat is a must. If you intend to use with your stove some locally bought petrol, you should be ready for the regular clogging of its head. If it is not self cleaning, take with you some thin springy wire to clean it. The best answer would be a gas stove but gas cartridges are not allowed in airlines and are almost impossible to come by even in Moscow. The walking boots should be strong and stiff enough to give good support to the ankles and withstand hours of walking not only on broad paths but over screes, snow (with crampons strapped on) and broken rock. There is no need for climbing boots, even if the ascent of Elbrus is planned. A set of clothes for any weather, hot in the valleys (up to +30°), cold and rainy high on the passes (+5-0°C), should be taken on the walks. Elbrus demands additional two or three woollen things, or preferably a light duvet jacket.

As to the medical aspect of Caucasian walks there is nothing special about it. You do not need to have any immunisations for travelling there. The standard medical kit, made at home, will do.

FOOD AND PORTERS

Agriculture (and therefore food) has always been a weak point of the Soviet System. The formula of success (and in general of prospering in the Soviet society - alas, it is still Soviet in many aspects) is as follows: if you know the right people, or know someone who knows them, and you pay them well, they will provide you with almost everything you need - salami, powder milk, some canned delicacies, freeze-dried food, and, maybe, this will cost you a little less than at home. If not, it may take you days running around town in an embittering and possibly fruitless search. And the quality will always be dubious. In the Caucasus fresh fruit, vegetables, meat and sausage are available in city bazaars. But then you will face the problem of how to keep and carry it. Sometimes they sell canned meat, fish and dried fruit at free price street sales in lesser towns along the main roads, but you can never be sure that in the end you will get what you need. And to cap it all, do not count on food shops in small towns and villages. Usually the choice there is unbelievably haphazard and meagre. Obviously, there are too many "ifs" and "buts" for such a serious question as food for a high level mountain walk, so the best answer is to calculate properly, buy freeze-dried food at home and to relieve this diet with fresh fruit and vegetables in towns and big valleys.

Mountain porters are a new institution for the Caucasus. The trekking season of 1991 proved that it can be successfully developed and unemployment, however cynical it may sound, can give the process a boost. When in the Caucasus do not try to hire porters yourself. The only thing to do is to go to the nearest mountaineering base, or best of all, to the rescue service headquarters of the area. Western goods, climbing and camping equipment in particular, are too much prized and coveted in the former Soviet Union to trust to the first person you meet without any references. As a matter of fact the chance of theft or robbery is fairly small, but it does exist and should not be ignored. Men recommended by the head of a base or rescue service will be good mountaineers and as such very helpful.

RESCUE SERVICE

There are two rescue services in the Caucasus. One belongs to an organization called "The council of tourism and excursions". Its main function is to check on groups of walkers whether they have the right route papers. Its rescuing function is more nominal than real. The other one is the rescue service at mountaineering bases. There is its office at each base and the headquarters in the two large mountaineering centres, Baksan and Dombay. If your route begins there, all the details of eventual rescue operations, including helicopter and its cost, can be talked over at the headquarters (the Russian letters on the signs pointing there are "КСМ").

If your route does not pass by any mountaineering base, your chances of getting fairly quick and professional help in case of an accident are not high. You should go to the nearest village. Very often they keep horses at "koshes", shepherds' huts up in the valleys, and shepherds will never refuse to bring down an injured or ill member of the group on a horse's back.

16

One thing should be borne in mind: there is no rescue service in the Caucasus, ready to act on your behalf at a moment's notice if you do not have "the right papers", and as a foreigner you cannot possibly have them. Both the systems, like many in Russia, are highly bureaucratic. In case of the climbing service, at mountaineering bases, it means that officially it exists only for climbers coming to those bases. The only guarantee that rescue operations will not be reluctant and therefore dangerously delayed is some preliminary arrangement with rescue service men. Nowadays many of them are very enterprising and open to any deal involving hard currency!

HOW TO DO IT

There are two different ways to organize your own walk in the Caucasus. For the independent, experienced high level walker and willing backpacker, ready to rough it, the task is the easiest. With the route in head and the map in hand it will not be more difficult than in any mountains elsewhere in the world. But you cannot make it in one day from home: to fly to Moscow, from there to Mineralny Vody (or Nalchik, Vladikhavkaz, Tbilisi), from there drive to the mountains and have enough time to walk to some convenient campsite up in the valley (it is the standard way Soviet backpackers do it) is not possible. The same on the way back. So, two or three nights in Moscow seem to be indispensable. You can book hotels there through Intourist Agency in London. When Mineralny Vody Airport gets international status and there is a morning flight there from Britain, then even this problem will vanish.

But if you don't enjoy backpacking and a comfortable hotel is a very welcome break for you from the hardships of the trail and a pack heavier than 5-7kg will kill all the joy of walking, then you have to face two problems. One is a hotel or rooms at some base in the Caucasus and the other is porters. And here again comes the formula for success: find the right people, who can do it. In recent years quite a few private companies and joint ventures dealing with foreign trekkers and climbers, have come into existence, not to mention freelance guides, ready to take you anywhere and be your booking agent, cook, porter and interpreter as well, charging for all this rather modestly. At this time of fast economic changes in Russia, it is difficult for the authors to be specific on the subject and give any names. Several British travel companies now do Caucasus treks but if you wish to do your own thing they may be prepared to help with contacts and you could write or fax the latter. It should be done well in advance of your planned trip to the Caucasus, 3 to 4 months preferably.

Note that paid accommodation is a highly unusual thing at Caucasian villages. So, walking outside the few civilized valleys with hotels, tourist and climbing bases you should not count on anything more than camping.

SOME USEFUL PHRASES

Please ? - Pojálusta

How do you do - Zdrávstvuyte

Thank you - Spasíbo

We are English - My anglichane

What is your name? - Kak vas zovút?

Goodbye - Dosvidánya

How much is it? - Skólko éto stóit? Or just - Skólko?

Where is a grocery here? - Gde zdes prodovólstveniy magazín?

Does this bus go to...? - Étot avtóbus idét v...?

Where is the bus station? - Gde zdes avtostántsiya?

How many kilometres (hours) to...? - Skólko kilométrov (chasóv) do...?

When does a bus leave for...? - Kogdá idét avtóbus do...?

We need to get to... - Nam nújno popást v...

What is the name of this valley, river, mountain, hotel, pass, village? - Kak nazyváetsya éta dolína, reká, gorá, gostínitsa, étot perevál, posélok?

We need one (two, three) rooms for one (two, three) day(s). ? - Nam nújen odín (nam nujny dvá, trí) nómer(a) na odín (dvá, trí) dnya.

Breakfast (dinner, supper) for two (three, four, five, six), please. - Záftrak na dvoíkh (troíkh, chetverykh, pyaterykh, shesterykh), pojálusta.

Can we camp here? - Mójno zdes stávit palátki?

Where is the nearest campsite, bridge, village, climbing base? - Gde zdes blijáyshie nochévki; blijáyshiy most, posélok, alpláger?

Where is drinking water here? - Gde zdes pityeváya vodá?

Where can we buy petrol? - Gde mójno kupít benzín?

Where is the wading place here? - Gde zdes perepráva?

Show us on the map where we are. - Pokajíte na kárte gde my.

We need the ... pass, river, valley. - Nam nújen ... perevál, reká, dolína.

We need a permit for travelling in the Reserve - Nam nújno razreshéniye dlyá prokhóda v zapovédnik.

Is it possible to pass here; by this path, bank (left, right)? - Mójno zdes proytí; po étoy tropé, béregu (lévomu, právomu)?

How much do we have to pay? - Skólko my doljny?

Where is the Rescue Service here? - Nam nujny spasáteli (kaespé)

We have had an accident, we need help (doctor) - U nas neschástye, nam nújen vrach.

Keep in mind that, when stressed, Russian vowels have always the same pronunciation, regardless of their position. Unstressed, they lose much of this and are similar to any English unstressed vowel.
a - as *u* in "luck"; e - as *ye* in "yes"; i - as *i* in "tin"; o - as *o* in "pop" u - as *ou* in "could"; y - when not linked with another vowel is close to the Russian *i,* but sounds broader.

GEOGRAPHY, GEOLOGY AND ETHNOGRAPHY

Between the Black and Caspian Seas there stretches over a length of 1,100km the backbone of the Greater Caucasus, its main watershed (further in the book the Main Range), not cut through by any meridional valley. Its real length, counting all the curves, is about 1,500km, the widest part (180km) being at Mt Elbrus, the narrowest one (60km) along the Military Georgian Road connecting Vladikavkaz (former Ordjonikidze) and Tbiliski, capital of Georgia, via the Krestovy pass (2,379m). The Greater Caucasus is a complicated network of lower ranges, north and south of the Main Range. On the north it is Bokovoy, (a little lower than the Main, at some places even higher), then Skalisty (the average height is 3,300-3,500m), Pastbishny (about 1,500m) and Lesisty, as its name ("wooded") implies, the lowest. The average distance between the ranges is 15-20km. On the south side again a criss-crossed ladder of ranges comes down to green wooded hills, 50-80km away from the Main Range.

Some boring figures. Half of the region in its central part is heavily glaciated, 2,047 glaciers. Their combined area is about 1,780 square kilometres, Mt Elbrus alone holding 144sq km. The longest valley glacier, 12km, is the Bezengi, in the Bezengi area. More than 200 peaks reach a height of 4,000m, 30 out of them surpass 4,500m (15 the height of Mont Blanc), 7 are over 5,000m.

Almost all geographers are agreed that the Caucasus can be divided into three distinct sections, and this partition coincides roughly with the ethnographic and geological maps of the region. So, the first section is the

West Caucasus, from the Black Sea to Mt Elbrus (440km, the highest summit is Dombay-Ulghen peak (4,040m), then the Central Caucasus, from Mt Elbrus to Mt Kazbek (180km), all the mountains over 5,000m being there (Mt Elbrus, 5,642m, the highest), and the East Caucasus is from Mt Kazbek to Apsheron Peninsula of the Caspian Sea, 480km (Tebulosmta peak, 4,492m).

The West Caucasus, the lowest of the three, is made along its highest central line of granite, gneiss and crystalline shales, with parallel ranges to north and south of limestone, dolomite, argillaceous slates and sandstones. The Russian, westernmost, part of the West Caucasus, populated mainly by Russians and Ukrainians, is 270km long. It does not mean they always lived there. The tribe of the Ubykhs, akin to the Adygeis (the small Adygei autonomous region exists there on the north) occupied the southern side till the seventies of the last century. Having refused to submit to Russian colonization, they chose to go away to Turkey, where they died as a nation. The mountains are not high (2,000-3,000m) and rich in fairy-tale spots of romantic beauty of the Dolomites type. The walks, mostly without snow and ice, are easy technicallly but often tricky in navigation owing to numerous canyons, preventing simple ways along the rivers, and vigorous, dense vegetation. Further east, reaching Mt Elbrus, there follows the Karachai (on the north) and Abkhazian (on the south) Caucasus, the Karachai's language belonging to the Turkic group, the Abkhazian to the Adygei one. It should be mentioned that the Abkhazians proper do not exceed 18% of Abkhazia's total population, the rest are Georgians, Russians, Ukrainians and some lesser groups. Constitutionally Abkhazia is a part of Georgia. The full name of the northern republic is Karachai-Circassia, but in the mountains the prevailing nationality is the Karachais. Over the 115km stretch of the Main Range between the Labinsky pass and Mt Elbrus the mountains are much higher 3,600-4,000m), of the well-defined Alpine type, with relatively small (1-3km long) but numerous glaciers, covering all the Main Range, without noticeable gaps. The walks here are more varied: in one day from beeches and laurel cherries to lichens, rock and snow. The navigation on the northern side is straightforward almost everywhere, but on the southern, steeper one it is more complicated. The mountains are of exquisite Alpine scenery, of rich and abundant flora and fauna. One of the two reasonably developed recreation centres of the whole Caucasus, the Dombay, is there.

The 180km of the length of the Central Caucasus can be divided into two halves. The first one is made of granite, crystalline and partly argillaceous shales. People living on the northern and southern sides are the Balkars (the Turkic language group) and the Svans (the Svanian and

Georgian languages). The other half, ending at Mt Kazbek, consists of andesite, diabase and has the last and small spot of granite near Mt Kazbek. Predominant nationalities are the Ossets on the north and the Georgians on the south, with the small Osset Autonomous Republic wedging itself in Georgia. These 180km of the Main and Bokovoy ranges are the highest in Europe. Two, out of seven Caucasian summits over 5,000m, Mt Elbrus and Mt Kazbek (5,033m), mark the western and eastern edges of the section and the other five five-thousanders are about 65km to east of Mt Elbrus, in the Bezengi area. By comparison with the West Caucasus the mountains here are much more austere, with large glaciers, gigantic north faces and long northern valleys, rather modestly, if not scantily, wooded. Even technically easy walks involve long scree and glacier travelling without paths and demand a certain level of fitness and agility. For those loving dramatic Alpine scenery and the seclusion of ice and snow deserts of high mountains the Central Caucasus has much to offer. The second recreation and mountain sports centre is at the head of the Baksan river, under Mt Elbrus.

The East Caucasus is an unbelievable orographic and ethnographic jumble. The predominant rock all along the Main Range is argillaceous slate with some large outcrops of diabase, porphyrit and sandstone. The type of the main rock and the dryer climate than on the west determine the face of this part of the Caucasus, exceeding 4,000m at many points but, on the whole, with negligible glaciation. Gently curving ridges and a small scree several hundred metres long, unconquerable on the ascent, is the main kind of slope.

Each autonomous republic on the north is a cluster of small and tiny nationalities (speaking different languages), the enumerating of which would take half a page. The larger groups on the northern side are the Chechens and Ingushes, the Daghestans (a collective name for more than 30 national groups, living in the Daghestan Republic) and further east the Azerbaijanians. On the south it is Georgian groups, somewhat different in culture and history but united by a common language and more to the east the Azerbaijanians again. No centres comparable to those in the Baksan and Teberda Valleys can be found here but the region is fascinating for the lovers of age-old remote places with striking architecture and strange ways of life.

FLORA AND FAUNA

Mr Michael Almond writes: The flora and fauna of the Caucasus is interesting and varied, being rich in species that occur nowhere else (*endemic* species). The flora is affected by the climate: very wet on the western slopes facing the Black Sea and progressively drier as one travels east. The flora is similar in many respects to the adjacent areas of north-eastern Turkey. The south-west is warm and wet and hence the vegetation is luxuriant. Further east the climate is much drier. Also generally the south is more rich in vegetation than the north, on the lower slopes at least.

The forests have lots of ivy and wild vine and wild fruit trees - plum, peach, apple, pear. The lower slopes of the range are covered in dense forest, especially on the southern flanks, where deciduous species grow at medium and low altitudes. The south-western slopes facing the Black Sea, where the climate is best described as "temperate rain forest", are covered, to a height of about 800m, with mixed forests of oak, beech, chestnut, hornbeam, alder, lime, maple and ash. Under the trees flourish lilac-flowered rhododendron bushes *(Rhododendron ponticum)* and on the forest margins can be found the bright yellow azalea *(Rhododendron luteum)*. Above the deciduous forest there is mixed deciduous/coniferous forest, with the conifers becoming more dominant as height increases. There are few of the extensive pine forests of the Alps. On the southern slopes of the central Caucasus conifers are found from about 1,250 to about 2,300m above sea level. In the forests of the drier south-east the oak and the hornbeam are dominant in deciduous woodland; there are also dense coniferous forests in this area, however, sometimes up to a height of 2,300m. These forests are interspersed with rhododendron, birch and dwarf mountain ash.

On the edges of the forest and in clearings occur some of the most spectacular of the flowers to be found in the area. The yellow Turk's Cap lily *(Lilium monadelphum)* grows in the company of tall purple bellflowers *(Campanula latifolia)* and columbine *(Aquilegia olympica)*. Orchids include the fragrant orchid *(Gymnadenia conopsea)* and the butterfly orchid *(Platanthera chlorantha)*, together with various species of marsh orchid *(Dactylorhiza)*. In the woods are to be found several species of wintergreen and other shade loving species such as broomrape and herb Paris. The village of Mestia in Upper Svanetia is surrounded with yellow azalea *(Rhododendron luteum)* which flowers in early June. It is likely to make any honey produced in the area at that time unsafe for visitors to eat. In scrub and woodland east of the village are to be found wild strawberries, wild gooseberries, yellow cinquefoil, red helleborine *(Cephalanthera rubra)*, tall pink campion *(Silene)*, large yellow loosestrife *(Lysimachia punctata)*. Down by river there are white foxgloves, henbane *(Hyoscyamus niger)*, *Datura* (related to the potato) and hollyhocks *(Alcea)*.

Above the tree line there are sub-alpine meadows, which can be very lush, especially in the western Caucasus. They are full of herbaceous plants such as lilies, columbine, lousewort, delphinium, ranunculus, bell-flowers, orchids, masterwort *(Astrantia)*, campion, brightly coloured vetches, statuesque dark-maroon lousewort *(Pedicularis)*, bistort *(Polygonum bistorta)*, scabious, cornflowers, pansies and many others. Higher up, on steep hillsides, grow dense thickets of white rhododendron *(Rhododendron caucasicum)*. In the wet west this shrub can cover entire hillsides but it becomes scarcer the further east one goes.

Higher still (from about 2,000m upwards) are the true alpine meadows which consist of low-growing, mainly perennial, plants, many of which form rosettes or cushions. Many of these are of great interest to the alpine plant enthusiast. The Central Caucasus in particular is the home of such gems as spring gentians *(Gentiana verna ssp pontica)*, annual gentians *(Gentianella)*, Pyrenean gentians, *Gentiana septemfida* and the yellow *Gentiana oschtenica,* primula (the pretty pink *Primula algida* and *Primula auriculata,* the purple oxlip *(Primula elatior ssp meyeri)* and the rare white *(Primula bayerni)*, saxifrages, pink cinquefoil *(Potentilla oweriniana)* and yellow cinquefoil *(Potentilla ruprechtii)*, mats of sandwort *(Arenaria)*, bellflowers *(Campanula)*, chickweed *(Cerastium undulatifolium)*, fleabane *(Erigeron)*, dwarf forget-me-nots *(Myosotis)* the Snowdon Lily *(Lloydia serotina)*, rock-jasmine *(Androsace villosa, Androsace albana)*, whitlow grass *(Draba bryoides* - tight cushions on rocks and in turf, with little yellow flowers), yellow wild pansies *(Viola caucasica),* the bright yellow *Pulsatilla aurea, Corydalis conorhiza* and *Corydalis alpestris,* buttercups, fritillaries *(Fritillaria latifolia* and others), anemones (the white *Anemone impexe* and the lemon-yellow *Anemone speciosa)*, prophet flower *(Arnebia pulchra)*, *Trollius ranunculinus* (same family as Globe Flower from Europe, but more the shape of a big buttercup), and many others too numerous to mention.

In such seemingly inhospitable terrain as the lunar-like landscape around the Elbrus cable-car middle station you can find the following in flower in July: bellflowers (3 types), *Aster alpinus,* whitlow grass *(Draba rigida)*, saxifrages *(Saxifraga juniperifolius* or similar, *S cotyledon, S flagellaris,* and another white species), pink cornflowers, *Jurinella moschus* (a prostrate, thistle-like flower), yellow mountain pansies, *Daphne glomerata,* ragwort, dog-daises *(Anthemis)*, catsfoot *(Antennaria)*, sandwort *(Arenaria)*. Even among the desolation of the top station of the Elbrus cable car several species of saxifrage can be found in flower in July.

The fauna of the Caucasus, like the flora, comprises a mixture of European and Asiatic species. At the end of the 19th century, the Caucasus was reported to be home to bear, wolf, wild boar, lynx, jackal, hyena, leopard, ibex, chamois, wild goat, wild sheep (mouflon) and bison and it is likely that all of these are still present with the exception of the hyena, leopard and bison. The pheasant is named after the River Phasis in western Georgia. Squirrels, larger and darker than our own red squirrel, abound in the forests and the ermine can be found in the higher mountains, occupying the same niche as the marmot of the Alps. Bird life, particularly birds of prey, is also plentiful.

A few words have to be added to Mr Almond's article. A very pleasurable feature of the Caucasian flora is the strips of barbery, dog-rose, cornel, honeysuckle, sea-buckthorn in up-valleys (mainly northern ones) and fields of bilberry bushes and of wild strawberries lower down in the forest. The tough rhododendron (the relic of Tertiary Era) covering in June vast slopes under screes and moraines with white and yellowish flowers is as ubiquitous as pine trees on the northern side.

Unfortunately, the authors (of the guidebook) must disappoint those who hope, on coming to the Caucasus, to see in the first valley they visit an ibex, wolf or lynx. It is possible, but for this you need to organize a special expedition to the remote, unpopulated parts of the mountains. An easy and scenic route (and the authors always try to pick these) is inevitably a popular route, but alas, not with wild life! In all the areas covered in the guidebook you are guaranteed to see in abundance the Caucasian goat (endemic to the Caucasus but resembling strikingly the chamois) which usually travels in flocks of 5-7 heads, and, if you are not too active and noisy at bivouacs, a charming creature, the weasel, is highly likely to come looking for your leavings. For Caucasian brown bear, wolf, wild boar and Caucasian red deer you need to visit the Teberda Reserve. Bison (aurochs, to be exact) do live in the Caucasus, in the Kizgych Valley of the Arkhyz area, where there is a herd of 2,000 heads. Yak is a new settler with a status half-way between wild and domestic and can be met at the head of Ullukam, Daut and Bityuktyubekol Valleys. Do not expect much of the Balkar Reserve. It has existed for 15 years only and in addition to that the regulations (or, rather, their observance) are pretty slack. A guard carrying a rifle with a telescopic sight is quite common there, so the wild life within the confines of this reserve does not differ much from that elsewhere in the Caucasus!

To make up for this, bird life is rich and can be very interesting for the keen observer. Jackdaws with their smart red or yellow beaks are unfailing witnesses to your bivouacs above the tree-line and the melancholic evening whistle of the rock partridge (a Caucasian endemic) will accompany anyone near the snow-line. Eagle, golden eagle, hawk, and griffon vulture can be seen circling above the ridges almost every day, and small fry - redstart, chiff-chaff, partridge, Caucasian pine-grosbeak, different kinds of tits, chaffinch, thrush, bullfinch, rock bunting are easily observed, particularly with a field-glass. Larger species, the numerous inhabitants of forests - black cock, jay, wood pecker, pheasant, owl, cuckoo etc. - are more difficult to catch sight of, if you do not spy on them specially.

WEATHER

In general, Caucasian weather is much more stable than that of the Alps. Abrupt changes for the worse with ferocious blizzards and the temperature falling by 10-15°, typical of Western Alps, are highly unusual for the Caucasus. The most important factor for any traveller is the amount of precipitation. The westernmost part of the mountains, nearest to the Black Sea (the southern slopes) gets the heaviest precipitation - 2,500mm per annum and going to north and east the figures drop considerably. The town of Sukhumi receives 1,230mm; Arkhyz 860mm; Teberda 690mm (the Klukhlor pass 1,780mm); Uchkulan 430mm; the Main Range west of the Chiperazau pass to the Marukh pass about 1,800mm, east of the Chiperazau 1,000mm; west of the Marukh pass, the northern side receives 1,800mm, the southern one 2,200mm; Terskol about 600mm; Tyrnyauz 400mm.

Choosing an area for your walk take these figures into account. July and August are the best months all over the Caucasus. In the Central Caucasus sunshine by day and a cold starry sky at night may last two and even three weeks. A long spell of bad weather, which usually comes from the south-west is a rarity at this time of year. On the west, in the Dombay and Arkhyz it is more likely. But the chances of a cold front from the north bringing a sharp drop in temperature and heavy precipitations are negligible everywhere.

As to a less important factor, the temperature, there is no need to list any figures. Suffice it to say that on a good summer day, walking in the valleys (and even over the Alpine meadows at 3,000m), you can wear shorts and a shirt. On high passes (3,400-3,700m), in the same weather, light trousers and a jacket will be added to that, in bad weather, or early in the morning warm underwear and a sweater will be quite enough. Night temperatures at 3,000-3,500m can drop to -5 -10°C, hardly any lower; at 1,500-2,000m they usually fall to +5 -10°C.

The higher a mountain the more clouds on it. Mt Elbrus and the Bezengi wall in particular are quite liable to local afternoon weather disturbances. Good waterproof clothes and an early start are the best answer to this.

HISTORY, CULTURE AND RELIGION

For many centuries the Caucasus was a real crossroads of civilizations, where different cultures from the Mediterranean, Near East, Middle Asia and Eastern Europe met. There the West touched the East and the North the South. The peoples of the Caucasus have many words in their languages, borrowed at different times from the Greeks, Romans, Arabs, Turks and Persians. But no single outside influence became dominant and each Caucasian culture was formed first and foremost as specific and local, even though they all have quite a lot in common.

Contrary to what many people in the West would think, the Caucasus is not, and has never been, "Russian", if population and culture are meant. For nearly a century and a half it was under Russian protection and in Russian possession; for 70 Communistic years it was a part of the monstrous Soviet State (and still all the North Caucasus is a part of the Russian Federation), but only one quarter of its total length, its westernmost and lowest part, is Russian, ie. not only belongs to Russia constitutionally but is populated mainly by Russians. In the rest of the Caucasus most Russians live in the big cities and mostly to the north of the Main Range. The North Caucasus is a chain of small autonomous republics, from west to east: Karachai-Circassia, Kabardin-Balkar, North Ossetia, Chechen-Ingush and Daghestan. The prevailing religious denomination there is Islam (except North Ossetia). To the south of the Main Range, in Transcaucasia, it is Christianity in Georgia and Armenia (with a much longer history than that of Russia!) and Islam again in Azerbaijan.

Karachai-Circassia and Kabardin-Balkar together with Georgia in the south occupy the highest and most spectacular part of the Greater Caucasus and all the routes of this guidebook lie on this territory.

The names and latest history of the two first are the result of the fearless Bolshevist strategy of replanning and remaking the whole political, social and domestic life in the Caucasus (as anywhere else), which apparently had been absolutely wrong before they came to power! As a matter of fact, the Karachais and Balkars, as well as the Kabardins and Circassians, are much more related to one another than the partner with whom they were united by Moscow. So, the Kabardins cannot understand the Balkars because of a profound difference in their languages and have to use Russian. It is the same with the Karachais and Circassians, whereas the Karachais and the Balkars, who, from time immemorial have been living high in the mountains, have no difficulty in conversing.

The origin of the peoples of the North Caucasus has been a constant mystery to the historians. Many archaeological finds in the Dombay area (the West Caucasus), in the Malka, Chegem and Baksan Valleys show that

26

Verkhny Chegem village. Old sepulchres

people who lived there in the mountains ("the Koban culture") were already using bronze and iron tools at the beginning of the first millenium BC. They had developed ties with the Mediterranean civilization. The main trading way was over the Klukhor pass in the West Caucasus, which connected the lands to the north of the Main Range with the ancient Greek colony of Dioscurias on the shore of the Black Sea, and it was very busy as far back as the 7th century BC. The trade was so active that the colony maintained 300 interpreters for visitors from the north.

Not much is known however about the Koban culture itself. Even the question of the language the natives of the North Caucasus spoke when the nomad tribes from the steppes arrived there has not yet been solved by the historians. The modern language the Karachais and Balkars speak was formed under a strong Turkic influence and belongs to the Turkic languages, whereas the one of the Kabardins and Circassians relates to the Abkhazian-Adyge group of Iberian-Caucasian languages.

The ancestors of the Kabardins and Circassians were the Adyge, an ancient people who lived on the plains to the north of the western part of the Caucasus and the Abazini from the coast of the Black Sea. After two succeeding invasions into the North Caucasus, Ghengiz Khan's in 1222 and Timur's in 1396, with following devastation of the Alan state, the Adyge and Abazini moved in and settled in the foothills. Even now the Kabardins call themselves "adyge".

There were three major waves of the nomad migration to the West and Central Caucasus: the Scythians who came from the Black Sea coast in the 8th century BC and stayed till the 3rd century, the Sarmatians (3rd century BC to 1st century AD) and the Alans who, together with the Kipchaks, played the main role in forming the Karachai and Balkar nationalities (1st to 14th centuries). Besides that there were the Huns, Pechenegs, Crimean Tatars, Khazars, Mongols and Bulgarians who have all left their mark and formed the layers round the local Koban ethnic group. The raids of Turkic tribes (Kipchak-Polovtsy) were quite frequent in the 11th century, and later came the mass penetration into the upper reaches of the Kuban River of their descendants, the Nogais from the Volga River. The process went on till the 19th century.

Of all the migrating peoples who came to the North Caucasus, the deepest traces were left by the Alans. To this day the Mingrelians living south of the Karachai territory call the latter "Alans", and in the Karachai language itself the word has survived and now means "friend". The first nomad Alans appeared and settled in the North Caucasus in the 1st century

Verkhny Chegem village in the Chegem valley

Ushguly village in Upper Svanetia
Adyrsu valley, the Old Djaylyk hotel

BC. The Huns' invasion in the 4th century drove some of them deep into the mountains and the rest found their home as far to the west as the Pyrenees. But rising gradually, by the 10th century the powerful Alan state had spread almost all over the North Caucasus. They traded actively with Transcaucasia, Byzantia, Near East and Russia. Under Georgian influence the Alan nobility tended to take Christianity, and the ruins of two Byzantine cathedrals in the Zelenchuk Valley, built at the time, are the evidence of this. There were attempts to create the Alan written language, based on the Greek alphabet but many Arab inscriptions of the period tell much about one more strong cultural influence.

In 1222 Ghengiz Khan put an end to the thriving state. The Alans divided again, most of them went to Byzantia, the remnants were forced into the mountains. In 1396 Timur came and crushed what was alive of the Alan culture. The Alans were shoved even higher, almost to the glaciers. After the Tartars had left the foothills were taken by the Abazini and Adyge who formed the present Circassian and Kabardin people.

As early as the end of the 15th century Russian peasants used to flee from their serfdom to the lower reaches of the Terek River but the first official links of the North Caucasus with Russia date back to 1557, when the Kabardins, tired of the harassing raids of Crimean khans and of the incessant internecine warfare, expressed their wish to join the Russian state. In 1561 Tsar Ivan the Terrible married Maria Temrukovna, a daughter of the Kabardinian prince. Thus Russia got a new stronghold on the south against invasions from the Crimea and Turkey. The Balkars took their time to decide and joined Russia much later, in 1827.

The Russian massive military and economic activity in the North Caucasus, which started at the beginning of the 19th century, was not something Iran and Turkey (with Britain behind them) could easily put up with. They stirred up resentment among the Adyge, Chechen and Daghestan local lords against the Russian presence on their soil, and it was not difficult, because many felt offended by the laws the Russians were introducing in their attempt to bring some order to the wild Caucasus. So the famous epoch of "the Conquest of the Caucasus" began in the 1820s and was going on till 1864, when the last breeding ground of resistance was quenched. The main figure of that epoch was Shamil who, declaring Holy War against the infidel, managed to unite all the anti-Russian forces into the Imamat of which he was Imam. A clever politician, he had made many promises to Turkey and as a result could for years get almost unconditional support (with considerable help from Britain). During the Crimean war between Britain and Russia he tried to break through Georgia and Azerbaijan to Turkey but failed.

There was no front line in the Caucasian war. Fanatical, brave and cruel mountaineers were waging a guerilla warfare against Russian heavy and slow military expeditions. Some of these tried to use the inefficient and in some cases blatantly stupid tactics of scorched earth. In the hope of depriving the guerillas of their cover they would fell forests over vast territories, which could not, of course, add much to good feelings towards the Russians among the natives. It was not so much the military success of those slug-slow expeditions as the growing discontent of rank and file tribesmen with the atrocious and predatory ways of many of Shamil's deputies, "naibs", and the cunning use that was made of this discontent, that in the end helped the Russians to win over the majority of the natives to their side. So, the lesser evil was chosen. In 1859 Shamil with his remaining supporters was surrounded in Gunib, a village in the mountains of Daghestan, and after a 15 days' siege he had to surrender.

Russian rule brought to an end countless blood feuds and the slave trade, and initiated some economic movement in the region. Roads were built, towns founded, literacy introduced. The town of Nalchik, now the capital of Kabardino-Balkaria, which started in 1818 as a Russian military settlement, became by 1863 a prosperous agricultural centre where new species of fruit trees were brought from Georgia and the Crimea by Russian gardening specialists. Ironically enough, that first harbinger of progress, Nalchik military settlement, had such an austere ruling order that it was not very far from slavery. Children of 7 years old were taken to military schools; at 20 they became soldiers and had to be in the service for 15 years. Time free from military activity was to be spent cultivating the land.

The Soviet period in the Caucasus did not differ much from that in any other part of the Soviet Empire. The native nobility and Tsar's governors were replaced with the Party functionaries, and industrial development was forced on, whatever the price. Stalin's policy of "peoples' friendship", that is of uniting different nationalities without asking whether they want it, has resulted in many delayed-action bombs of national conflicts in the Caucasus. Nagorny Karabakh is just one example. The dictator never indulged in slow and surreptitious ways of dealing with his subjects, either individuals or whole nations. When at the end of the Second World War he came for some reason to be displeased with the Balkars, Kar chais, Chechens and Inguishes, in 24 hours hundreds of military lorries were brought onto the mountains, the villages of the "guilty peoples" were surrounded and all the population, from babes to war heroes, were deported to the arid steppes of Kazakhstan in Central Asia. It was only after Stalin's death in 1953 that some of them could return to their homeland. The ruins

Georgia

On the north the country is bordered by the Main Range of the Caucasus, on the south by Azerbaijan, Armenia and Turkey. The variety of Georgian landscapes and vegetation is amazing: from ice, rocks and lichen to palms, tangerines and a warm sea. And all this can be seen during one day's journey.

The Georgian people belong to the oldest races of the world. The Georgians claim that they go back to Karthlos, the brother of Haik (great-great-grandson of Noah) and call themselves Karthlians and their country Sakartvelo, or Karthli. The name Georgia was given by Europeans from St George, the country's patron saint. The land was known to the Greeks and open to Greek influence. It was there that Prometheus was chained by the gods to Mount Kazbek and an eagle was sent to tear at his liver. And the Argonauts came there, to Kolkhida in search of the Golden Fleece. We know from the Greeks that as far back as the 6th century BC it was a prosperous land of highly developed agriculture with many towns, bazaars, good roads and bridges. In the 1st century AD Rome recognized Iberia (another old name for the land), as an ally. About the year AD 330 Georgia was converted to Christianity. The country became an outpost of Christian civilization in the Middle East. But then there followed centuries of Persian and Arabic invasions and of endless fights against them. Only during the time of David the Builder and his great-grand-daughter Tamara (11-12th century) was Georgia entirely independent and spread from the Black Sea to the Caspian Sea. Then invasions began all over again - the Mongols, and after them, in the 15-16th century, Turkey and Persia. People were killed, enslaved or exiled by hundreds of thousands.

Because of this, at the end of the 15th century Georgian princes made the first attempt to get Russian protection, but Russia was not strong enough at the time. In 1783, however, Georgia and Russia concluded a Treaty by which the latter was to protect the eastern part of Georgia. In 1795 Transcaucasia saw a recurrent Persian raid, this time disastrous. The Georgian army was routed, the capital Tiflis destroyed to the last house and more than 20 thousand people were captured and sold as slaves. That was too much for the Russian emperors, seeking to fortify Russia's position on the Black Sea and in the Middle and Near East. In 1801 Emperor Alexander I signed a manifesto granting Eastern Georgia Russian citizenship. The wars with Persia (1804-1813) and Turkey (1828-1829) were fruitful for Russia: all the western parts of Georgia were brought under control. The first attempt by the Georgians to restore self-government was made in 1920-1921, but the desire to be democratic and independent was cut short by the Bolsheviks, who could put up with the words but disliked the action utterly.

Upper Svanetia

Some walks in the Central Caucasus start and end at Mestia, the capital of Upper Svanetia, which is a region of Georgia. The place is unique, a sort of ethnographic and cultural sanctuary of the Caucasus. Try and find another place in Europe (may be in the whole world), where the natives saw the wheel for the first time in their life only in 1937!

The ancestors of the Svans were the Karthlians who at one time populated Asia Minor, hence some similarity between the Svanian and Persian languages and between Syrian ornament designs and those of the Svans. It was about 1000 BC, that they appeared in the territory we call now Georgia, but the date they settled in Svanetia is not known. The Karthlians had many cultural connections with Palestine, Syria, Mesopotamia.

The first mention of the Svans was made in the 1st century AD by Roman historians who highly praised their fighting qualities. But there are no reliable sources dealing with the history of the Svans before the 10th century AD. All the parchments and icons only date as far back as this, although it was as early as 523 that Christianity made its way there. Even so, the ancient pagan beliefs and customs of the Svans have lived to this day and some traces of them can be found in everyday life. The sacrificing of sheep on the days of great religious events is just one example.

By the beginning of the 12th century. Georgia had been united by David the Builder, who became its first monarch. During 11-13th centuries its influence spread over Mesopotamia, Persia and all Asia Minor. It was the Georgian Golden Age, the time for arts blossoming forth, churches being built and enriched with frescoes, for icons being painted or chased, for parchments being written. Most of the churches we can see now were built at the time. Then there came the Mongol invasion and a slow disintegration of the Georgian state. Upper Svanetia remained the last and only unconquered Georgian land. Guarded on all sides by high mountain barriers, the only way to it was up the Ingury Gorge with its narrow, dangerous path, easily aimed at from the commanding heights. For centuries the land served as a treasury where Georgian religious and cultural riches, saved from the marauding enemy, were stored. There followed years and years of a stubborn fight against the neighbouring feudal lords, of endless internal blood feuds and of almost a total isolation from the outside world. It was broken only in the thirties of the last century after Georgia had been made a part of the Russian Empire. But the Svans were never easy to push, and more than once the Tsar's governors had to flee down the Ingury Gorge. The last one was driven out in 1905. And it was not until 1924 (two years after the Civil War ended!), that the Bolsheviks managed to suppress the Svans' resistance.

Although a part of Georgia, Svanetia differed greatly from it. The Svanian language has very little in common with Georgian and their histories, even if parallel, seldom mixed. In Georgia the tribal system was changed for the monarchy in the 3rd century BC; in Svanetia it lived on to see the 20th century. And it was only in 1937, that the Svans tried a totally new device, the wheel. For centuries they used, and still use, wooden sledges, dragged by bulls. A Svanian tribe usually comprised, and still comprises, a village, about 30 households ("smokes"), that is 200-300 people, and all domestic problems were discussed and solved by common consent. Houses and towers were built jointly.

The most remarkable feature of all the Svanian villages are their stone towers. In 1887 Freshfield counted 80 of them in Mestia only (the capital). Since then their number has much diminished. The only function of this impressive structure is to stand a siege or to hide someone of a family from his revengeful enemies. Most of the towers were built during the 11-12th centuries and now nobody knows exactly what was the method of construction. The guess is that wooden scaffolding was put around in spiral fashion and huge stones were hoisted by bulls. There are several floors in each tower, connected by hatches and ladders which could be pulled up, thus blocking access.

A blood feud might occur not only between some neighbouring tribes, but within a tribe itself, between its households. Some rude words, or a kick at a neighbour's dog could easily stir up a quarrel lasting twenty or thirty years with some ten or fifteen dead in the end. One famous feud lasted more than 100 years, and the final score was 14-14. Even quite recently feuds were still so common that from 1917 to 1925 600 men were killed in domestic guerrilla warfare out of a population of 12,000. The result is that the black mourning dress Svanian women wore for their dead men became an everyday one. A feud could be stopped by a local court, comprising 12 relatives of the killer and 13 of the killed. In this case a huge ransom had to be paid in land or in cattle. So it is easy to understand why politeness is the inborn Svanian virtue and the strongest invective in Svanian language is "ᴀ ᴏl".

Svanian churches are worth a special mention. They are not the kind Europeans are used to seeing all over the world. Most of them are small, sometimes 5 or 6 square metres in all. The Svans are not ardent worshippers and their churches were not so much for praying inside as for keeping safely icons and crosses, as well as any objects they considered sacred. An

33

aluminium mug or a cheap religious picture, bought at the nearest bazaar, are a very normal thing there. The way the austere Svans treat their clergy seems bizarre: the churches are guarded so rigorously that even the clergymen have no free entrance and the keys are kept by three old and esteemed local men. Every village has its own church. For example, at the village of Lagami (a part of Mestia) the festival is held in February. A snow tower is built and men hoping for a son must come in the morning and lay its foundation. All the people from Mestia gather here, then the guests attack the tower and the locals defend it. "The battle" ends in a round dance and a prayer-song addressed to the local saint.

Alas, the transportation and accommodation in this wonderful land leave much to be desired, especially the former. In Mestia you can count on the roof of the two storey Tetnuldi hotel (at the town's eastern edge), smart-looking but dilapidated inside (sleeps 70) and the Ushba mountaineering base (Rescue Service); a long two storey barn-like building, $2^{1}/_{2}$km east of the town, on the wooded slope above the valley floor. It is more spacious but its grade is much lower than that of the Tetnuldi.

Separate regular bus services (with the time-tables almost inaccessible) connect the town with the villages of Mazeri in the Dolra Valley, Jabeshi in the Mulkhra Valley and Nakra in the Nakra Valley. There are several more or less reliable buses a day (about 4 hours drive) and several flights a day (if it is a clear one) of small planes or helicopters to the town of Zugdidi. You can get by those buses to Khaishi Village on the Ingury Road, near the mouth of the Nenskra River. The only possibility to go to the village of Ushguly (Route 2. General Information) is to charter a bus or truck, which is by no means a minor task.

There is a choice of 12 routes over the Main Range, connecting Mestia with the northern valleys, from the two Semi-Upper Tsanner Passes (Route 25) on the east to the Chiperkarachai Pass (Route 6) on the west. The shortest (and transport trouble free) route is over the Mestiysky Pass (Route 2), the easiest one is the Donguzorun Pass (Route 6).

There is a post office, small market and two or three food shops in Mestia. Going to the post office, do not be too optimistic. Even Moscow can prove to be too far for reliable communication!

The Routes

Baksan Valley

The valley occupies half the territory of Kabardino-Balkaria and the latter represents the highest part of the Central Caucasus, with all the summits over 5,000m, except Kazbek. The upper part of the valley runs virtually east-west and is bordered on the south by the Main Range with its northern branch, the Adyrsu range, extending from Sarykol peak at the head of the Adyrsu Valley. The northern border is Mt Elbrus and its eastern ridges. The upper reaches of this long, spacious and (above 1,700-1,800m) richly wooded valley, from the town of Tyrnyauz to the foot of Elbrus, are the scene of the busiest mountaineering activity: climbing, walking, skiing and paragliding. The place is highly civilized by Soviet standards, with more-or-less developed recreation facilities, ie. a metalled road coming close to the Main Range, some passable hotels, cableways and some huts on the walking routes.

The part of the valley covered by this guidebook stretches for 43km from the town of Tyrnyauz (1,200m) to the Azau Glade (2,200m) at the foot of Elbrus. There is a regular bus service along the valley, connecting Mineralny Vody Airport with Terskol, the uppermost town of the valley (6 runs a day, 5 hours' drive) and 7 buses a day run (3½ hours) from Nalchik, the capital of Kabardino-Balkaria, to Terskol and Tyrnyauz (10 or 12 runs, 2½ hours). The last runs of the day are about 3.00-4.00pm, and normally even at the peak of the season after 6.00-7.00pm the traffic in the valley, except for some chance trucks or private cars, virtually comes to a halt till morning. Taxis can be hired both at Mineralny Vody and Nalchik.

The road is a string of small towns, villages and (higher up) of touring and mountaineering bases and hotels. Post offices with long-distance telephone service (do not expect more than Moscow; no international calls!) can be found in Tyrnyauz, Elbrus (17km down from Terskol) and Terskol itself. The best hotel of the valley is the former "dacha" of the Central Committee of the late Communist Party (3km up the Adylsu Valley). The second best is the Itkol hotel (3½ km down from Terskol). The staff is trained for "foreign service" and the kitchen is fairly good. The third one is 1½ km up the Donguzorun Valley on the Cheget Glade.

The valley boasts two cableways. One is on Elbrus, two runs of cable cars and a chair-lift above, up to 3,750m. The lower station is on the Azau

Glade (2,200m), the intermediate one is Stary Krugozor (2,920m) and Mir Station at 3,470m. The second cableway is a couple of chair-lifts (single and double seats) on the Cheget Glade (2,100m) bringing you to a shoulder (3,050m) on the eastern ridge of a peak, facing Elbrus across the Baksan Valley, with a very long Balkarian name: Donguzorun-azau-gitche-cheget-cara-bashy, shortened to just Lesser Donguzorun. Both the cableways operate from 9.00am to 3.00pm, Monday is a day off.

To count all the huts in this mountaineering and skiing centre only requires the fingers of one hand. The largest is the Refuge of 11, a fairly comfortable three-storey hotel (with carpets in the corridors) high on the slope of Elbrus (4,200m), on the voie normale. There are dormitories for two and four with pillows and blankets (or wadding filled sleeping bags), but no linen and washing facilities. All meals are self-prepared on your own stove and there are no purchasable foodstuffs. The two other huts in the Adyrsu and Adyslu Valleys are just unwardened cabins with plank beds. In all the upper reaches of the Baksan Valley camping is prohibited, except for the official campsites near the road, dusty and uncomfortable. A relatively good one is on the Cheget Glade.

Nowadays accommodation at the mountaineering and touring bases is possible for any traveller. In many cases it is just summer cottages with rooms for four and without private facilities. Hot water in the common shower room is available during certain hours of the day. There is no regular bus service up the side valleys, where most bases are situated.

It should be noted that some business-minded managers with a view to future profits in hard currency are trying to rebuild and partly refurnish their premises, making them suitable for foreign tourists.

The Baksan Valley has quite a number of branch valleys, joining it from the north and south. Half of them are declared by many Russian guidebooks to be "the most beautiful in the Northern Caucasus". And not without reason. All the interesting side-valleys are described briefly:

Tyutyusu Valley. 4km up from Tyrnyauz. The valley, wooded, beautiful and uninhabited, connects Baksan and Chegem via the Kilar Pass (Route 1). The upper part offers the spectacular view of the north walls of Tyutyu (4,460m) and Djaylyk (4,540m) peaks.

Adyrsu Valley. Further to the west, 20km up from Tyrnyauz. It has a 12km long jeep road, leading to two large mountaineering bases (2,400m) and has many more climbers, walkers and in winter skiers. When you emerge from its lower, narrow and woody part after a long and sweaty walk up the road and see the shining north face of Ullutau across the vast space of its

37

head, then you will recall the guidebook's words and agree that this one is "the most". Until you get in some other one! Luckily, there is no easy access to the valley because there is a canyon at the Adyrsu river's mouth (1,600m) and no motorable way up. To get on to the road in the valley you have to use a car-lift, which is almost in the private possession of the local people who operate it. It is said to work from 8.00am till 7.00pm. It is not a problem to make it on foot, just 400 iron steps. The upper part of the valley is so broad and spacious, that even the roofs of two mountaineering bases somehow cannot make themselves conspicuous. There are many good places for camping, but the best one is on the left bank, in the pine grove, right opposite the ruins of the old Djaylyk base (on the right bank), destroyed by a mud and stone avalanche in 1983. To get there use the bridges near the new Djaylyk or Ullutau bases.

Two passes connect the valley with its neighbours: Mestiysky (Route 2), leads across the Main Range to the Lekzyr glacier and Upper Svanetia (Georgia), and Koyavganaush (Route 3) to the Adylsu Valley.

The Mestiysky hut at the foot of its namesake pass, at 3,150m, can take 16 people on its plank beds. Quite a remarkable feature of the valley is the Old Djaylyk hotel, the first private one in the Elbrus area, and a very comfortable and friendly place to put up at. Sleeps 18 persons, situated halfway between Djaylyk and Ullutau bases (the right bank, 30 minutes walk from each other). The nearest village is Upper Baksan in the Baksan Valley, opposite the mouth.

Adylsu Valley. This has much to offer to those, who care about meetings and talks with fellow walkers. It is nearly three times shorter than the Adyrsu, with no devices at its beginning, shutting out chance vehicles. There are four mountaineering bases, a hotel and summer camps there, so travelling traffic is rather substantial. The head of the main valley cannot boast scenery like that of Tyutyusu or Adyrsu, but the upper parts of its three left side branch valleys, Shkhelda, Kashkatash and Bashkara, are well worth visiting and taking in the views. There is the long north wall of Shkhelda Peak (4,320m), closing the valley on the south and, may be, the high, faraway, elusive Ushba (4,710m). The cirque of the Bashkara glacier is a rare exception for rather a long stretch of the Main Range. It is a mountain cul-de-sac with no passes on its abrupt ridges, linking Ullukara (4,300m), Bashkara (4,240m) and Djantugan (3,990m) peaks.

The first base is Adylsu, in the forest (1,800m) on the left bank, close to the road in the Baksan Valley, the second one, Shkhelda (1,900m) is 3km from the latter, up a steep road. The Rescue Service of the Elbrus area is located there. The metalled road goes up one more kilometre, turns sharply right and ends at the former Central Committee's "dacha", now a high class hotel. To the left of the road, down in the forest is the Elbrus base. And the last one, Djantugan (2,130m), is at the end of the jeep-road (1$^{1}/_{2}$km from the "dacha"), climbing the right side of the main valley. On the left bank of the Adylsu River, in the pine forest, opposite the base, is a well known campsite, the Glade of Koshes. The next one, called the Green Hotel, is at the head of the valley, near the right bank moraine of the Bashkara glacier (2-2$^{1}/_{2}$hours walk from Djantugan base). You will find there the second and the last hut (for 16 people) in the whole Elbrus area. A good easy climb and a good viewpoint is Gumachy peak (3,805m), in the left corner of the upper basin of the Djankuat glacier (return time 8-9 hours). The Koyavganaush Pass (Route 3) is the way to the Adyrsu Valley across the Adylsu Range. An exciting walk to Upper Svanetia under the walls of Ushba (with an easy ascent of Shurovsky peak) can be made early in the season across the Ushbinsky Pass (4,100m) through the Shkhelda Valley (Route 4). The other pass there is Akhsu (Route 5), to Svanetia as well. The nearest village is Teguenekly, in the Baksan Valley, 1$^{1}/_{2}$km from the mouth, upstream. The nearest post office is at Elbrus village, 4km downstream.

Yusengy Valley. The second easiest pass (Route 4), leading to Upper Svanetia, the Becho Pass at the head of this valley, was used for decades as a short and beautiful "caravan way" to the coast of the Black Sea. And for decades, each summer day between 9.00 and 10.00am one could observe a curious scene on the saddle of the Becho Pass. A large and colourful group of trekkers, of all ages and bodily constitutions taking off, with relief, their nailed boots and a couple of burly natives, shoving the latter into sacks and strapping them to donkeys' backs. Then the party would split. The donkeys would retrace the way to the Northern Refuge (now just ruins) and the trekkers, relieved of their boots (2$^{1}/_{2}$kg each), would briskly go down to the Southern one (now a kosh).

There is a good path on the right bank all the way to the Yusengy glacier under the Becho Pass. In the Baksan Valley the path begins 100m downstream from the bridge over the Baksan River (1,850m, 4km down from the Itkol Hotel), goes for 1km along the right bank of the latter, then turns steeply left into the Yusengy Valley. Suitable campsites can be found either closer to Baksan or in the last upper third of the valley. There us a mountaineering base, "Baksan", where the Yusengy River flows into the Baksan, on the left bank of the former.

Donguzorun Valley. The Donguzorun River is the last right tributary of the Baksan (or the first if you look downstream) and the valley is the most popular caravan way, even though not the shortest one, from the Baksan Valley to Upper Svanetia. It goes across the Donguzorun Pass (Routes 6, 7) into the Nakra Valley. The latter joins the Ingury Valley with a road in it up to the town of Mestia and down to Sukhumi. The second pass, the Donguzorun West (Route 9) leads into the Nenskra Valley which, owing to its length, is a day or two longer way to Mestia.

The road into the Donguzorun Valley branches off from the main road in the Baksan, 2km down from the town of Terskol, goes over a bridge across the Baksan River and comes to the Cheget Glade (2,100m) with the seven storeyed Cheget Hotel, small fruit and woollies bazaar, two cafes (or, rather, take-aways) and the two lower stations of single and double chair-lifts. The hotel has rooms for two and three, combined in one apartment with shared private facilities, a restaurant with rather unreliable service and canteen.

The chair-lifts work from 9.00am till 3.00pm and Monday is a day off. The first lift to "Café Ai" station (2,750m) takes 15 minutes. There is one more lift to a shoulder on the ridge (3,050m), but it is just a view point for Mt Elbrus across the deep and green Baksan Valley. A wide path goes up through the Donguzorun Valley in view of the formidable north walls of Donguzorun (4,457m) and Nakra (4,277m) peaks, past a large torquoise lake under the former, up to the foot of the Donguzorun Pass. In its upper part the valley is uninhabited and, despite its popularity, cannot offer anything in terms of accommodation, except the ugly ruins of two large huts which served for many years the trek across the Donguzorun Pass.

Azau Valley. The Azau River, interflowing with the Garabashi makes the Baksan River itself. The Main Range and the ridge connecting it to Mt Elbrus, form the head of the gorge and are low and eroded, thus offering fairly easy ways across. There are three passes there: Chiperazau (Route 10) leads to the Nenskra Valley, Azau (Route 11) to the upper reaches of the Ullukam Valley on the northern side of the West Caucasus and Ekho Voyny (Route 12) to the Khotyutau snow-field (and to the Khotyutau Pass itself, Route 17), a large plateau to the south of Mt Elbrus. There is a clear path in the gorge, but to get to the campsite, a starting point for all three passes, it is necessary to cross the body of the Bolshoi Azau glacier, covered with black volcanic gravel, very awkward for walking. Besides, because of steep eroded slopes, the gorge is notorious for stone falls when it rains heavily. For several hundred metres of its narrowest part its left volcanic side is a grandiose 200m high wall, made of black basalt hexahedrons. To get into the gorge turn left from the lower station of Elbrus

40

cable way (where the road in the Baksan Valley reaches its highest and final point, 2,200m) and descend to the Azau River. There find the path and turn right.

Irikchat Valley. Another three branch valleys with good walks in them join the Baksan Valley from the north, to the east of Mt Elbrus. This area is in the weather shade of this huge mountain and gets much less snow and rain than other parts of the Elbrus area, so the valleys there are drier and the weather is usually better. Also, the snowline is higher and therefore long scree slopes are very typical for the routes there. The first of the three, joining the Baksan Valley just opposite the village of Elbrus, is the Irikchat: long, uninhabited and beautiful, with the white cone of Mt Elbrus dominating the scenery. There is a pass at its head to the upper reaches of the Malka River (north of Mt Elbrus) the Irikchat (Route 14). To get on the path along the left bank of the Irikchat River turn left from the main road in the Baksan Valley (facing downstream) 400-500m short of the petrol station (to the right of the road) and by a narrow street of the village go to the mountain side. Then turn right, cross the Irikchat by way of a footbridge to the left bank and pick up a path, climbing into the valley above the gorge.

Syltransu and Kyrtyk Valleys. The next two valleys, the Syltransu and Kyrtyk, meet the Baksan Valley at the village of Upper Baksan, exactly opposite the mouth of the Adyrsu River on the south side. The first one has at its head the largest and highest lake in the Central Caucasus, Syltrankel (30 square km, 2,950m), set in an amphitheatre of shapely snowy peaks and a low (by Caucasian standards) pass, Syltran, (Route 13), leading to a northern neighbour valley, the Kyrtyk. This one is long and dry not much frequented by climbers and walkers. There is a cave town created by prehistoric man at the foot of Ulluckaya Rock (2,860m) on the left bank, 9km from the mouth, and two passes connect the Valley with the Malka Valley's head. One leads on to the largest ice-field in the Caucasus, Djikaughenkez, under Mt Elbrus (Route 18), the other one to the Islamchat Valley (Route 13), which, in its turn, is a way to the vast green basin at the northern foot of Mt Elbrus, closed on all sides except for a narrow gorge at its north-east corner cut by the Malka River.

ROUTE 1: From the Baksan Valley through the Tyutyusu Valley, via the Kilar Pass (1B, 3,850m, between Kenchat and Orelyu Peaks) to Bashil Tourist Base in Bashilauzsu Valley (the left source valley of Chegem Valley). *(See maps 11 & 13)*

The route takes 3 days, the first and second demand 7-8 hours of walking each and the third 4-5 hours. On the western side of the pass there is a reasonably crevassed glacier, a bergschrund, normally with solid bridges, a snow slope, 30m 35°, which turns into ice in late August, and 30m of easy rock scrambling. On the eastern side - a snow (or ice in August) slope, 10m, 30°. The best conditions for crossing the pass are from mid-June till late July. Rope, crampons and ice-axe required.

Stage 1. The mouth of the Tyutyusu River, flowing into the Baksan, is 4km upstream from the town of Tyrnyauz. From the road in the Baksan Valley turn on the rough track, going along the right bank of the Tyutyusu, come to a suspension bridge, cross it to the left bank and follow a road there. It soon comes to a ford for vehicles. Cross the river again by a fairly flimsy footbridge to the right bank and 2 hours after this come to the end of the road with a kosh in sight. In case the footbridge is swept by high water, return to the suspension bridge (it will take 20 minutes), cross it and follow a path, which climbs steeply for 50-60m and then goes almost level above the river in the forest. At one particular place it descends into a ravine and then surmounts its left side, which is a rock step, 5m high, 45°. After this it meets the road on the right bank.

On reaching the kosh follow the path and in $2^{1}/2$ hours you come to the tree line. A good campsite is available there (2,600m). Five hours from the Baksan. A giant rock step, 500m high, with grassy old moraines descending from it is seen on the south-east. The Tyutyu glacier is behind the step, hidden from view. Go to the south along the path on the right bank, wade or cross by stepping stones the stream from the West Kayarta and Orelyu glaciers on the left, cross the old grassy terminal moraine of the Tyutyu glacier and come on to the crest of its right bank moraine. There are small cairns there marking the way.

Two and a half kilometres from the giant rock step, at the head of the Tyutyu glacier the latter is joined by the West Kenchat glacier, its terminal moraine merging with the Tyutyu glacier's right bank moraine. There the path turns sharply left and ascends the West Kenchat's terminal moraine to reach a sandy campsite by a stream (3,400m), $2^{1}/2$ hours from the campsite at 2,600m. The total time is $7^{1}/2$ -8 hours. To the south-west the eye-catching view of the great north walls of Djaylyk (4,540m) and Tyutyu (4,460m) peaks is offered.

Stage 2. Early start. From the campsite go to the north-east, climb on to the right bank moraine of the West Kenchat glacier, go along it, then, where practiable, turn to the dry glacier. Rope up. Having gained its middle level part, go south-east, to its left bank, skirting a big rock island (crevasses). In the upper basin of the glacier go to the saddle which is seen to the south-east, aiming at its left side where there are good bridges over the bergschrund. Cross it and climb the steepening slope, bearing slightly to the right and heading for the centre of the saddle. The upper part of the snow slope (35°) is followed by some loose rocks (30-40m, 45°). From the saddle a good view back is afforded of the vast upper reaches of the Tyutsusu Valley and of Mt Elbrus far on the west, 5½ hours from the campsite.

There is a fairly steep snow pitch (or ice late in the season), 30°, 10m on the eastern side of the saddle. On descending this cross to the east (roped) upper basin of the South Kenchat glacier, keeping to the eastern ridge of Kenchat Peak. Having gained a big rock island (30 minutes from the saddle) turn north-east and leave it to your left, as well as the other one at the junction of the northern and southern branches of the South Kenchat glacier. Walk over dry glacier to the left bank moraine, which turns east. Follow it and keep that direction over the hills of moraine debris until you come to the right bank of the Kenchat stream. The campsite is on its left bank under a waterfall, by a small tarn (3,400m) 2½ hours from the pass.

Stage 3. From the campsite follow the path down the left bank (cairns). It descends the rock step separating the hanging valley of the South Kenchat glacier and the Djaylyk Valley and comes to the confluence of the Kenchat and Djaylyk streams. To get to the Bashil tourist base follow the path on the left bank of the Djaylyk stream, which meets the Bashilauzsu River. Cross the latter by way of a bridge and go down along the road the last 1½km. 5 hours from the campsite.

ROUTE 2: From the Adyrsu Valley to the Town of Mestia, the Capital of Upper Svanetia, via the Mestiysky Pass (3,860m, 2A, on the Main Range, at the Head of the Adyrsu Valley). *(See maps 13 & 15)*

There are three relatively easy ways from the Baksan Valley to Mestia. From west to east: the Donguzorun, Becho and Mestiysky Passes. Among them the last is the highest and hardest. Though not much harder in its upper part than the Becho, the glacier approaches, especially on the south side, are considerably longer. The only technical section is on the northern side, a 100-120m snow slope of 30°. Late in the season it turns into ice, so for those not willing to be involved in climbing ice, cutting steps or frontpointing, the deadline for easy crossing is the middle of July. If you are not an expert in snow climbing either, it is always possible to hire a couple of experienced climbers down in the valley to guide you. Good steps in snow, made in the afternoon, can be used in the morning as a comfortable ladder. The route has two very good advantages over the other two. One is you will not need a bus or truck to get to Mestia after the pass, which means one big problem less, for in Upper Svanetia it may turn out to be even bigger than walking over any pass! The second one is the dramatic, savage high mountain scenery around one of the largest glaciers of the Caucasus, the Lekzyr. Its east to west dimension is 16km. You may need to add to your equipment a pair of crampons, not so much for safety as for comfort.

The town of Mestia lies in the heart of the Greater Caucasus, in a wide green valley between the snow-clad Svanetsky Range and the Main Range, only 10km from the latter. On the east the town is guarded by twin-giants, the white pyramids of Tetnuld Peak (4,974m, the first ascent made in 1887 by W.D.Freshfield, quite an easy and tempting climbing option) and Gestola Peak (4,860m. W.D.Donkin and C.T.Dent in 1886).

There are two places worth visiting. One is the ethnographic museum of Mestia, which is full of the relics of the long, austere and isolated life of the Svans: ancient agricultural implements, weapons, dress, household articles, icons and manuscripts. Also there is a separate hall, which contains all the material on the climbing activity of the Svans from the very beginning. The second place you should not miss is Mikhail Hergiany's memorial estate. No mountain region of the former USSR can equal Upper Svanetia in the number of native climbers and the best ones at that. Only here you can find a monument to a climber and his memorial estate. The climber is Mikhail Hergiany, a great man of Soviet mountaineering, "one of the best climbers of all times" (Jean Franco). The estate is also a kind of museum of old Svanian domestic life. The house, with its massive walls made of stone with narrow slits instead of windows, was built to give shelter not only from rains and frosts, but from bullets as well. In fact it was a fortress. The ground floor is a large, dark room with a wooden enclosure for cattle, long benches and a huge cauldron hanging from the ceiling by chains. During long winters all the family lived here, the only warmth and light provided by the fire under the cauldron.

When in Mestia, try to find a car and get to Ushguly, the remotest and highest village at the river-head of Ingury, under Shkhara Peak (5,200m), 2 hours' drive. It is a Svanian history and ethnography natural reserve in the open, with clusters of black towers and houses of 10-12th century, ancient churches, steep, narrow, winding alleys, naked mountains on both sides and the white barrier of the Bezengi Wall on the north. For many years the village was the safest place for the persecuted and for religious and cultural values... The famous Svanian hospitality attains here its climax. This is because the villagers feel they have to atone their collective sin against hospitality, committed in 1547, when one of the princes Dadeshkeliany, who for four centuries had tried to subjugate the village, was invited as a guest and killed while feasting. No one wished to take the whole responsibility, so all the men scraped their bullets to get some lead, one bullet was cast, a rifle was tied to a tree, a rope to the trigger and only then the men all together pulled the rope.

Stage 1. The path to the Mestiysky hut, at the foot of the Mestiysky Pass, goes along the right bank of the Adyrsu River. Both the mountaineering bases are on this bank as well. It is possible to camp in the grove on the left bank, midway between the Djaylyk and Ullutau bases, then you go upstream to the bridge and cross the river to the right bank.

Climbing old moraines the path takes you in 3 hours to the lower Mestiysky campsite on the right bank of a stream, with a signpost, pointing to some local passes. To the NE, the Mestiysky Hut is located on top of a rock buttress, called Kyt (Whale), separating two glaciers. There is a path, going straight ahead and down to the foot of that buttress and another one which crosses the stream and after 50-60m on its left bank turns right and climbs steeply up a dusty scree slope (100m). Follow this path which further on skirts the snout of the East Adyrsu glacier (a cave can be seen, from which a torrent flows). Gradually it turns right and goes along the right side moraine for 300-400m. At a convenient place turn right and cross the covering moraine, then the dry glacier.

Head for the lowest left side of the Kyt buttress. There are two or three narrow crevasses just before rock debris is reached. Skirt them to their left or jump over. In 10-15 minutes a path will take you to the hut (3,150m, 5 hours from Ullutau base). If it is occupied, there are many sites around for tents. Water for cooking is to S down the slope, towards the pass. At night the temperature may fall below zero. High mountain scenery is on all sides, except down the valley: glaciers, snow cirques, rock walls and ridges. To the right (looking S) the huge north wall of Ullutau (4,200m) looms.

Camping on the Lekzyr glacier

Stage 2. An early start is highly desirable to avoid soft snow on the south side. Go S over moraine debris to the foot of a snow slope (25-30°, 100-120m) leading to the pass. It may be necessary to put on crampons and rope up to ascend this slope. Keep to the right of two rock islands, then slightly to the left, to avoid the steepest part. If the steps, prepared in advance, are large enough, there is no need for crampons. Further up there are two ways to the saddle - right or left of the isolated rock ridge, going SE to the pass. If there is enough snow for good bridges over three large crevasses, the right one is more logical and preferable. If not, turn left, climb a snow slope of 30° (50-60m), turn right and walk to the saddle leaving the ridge to your right.

The saddle is a vast snow plateau (2¹/₂ hours from the hut). The view to S is the immense upper snow fields of the east branch of the Lekzyr glacier (16km long in E-W direction). Directly opposite, Bashil (4,260m), Tot (4,000m) and lower down, Svergar (4,110m) peaks fill the view with the severe splendour of their jagged airy ridges and abrupt north faces. To the right the famous Ushba is seen in the distance to SWW.

Turn right and walk on snow along Ullutau's south slopes then follow a gentle snow arête. Descend by a short slope (25°) and then a wide snow couloir (15-20°) for 250-300m. Aim for the lower end of the moraine, bordering the slope on the right. In the lowest part of the slope there may be one or two narrow crevasses. There is a path, going along the crest of the moraine ($2^1/2$ hours from the saddle) with two small campsites to the right.

Where the path ends, descend on to another snow slope with quite a number of crevasses at its foot. But here the snow of spring avalanches is very compact, so there are no treacherous bridges and it is easy to find a way among the crevasses. When on the dry glacier, go W, keeping an eye on the rocky mountain side to your right. Having come to a waterfall 25-30m high, turn left at right angles and cross the medial moraine. A suitable campsite (gravel on ice) is reached 100-120m from the edge of the moraine. A chain of small cairns marks the way ($5^1/2$-6 hours from the saddle).

Stage 3. Reverse the way to the edge of the moraine and walk down over the dry glacier. To W the confluence of three glacier branches, from E, W and N, can be seen. This is the Krest (cross) of Lekzyr. 300-400m before you reach it turn left and go SW, crossing the medial moraine (awkward, unstable boulders). Trying not to lose height too quickly, aim at the left bank moraine of the main, short body of the Lekzyr glacier flowing to S. Follow this moraine for about 40 minutes, then descend a scree slope leading down to the Tyuibry River.

There is a path on its left bank, going through a maze of big blocks in a narrow gorge. Close to the river there is a place for two or three tents. A green valley opens up ahead after the gorge ($2^1/2$ hours from the campsite). The path turns left and climbs up some slabs and then, less discernible, it goes through shrubs and boulders for 200m. Here there are two options. To the left 300m up the slope you can see the high embankment of an old moraine and at its right end, behind it, an abrupt rock wall 20-30m high. To reach there follow a poorly defined path through dense bushes. There is a good track (and a site for two tents) on the crest. The other option is to go on descending to the river and follow a very poor path leading to a tree trunk across the Murkvan river, flowing into the Tyuibry from the left. This crossing will demand organizing rope hand rails and belaying. Then follow the path along the left bank.

The upper option path goes to the right in woods and soon turns left up the Murkvam Valley. Head for the nearest snow bridge over the river, cross it to the path on the left bank and follow it down ($1^1/2$ hours from the gorge). In 1 hour a suspension bridge across the Mestiachala River (formed by the Tyuibry and Chalaat Rivers) is reached, where a jeep road going to Mestia ($1^1/2$ hours) begins. Six hours from the campsite to Mestia.

ROUTE 3: From the Djantugan Mountaineering Base in the Adylsu Valley to the Adyrsu Valley via the Koyavganaush Pass (1A, 3,500m, under Koyavganaush Peak, on its South Ridge). *(See map 13)*

The shortest and easiest way between the upper reaches of the valleys, without much glacier travelling. The main difficulty is a slope on the eastern side of the pass (25-30°, 200-250m), snow the first half of the season, later small scree, comfortable for descending. So, the best time for crossing is late July and August. Necessary equipment: crampons, ice-axe or ski poles. Very awarding views of many impressive peaks are offered from the pass: Ullukara (4,300m) and Bashkara (4,240m) to the west, Djaylyk (4,540m) to the east and Ullutau (4,200m) at the head of the Adyrsu Valley.

If you are short of time it is quite practicable to make the route in one day. If not, it is preferable to break it into two easy stages to be able to camp under the pass and enjoy better morning weather when on the saddle.

Stage 1. From the Djantugan base follow a well-trodden path in the forest along the right bank of the Adylsu River, past koshes and summer tourist camps. Soon the path rises and leaves the trees behind. In 40 minutes it crosses a torrent after which it divides. The left branch goes along the right bank of the Djankuat River, the right one, after crossing the latter by a footbridge, climbs the big and long right side moraine of the Bashkara glacier and goes along its crest. The left path is rather exciting. For 30-40m it clings to a steep rock slope, 3-4m above the roaring river, with a cable handrail in some places. The other variant is quieter and more interesting for its views, even though it means gaining and losing some height.

Further up you may choose between taking the path on the left bank of the Djankuat River or following the crest. Where the moraine turns sharply to the right there is a large green meadow called "the Green Hotel", a comfortable campsite (2,400m) 2 hours from the base. There is a hut here, a property of the Djantugan base, and two wooden cottages, the glaciological base of Moscow University.

Descend from the moraine to the meadow and follow the path, going from the cottages to the south-east, towards the Djankuat glacier. Cross the stream outflowing from the glacier and head for the lower end of its right side moraine. A path climbs a steep eroded slope to the pocket behind the moraine, turns right, goes past steep rocks on the left, turns left and follows up the right bank of a stream. Climb a grass and scree slope, bearing to the

On the Koyavganaush Pass. The head of the Adyrsu Valley in the distance

left and in 30-40 minutes find a suitable place for a campsite on a grassy shelf, 1$^1/_2$ hours from the Green Hotel.

Stage 2. Head east, up screes, to the moraines barring the way to the upper basin of a small, uncrevassed, glacier. The ridge enclosing the basin is high, without any depressions except to the east where you can see the high and abrupt rock step of Koyavgan Peak dropping down to the saddle of the Koyavganaush Pass. Further to the right there follow some rocks sticking out of the ridge and another saddle, a false one, because of a big snow cornice hanging on the eastern side. A slope of 20-25°, scree and snow, leads to the left saddle, 1$^1/_2$-2 hours from the campsite.

The straightforward descent of the eastern slope to the glacier (snow and scree) takes 20-30 minutes. While going down watch the rocks of Koyavgan Peak for falling stones. The mountain is notorious for this hazard, especially late in the day. Once on the glacier turn left into the narrow valley. There is a path on the left side moraine leading to the floor of the Adyrsu Valley. Two hours from the pass. To get to the right bank of

Ushbinsky Pass seen from Ushba glacier

the Adyrsu River you have to walk up or down to a bridge for 20 minutes. If you want to get to the Djaylyk mountaineering base go down, to the Ullutau base - up. There is a nice campsite, even though not too tidy, in a grove of pine trees 10 minutes walk up the left bank.

ROUTE 4: From the Baksan Valley to the Dolra Valley and to the Town of Mestia via the Becho Pass (1B, 3,375m, at the Head of the Yusengy Valley) - or back to the Baksan via the Ushbinsky Pass (3A, 4,100m, between Mt Ushba and Shkhelda Peak). *(See maps 12 & 15*

This route is a feast for those who love really high, awe inspiring mountain scenery. It is the only one which is relatively easy, giving an opportunity to see Mt Ushba in close proximity.

In his chapter on the Caucasus in The Mountains of Europe *Vic Saunders says of Ushba "It is hard not to be too superlative about this mountain, which is one of the most beautiful in the world." Well, the authors of this guidebook have seen it many more times than Vic Saunders but could never feel it was "beautiful". If it is so, its beauty is of the sort that a huge snake could claim. No other Caucasian mountain (with the possible exception of Mt Elbrus) has on its account so much of men's worship, fear and hopes as Ushba. A beauty, witch, monster, killer, all this is said about her (for the Svans it is always "she", never "it"), towering her two uncomparable fangs to 4,710m and exceeding by 300m her not in the least small or timid neighbours - Shkhelda (4,320m) and Chatyn (4,405m) peaks. It was this mountain who, at the beginning of this century, united her British conquerors into the club of "the ushbists".*

There is rather a large glacier, with some crevasses, on the north side of the Becho Pass and a snow slope of 25°, 100m, under its saddle. The south side is patches of snow, 20-25° and scree slopes with a small inoffensive glacier lower down and a good path on a shelf high above a canyon. Being a caravan way from the North Caucasus to Georgia, the pass is normally secured with discernable tracks on the glaciers on both sides. It takes a full day to cross it "from grass to grass"; from one valley to the other.

The Ushbinsky Pass is among the few in the Caucasus over 4,000m. Its grade, 3A, misses the hardest 3B by one subgrade. There are two long ice-falls on both sides of the pass which in late July and August may demand rather developed climbing techniques, including abseiling into wide, long crevasses which stretch from wall to wall. But in late May and in June these

51

difficulties are brought down to a surprisingly low level of 1B - 2A by thick winter snow covering the ice-falls. Rock-fall danger is almost non-existent at this time of year. Nonetheless the latter has its own disadvantages, for the weather is much less stable than in July and August and in the afternoon that deep snow may soften and slow down walking. So, an early start (5.00am) should be the rule.

Two options can be suggested: a rest day at the campsite behind the right bank moraine of the Ushba glacier and, when camping on the pass, the ascent of Shurovsky Peak (4,259m), standing at the northern end of the Ushbinsky plateau, a quick and easy snow plod (1-1½ hours) rewarded enormously with a superb view of the plateau, Mt Ushba (4,710m) and Chatyn Peak (4,405m). The route can take from 5 to 7 days, depending on the two options. Necessary equipment is rope, ice-axe, crampons.

Stage 1. Two kilometres up the valley from Teghenekly Village there is a bridge over the Baksan River. A hundred or so metres down from that, on the right bank, turn south on a wide path going through the Yusenghy Valley. Walk 15 minutes along the gently sloping path, then turn to the left where it climbs steeply a clearing in the forest. To the right there is a small pyramid: the Second World War memorial. Soon the valley narrows and the path goes high above the river, keeping the same steady incline. This pleasant walk on a broad path in the shade of the forest takes 1½ hours. Above the treeline the valley broadens and the Main Range opens ahead to the south. The Becho Pass is seen there as an insignificant depression on the long eastern ridge of Donguzorun Peak, to the extreme left.

Another hour takes you to the ruins of the old Northern refuge (2,430m) (below, to the right near the river) where the trekkers used to spend a night before crossing the Becho Pass. To be better positioned for the next day, a sensible thing to do is to follow the path for 40-50 minutes more and camp on a meadow on the right bank, half-way between the kosh standing to the left of the path and the lower end of the right side moraine of the Yusenghy glacier. The glacier is seen at the end of the green flat floor of the valley.

Stage 2. An early start (5.00-5.30am) is advisable to avoid soft snow on the crevassed Yusenghy glacier. The path goes south, crossing some minor streams from the left and having crossed a bigger one shortly before the lower end of the moraine, climbs on to its crest. The moraine turns gradually east, then merges with the slope and the path goes fairly steeply through the screes and loose rocks of the mountainside high above the glacier. Finally it levels and traverses to its upper basin. Two hours.

Yusengy Valley. Becho Pass in the distance

Rope up and cross the glacier in a wide loop from south-east to south-west, under the slopes walling it. Watch the two hanging glaciers on the left for falling seracs. There is a snow spur with some rocks jutting from it, extending from the Main Range to the north and abutting an ice-fall. Aim at its upper part and begin to climb the snow slope leading to it. On the spur turn left, climb straight up and where it levels out head south-east-south to the saddle. 3½-4 hours from the camp site. The rocks on the saddle are studded with memorial tablets dedicated to the fight between Russian and German troops during the Second World War. Several tent sites are available for emergency camping.

Descend a path to the upper basin of the Kerunda glacier (without crevasses), cross it south-east, to the rock face forming the left side of the gorge into which the glacier flows. There is a good path on the face's flank going up to a tiny saddle on the ridge. From the saddle it goes to the left and down by steep hairpin bends, over screes and rock outcrops, lower down among rhododendrons. To the right, high above the valley, the hanging ice wall of the Dolra glacier attracts attention. From the pass to a camp site behind the left side old moraine down in the valley 2½-3 hours. Total time is 6-7 hours.

In May and June (some years well into July) the path on the flank above
the Kerunda glacier is blocked by winter snow and impassable. Then the
only way down is over the glacier along its right bank. The descent is not
too steep (except one snow slope of 30°, 20-25m) and takes less time than
by the path.

Stage 3. The path goes along the moraine and descends to the floor of the
Becho Valley. To the kosh at the confluence of the Becho and Kvish Rivers
(2,300m), 1$\frac{1}{2}$ hours. There turn left and follow the path on the left side of
the Dolra gorge, high above the river, over meadows and through lush
southern vegetation. In many places the river is covered by spring avalanche
snow till late in summer. At two particular spots the path crosses rather
steep (30°) eroded slopes, 20-25m wide.

In 1$\frac{1}{2}$ hours after the confluence you get to a place where the path
comes closest to the river. There is a kosh there, in the woods to the left and
the grey sheer walls of Mazeri Peak (3,900m) and the powerful yellowish
waterfall of the Ushba River are seen above the valley. **The descent to
Mazeri Village and Mestia starts here - see below. For the return to
Baksan continue as follows:** Turn north on a poor path going past the kosh
in tall weeds and beech forest along the right bank of the Ushba River. Two
hours over rough terrain (brushwoods, stream crossings and boulders) the
hanging valley from where the river falls is reached (2,400m). The
waterfall is a sight well worth making a small detour to the right to
contemplate - a tunnel chiselled by the torrent in living rock and persistent
boulder bombardment. Follow the path north-east along the Ushba glacier
over moraines and cross the South Shkhelda glacier (dry and level here) to
the junction of its left bank moraine and the right bank moraine of the Ushba
glacier. A comfortable campsite is in the pocket, right inside the corner (2,900m).

[A descent can be made to Mazeri Village as follows. From the kosh
under Mazeri Peak go on the path, which soon comes to the right bank
by a bridge, rises and runs through the forest high above the river. A
forest track takes over and brings you to the wide floor of the valley. The
snow-clad Svanetsky range opens on the south. The track leads to a
bridge over the Dolra to the left bank with the large, two-storey building
and from there runs due south over a meadowland to the scattered
houses of Mazeri Village. 1$\frac{1}{2}$-2 hours from the kosh, 4$\frac{1}{2}$-5 hours total
time. There a bus service to Mestia, but do not lose any opportunity to
get a lift. The best place for this is by the road at the southernmost edge
of the village. It takes about one hour to drive to Mestia.]

Mt Ushba and Shkhelda Peak from the west

Stage 4. Early start. Go on the path along the crest of the right bank moraine of the Ushba glacier, descend on to the glacier and keep to its right bank to reach the ice-fall with an island of glacial slabs at its foot, on the right side. In late May or early June the fall is just a long bumpy snow slope of 25° on the average, allowing a straightforward ascent without any route-finding problems. But still, watch the slopes of Shkhelda Peak on the left for falling stones. All the way to the pass the faces of Ushba will loom to the right, arrogant, defiant, of incredible height and steepness. The direction is north. On reaching the upper basin turn slightly east, to Shkhelda's low east ridge. As a matter of fact the pass does not have any saddle. The ridge drops in a sheer wall to the northern ice-fall. Find a suitable flat snow patch and camp. A snow shovel could be very useful for digging a hole for the tent or making a snow wall. The place can be very windy. 4¹/₂ -5 hours.

Stage 5. To the east and 100m higher lies the Ushbinsky plateau. To descend the northern ice-fall climb up in the direction of Ushba 200m, turn left to the north, find a way between some big seracs, through a safe "moat", then turn left again, north-west, and follow a slight depression in the ice-

Mt Ushba and Chatyn Peak seen from helicopter from the north-east

fall. Lower down the average steepness is 25°, some short sections up to 30-35°. There can be a 3-4m high wall of 45° at the upper part. Once on the easy snow at the foot of the ice-fall cross to the north-east the right-hand tributary glacier under its ice-fall, without losing much height and heading for a low rock and scree spur bordering the tributary on the north. There are numerous tent sites on top of it (3,200m). 2-3 hours from the pass.

If you decide against climbing Shurovsky Peak, which with the descent takes 2-2¹/₂ hours, or the weather is not good enough for this, then there is no need for camping - continue with Stage 6.

Stage 6. Descend on to the Shkhelda glacier and walk west-north-west keeping to its right side. There are some crevasses easily skirted. To the left the North face of Shkhelda Peak (4,320m) with its towers and rock spires unrolls by degrees. Continue to the place where the glacier (dry here) turns to north (1¹/₂ hours).

Cross it to the north-east over moraine hills to a path going down along the left bank. Nearing the snout the path may disappear among big blocks. Climb higher to the left; it will be there. The snout is bypassed to its left.

Keep closer to the mountainside and when the black ice wall of the snout has been left 100m behind turn to the right and climb down an awkward steep loose scree, 30m high. 2½-3 hours.

Once on level ground the path winds through a "forest" of huge blocks (the debris of quite a recent stone avalanche from the left mountainside) past a small lake with flat sandy banks, on to the alpine meadows and steeply through the woods to the road in the Adylsu Valley (1½ hours). One more hour down to the Baksan. While still on the path in the Shkhelda Valley, having come to a fence with a stile on it, turn left and walk to the road along the fence, unless you need the Shkhelda climbing base which is behind that fence. They do not like flocks of walkers streaming through their territory! Total time is 5½-6 hours.

ROUTE 5: From the Dolra Valley to the Baksan via the Akhsu Pass (2A, 3,830m, between Akhsu and Yusengy Uzlovaya Peaks) and through the Shkhelda Valley. *(See maps 12 & 15)*

The pass was first crossed in 1889 by Freshfield. The easiest and most logical way to do the route is to cross the pass from south to north. The descent on the south side of a steep snow slope (40°, 150m), the main and only difficult, may be rather tricky for an average high level walker, whereas climbing up it is much easier technically and psychologically. The route takes 2 days and the necessary equipment is rope, crampons, ice-axe. Combined with the Becho Pass crossed from north to south (Route 4) it makes a good 4 days' circuit and gives an opportunity to see the impressive, five kilometres long, north face of Shkhelda Peak (4,370m) and from afar, Mt Ushba (4,710m). Good snow conditions hold normally till mid-July, so this is the deadline for a safe and enjoyable walk over the pass before the snow turns to ice.

Stage 1. From the campsite (2,400m) at the foot of the Becho Pass on the south side an old moraine with some grass on its lower part can be seen going up to the north-east, rounding a spur and turning to the left. There is a campsite (2,800m) in the pocket between the spur and the moraine, gained in 1 hour. It is a starting point and the start should be early indeed, 5.00am, not later, so that you can be under the snow pitch at about 8.00am. From the campsite climb the moraine and come on to the Kvamp glacier, narrow and walled on both sides by rock faces. Go north-east, keeping to its middle part, dry, then higher up covered with snow (rope up). To avoid

57

Adylsu Valley from helicopter

crevasses when nearing the pass come closer to the glacier's right bank. Three hours to get to the foot of the snow pitch. There may be a bergschrund of negligible proportions, if any at all. Find a safe place to cross it and climb the pitch (150m, 40°). After 10.00am there will be the danger of stonefall from the Yusengy Uzlovaya Peak to the left, so it is highly advisable to get to the saddle before that time. 4-4¹/₂ hours from the campsite.

Do not descend straight to the snow basin under the saddle. Go (roped up) north-east, then east, traversing the snow slopes of Akhsu Peak on your right and descend (snow of 25°) on to the upper cirque of the right branch of the Akhsu glacier. At a pinch there is a campsite on the rock island between the two branches (3,700m). Walk down, leaving the icefall under the walls of the island and the icefall of the left branch to your left and go north aiming at the left bank moraine of the glacier. The campsite is in the pocket behind the moraine (3,200m).

Stage 2. Go down the path along the crest of the moraine to the junction of the Akhsu and Shkhelda glaciers. There the path comes down, turns to the left and goes through moraine rubble along the Shkhelda glacier's left side, under the eroded slopes on the left. For further descent see Route 4. Total time from the campsite to the Shkhelda mountaineering base is 4-4½ hours.

ROUTE 6: From the Baksan to the Head of the Nakra Valley via the Donguzorun Pass (1A, 3,160m, on the West Ridge of Nakra Peak, the Main Range); to the Upper Reaches of Nenskra Valley via the Bassa Pass (1A, 3,057m, on the Shtavler Range); to the Head of the Ullukam Valley via the Chiperkarachai Pass (1A, 3,292m, the Main Range) and back to the Head of the Baksan Valley via the Khotyutau Pass (Route 17) *(See maps 1, 9 & 12)*

A circular trek connecting the Baksan with two valleys to the south of the Main Range and a northern one in the West Caucasus. An easy walk through uninhabited valleys above the tree line, over easy and relatively low passes with small glaciers (except for the last pass) and many screes, meadows, clear streams and mild scenery. The Donguzorun and Chiperkarachai passes were known to the local people from time immemorial. The first description of the former was made in 1868 by W.D.Freshfield. There was a slow but dogged fight during 1942 between German and Soviet troops for control over these passes. So there are an impressive number of memorial tablets on them and many rusty remains of the War on the neighbouring ridges. The walk takes 6 days, does not demand any climbing equipment and is practicable till late October.

Stage 1. 1½ km downstream from Terskol turn right, walk over the bridge across the Baksan River and ½km more to the lower station of the Cheget chair-lift (2,100m). The ride to the second station, "Ai Cafe", (2,750m) takes 15 minutes. The path into the Donguzorun Valley begins to the left of the station (looking up) on a grass slope and goes south-east, turning south and south-west, almost level. If the chair-lift is at a standstill (which is not a rare occurrence), take the tractor road zigzagging steeply south from the lower station. Walk up 30-40 minutes and after a straight run along the valley, where the road turns sharply to the right, go ahead to the south-west on a path branching off to the left. It passes a kosh and joins the upper path. One hour from the upper station (two from the lower one), the Medvejiy stream is reached, a left tributary of the Donguzorun River. After the crossing by a footbridge made of whatever was handy (a huge metal five-pointed red star is among the supports!) the path goes to the left and up through thick rhododendrons. When it forks, always take the right

Donguzorun Pass, the northern side

branch. One more hour to the ruins of the former North Refuge, which for many years served a trek across the Donguzorun Pass. Plenty of campsites around.

Stage 2. The pass is at the left corner of the valley's head (looking up) and not visible from the ruins. Follow the path to west. After a small tarn it begins to climb the right side scree slope turning gradually to the left. Higher up there are three snow ascents (up to 25°) with gentle terraces between them. Late in the summer patches of ice may appear. If all the slope has turned to ice (a very rare thing, as a matter of fact), make a loop to the left, skirting the glacier and scramble up the jumbled rocks and screes. 2½-3 hours from the ruins.

A V-shaped, treeless valley running to the left opens out to the south from the wide rocky saddle, studded with memorial tablets. The views from the pass are not particularly impressive but the descent south through rhododendrons and other flowers is a pure delight. Under the saddle the path going down over small screes is clear enough but soon it disappears on blocks and boulders. Keep to the right side there and from a small rock and scree cirque the way is straight down. The path is there, on a grass slope, zigzagging to the left. There is a good campsite on the floor of the valley (2 hours from the saddle). Follow the path on the left bank of the Nakra

Koyavganaush pass. Ullutau peak at the head of the Adyrsu valley is in the distance
Camping near the ruins of the north refuge under the Donguzorun pass

Two views of Donguzorun and Nakra peaks

River. In 30 minutes you cross a stream by stepping stones and in another 30 minutes there is a torrent from the Ledesht glacier with a plank footbridge. The valley curves to the left and widens. Find a suitable site and camp here.

Stage 3. 10-15 minutes walk takes you to a war memorial; a small metal pyramid to the right of the path. Cross the Nakra River by a bridge and go $1^{1}/2$km downstream. It is essential to find the path leading to the Bassa Pass and it is not visible from a distance. You just come across it in the bushes below a long narrow scree, coming down from the slope. Follow the path straight up past a waterfall to the left, over three consecutive grassy terraces, then climb a steep old left bank moraine, finally come on to the snow at its end, where it joins the snow basin under the pass. The saddle is seen to north-west with a scree leading to it, $3^{1}/2$ hours from the Nakra River. On the way up make sure not to turn into any gullies on your right. They lead to the False Bassa Pass, well known for its stone-fall danger.

The pass is a very good viewpoint. To the north Mt Elbrus raises its white cones high over the Main Range, relatively low there and to the south-east all the Dolra range is on display, from Nakra Peak to the Ingury Valley, far in the south. Descend north by the easy snow under the saddle, aiming at the lower end of the ridge, running to north-west and bordering on the right side the upper snow basin. From there walk in the same direction across another small, snow covered glacier to its right side ridge. Pick up a good path there, going down along the ridge to an old right bank moraine and descending to a scree terrace under the snouts of the two glaciers crossed before, and then to another one, grassy, with the standard pyramid of a war memorial. From there it takes 20 minutes to descend by a zigzagging path to the Nenskra River. Follow the path on the left bank upstream for another 15 minutes and camp on a wide meadow with clear streams.

Stage 4. Across the river, on the right side of the valley the hairpin bends of the path to the Chiperkarachai Pass can be seen between two tributary streams just opposite the campsite. The right one has in its bed a huge rectangular boulder. The path goes up the left bank of the left stream (looking up). You may get to Nenskra's right bank either by an avalanche snow bridge right here, which often holds till late August, or go down $1^{1}/2$km to a man-made one and then up again. It takes 2 hours to climb by the steep path to a large grassy hanging valley. The path goes north, crosses a stream, comes to the head of the valley, at a rocky terrace, turns left (west) and crosses it to reach the upper cirque (another 2 hours).

The pass with a snow gully leading to it is seen to the west. The path in the cirque is marked with cairns. $4^{1}/_{2}$ hours from the Nenskra River. A good view back to the south-east of the Shtavler range with the Bassa Pass is afforded from the saddle. Early in the season there may be an abrupt snow step under the saddle, on its western side. So, go to the right, past the dugouts, a reminder of the last war, and take a path, leading to a snow patch of 20°. Further down it goes over screes and loose rocks, keeping to the right side of the valley. In 2 hours an old, high right bank moraine is reached and in 30 minutes, the mouth of the first considerable right tributary of the east Kichkinekol River. There is a flat meadow for camping, shortly after the moraine and a comfortable campsite on the right bank of the river is 30-40 minutes from the mouth. Total time is $6^{1}/_{2}$-7 hours.

Stage 5. All the way down to Voroshilov Kosh (see Route 11, Stage 2) the path goes along the right bank of the East Kichkinekol River. It takes $2^{1}/_{2}$ hours to get there. There is a solid bridge over the Ullukam River. For the next stage to the Baksan Valley see Route 17. On this trek a very sensible thing to do is to walk to the head of the Ullukam Valley and camp at the foot of the Khotyutau Pass, where the path turns to the right (east), 3 hours from Voroshilov Kosh.

ROUTE 7: From Mestia to the Baksan Valley via the Donguzorun Pass (1A. 3,160m, on the West Ridge of Nakra Peak). *(See map 1)*

The easiest route, connecting upper Svanetia with the Elbrus Area is 3 days long. No special equipment is needed. For many years it was used as a trek by an All-Union tourist organisation, so there are well trodden paths on both sides of the Main Range. The two huts which served it on the north (in the Donguzorun Valley) and south (in the Nakra Valley) sides are abandoned now, and in addition the northern one has been destroyed by fire. Some rooms of the southern one (a two-storey wooden building on the right bank of the Nakra River) can be used as a bothy. The Nakra Valley is a very good and varied valley-walk; the Donguzorun, its northern counterpart, offers a great sight of two high north walls, and the pass itself is a simple walking affair, even in its worst condition late in the season.

Stage 1. It takes $1^{1}/_{2}$-2 hours by bus or truck down the Ingury Valley from Mestia to the mouth of the Nakra River. In theory there is a regular bus

Donguzorun Pass

service from the capital of Upper Svanetia to Nakra Village, 5km up the Nakra Valley, but the schedule seems to be different with each day. So it is most likely that you will have to make it on foot, 5km along a jeep road, through the beautiful, wooded lower reaches of the valley and through the village up to the southern hut (another 3km). 3 hours.

Stage 2. All the 14km from the hut to the foot of the pass a good wide path (the first $1^{1}/_{2}$-2km a forest track) goes on the left bank of the Nakra River. Above the tree line the valley turns to the right, north-east. 2km from the turn on the left side of the path stands a small memorial pyramid to Soviet soldiers who fought here during the Second World War. The river ramifies here on the wide even floor. Right ahead you can see that the valley forks, the left branch going north-north-east, the right one, the Ledesht Valley, west. 1km from the memorial the path divides as well. Follow the left one, which means crossing the Ledesht River by rather a precarious plank or twig bridge. There is a wide meadow on the other bank, covered by tall weeds (a former kosh site) with a narrow muddy path through it. Follow that path (another two stream crossings by stepping stones are made) until you see the path climb steeply up the slope to the right. A good campsite is here, among big blocks (2,500m). 1 hour from the bridge, 6 hours from the hut.

Stage 3. It takes 1 hour to walk to the upper scree cirque, from where the pass is seen to the north-west. The path is barely discernible, so keep to the slopes on your left until it appears again on a small scree under the saddle. The views from the pass are rather modest in both directions, in contrast with the rocks on the saddle itself, shining their numerous memorial tablets of different shapes and sizes. 2 hours from the campsite.

On the descent go to the right for 100m, then turn to the left and descend straight down (to avoid the steepest snow (25°) under the pass). If there are some ice patches or all the glacier (without any crevasses) is ice, traverse to the right to reach loose rocks and broken glacial slabs and from there scramble down to the path. 2 hours from the pass to the ruins of the northern hut. From the hut follow the path on the left mountainside and where it forks always take a left branch. In 30-40 minutes it veers to the left and descends to the tributary stream from the Medvejiy Valley. Cross it by an awkward, haphazard bridge with a cable as a handrail and a big metal red star as a support for feet. To the right, across the narrow valley, two north faces rise dramatically to 4,277m and 4,454m - of Nakra and Donguzorun Peaks, with a large greenish-turquoise lake under the latter. From the bridge the path climbs past a war memorial up to a grassy spur. Soon it forks, the left branch going up gently but steadily to the Ai Cafe chair lift station (2,750m, works till 3.00pm). It takes 20-25 minutes to get there, 15-20 minutes to queue and 15 minutes to ride down. If you take the right branch it will be 35-40 minutes to the Cheget Glade (2,100m) and the lower station. Another 20 minutes will bring you to the Baksan Valley.

ROUTE 8: From the Nakra Valley over the Dolra Range to the Dolra Valley via the Ledesht Pass (2A, 3,400m, between Nakra (4,277m) and Kvish (3,702m) Peaks. *(See maps 1 & 12)*

The walk takes 2 days, includes a lot of glacier travelling, but is quite straightforward, without much wandering among crevasses, and has a snow pitch (80m, 45°) on the western side of the saddle. So, rope, crampons and ice-axe are essential. Technically fairly demanding, it rewards lavishly with vast radiant snow landscapes and with a sight of ice-clad Nakra (4,277m) and Donguzorun (4,454m) peaks when crossing the Nakra plateau. The route can make a central part of a 5 days' circuit - the Baksan-Donguzorun-Nakra-Dolra-Baksan Valleys via the Donguzorun (Route 6), Ledesht and Becho (Route 4) passes.

Stage 1. The Ledesht stream is the biggest tributary on the left side of the Nakra River in its upper reaches (3km down from the campsite under the Donguzorun Pass). The good path on the left bank of the Nakra River crosses the stream 100m up from its mouth (2,150m) by a flimsy footbridge. There is a large patch of lush and high grass there, on the former kosh site on the right bank of the stream, and a path, branching off from the main one in the Nakra Valley is on the stream's left bank. It goes to the south-east, climbs into the mouth of the valley by a step and runs over meadows and through thick rhododendrons. Having crossed a side-stream at a huge black block you come to the level part of the valley with the two sources of the Ledesht stream, seen from there, the right one (orographically) flowing from the Ledesht glacier on the east and the left one, coming from the Leyrag glacier on the south-east.

Wade the left one and follow a path on the left bank of the right stream. The Ledesht glacier is fenced off by a band of glacier smoothed rocks. The way on to the glacier is between that band and the western spur of Ledesht Peak. Keep to the stream's left bank, climb a grass slope (up to 30°), then scramble up a section of broken rocks, find a wide ledge covered with scree under the spur and climb to the moraine under the glacier's snout (3,000m). $2^{1}/_{2}$ hours from the Nakra River. If necessary, sites for tents can be found there. The general direction is eastern-northerly.

Climb the cone of spring avalanche debris to reach the lower basin of the Ledesht glacier. There is an island of glacial slabs in the middle of the basin (with a sandy campsite on top of it). From the island go north and climb two or three oblique, inclined ice ledges (50m, 15-20°), leading to the upper basin. There are three saddles in the ridge, connecting Nakra and

Ledesht Peaks. Head north for the snowy pyramid of Nakra Peak and leave Kvish Peak (3,702m) to your right. The Ledesht Pass is on its northern ridge, close to the peak itself. 2 hours from the campsite at the snout to the foot of the pass. A snow slope, 80m, 45°, leads to the saddle. $^{1}/_{2}$-1$^{1}/_{2}$ hours. Half the Shtavler range is spread before the eyes to the west with the rock buttress of Kuarmash Peak in the centre and the low triangle of Nenskra Peak to its right, sticking out of the glaciers. To the east the wide spaces of the Nakra plateau open out with the white mass of Donguzorun peak at its north-east corner.

Descend on to the Nakra plateau by scree and snow and walk south, keeping to the Kvish and Ledesht Peaks' slopes. The first ice-fall of the Kvish glacier, flowing out of the upper snow basin is skirted on its right side. Then take the path on the right bank moraine. There are tent sites at its upper (3,100m) and lower (2,800m) ends. 3$^{1}/_{2}$ hours from the pass to the lower campsite.

Stage 3. The lower part of the glacier is an ice-fall, bordered on the right by steep rocks. From the campsite go south-west, leaving those rocks to your left and descend on to the West Kvish glacier, dry at this point. On the glacier turn left and walk straight down, keeping to the left of the central moraine. Lower down, where the snout of the glacier is squeezed by rock faces on both sides, go from the ice on to the screes under the left face and head for the snout of the Kvish glacier. Cross the stream flowing from under the snout where it divides into several shallow arms. There are cairns at the wading points. Walk down on the left bank of the stream to the place where it meets the stream from the West Kvish glacier. The place is marked with a huge round boulder on the same left bank with a campsite beside it (2,500m) and a fairly good path going down from there. 40 minutes from the campsite at 2,800m. In 1 hour it brings you, over moraine debris and gravel, to a short canyon, which is either passed above, or walked through close to the water, if the latter is not too high. There is a kosh on the left bank of the Dolra River, where it is formed by Becho and Kvish Rivers. A bridge over the Becho is upstream from the confluence. If it is swept away, go up along the Becho's right bank past a canyon and find an avalanche snow bridge above it. There is a beaten track on the left bank, leading up to the Becho (Route 4) and Akshu (Route 5) passes, and down to the Ushbinsky Pass and Mazery Village (Route 4). From the huge boulder to the kosh is 1$^{1}/_{2}$ hour's walk.

ROUTE 9: From the Baksan through the Donguzorun Valley via the Donguzorun West Pass (1B, 3,260m, on the Main Range, to the West of the Donguzorun Pass) to the Nenskra Valley. *(See maps 1 & 9)*

A relatively easy walk with a snow slope of 20° on the eastern side of the pass and a short snow descent of 30° on the western one as a technical part of the route. The necessary equipment is rope, ice-axe, crampons.

It is 2 hours walk from the Ai Cafe station of the Cheget chair-lift to the ruins of the Northern hut under the Donguzorun Pass (Route 6) and from there to cross the Donguzorun West Pass to the head of the Nenskra Valley takes 5-5½ hours. So it is quite possible to make it in one day, but bearing in mind the chair-lift which does not start until 9.00am and the 2-2½ hours needed to get from the ruins to the pass, you will certainly not be on the saddle earlier than 2.00pm. That means taking chances on soft snow over crevasses, not to mention plodding through it. So it is better to break the route into two stages.

For those partial to valley treks, to walk down the Nenskra Valley, which is 50km long, may be quite interesting, even through a little monotonous and hot. At Chubery Village (43km from the war memorial at the head of the valley) it is possible to get a lift or try to hire a truck to Khaishy Village, which is on the road in the Ingury Valley. There is a regular bus service in that valley between the town of Mestia (3 hours bus drive upstream from Khaishy) and the town of Zugdidi (2 hours downstream), 5 runs a day. But the buses are small and more often than not overcrowded, the schedule is rambling and, moreover, very difficult to get any information about. The chance of hiring a vehicle at the village is rather slim. Were it not for the transport problem, the drive itself to Mestia high over the river (at some places breathtakingly high!) along the scenic Ingury Valley with clusters of small villages scattered on its green slopes, could be a treat to the traveller.

Hopefully, with the advent of the free enterprise spirit to that remote and stubborn soil, the situation with travelling facilities will improve, but as in the case of the wheel, which came there only in 1937, it may take some time.

The bus and train service between Zugdidi and Sukhumi (and its airport) is quite regular and reliable, about 8 runs a day, 2 hours drive. The same applies between Zugdidi and the capital of Georgia, Tbilisi (airport), 7-8 hours drive.

Those who prefer alpine meadows, rocks and snow and do not want to walk all the way down the Nenskra Valley can choose among the following possibilities:

1.   To cross the Shtavler Range by the Bassa Pass (Route 6) and get into the Nakra Valley with the Donguzorun Pass, leading from there to the Baksan (Route 7) and the Ledesht Pass, leading to the Dolra Valley (Route 8).

2.   To walk down to the mouth of the Dalar River, Nenskra's right side tributary, go up that valley and cross the Main Range to the northern slopes of the West Caucasus (Route 28).

3.   To cross the Main Range again, back to the north by the Chiperkarachai Pass leading from the Nenskra Valley to the head of the Ullukam Valley, the eastern part of the West Caucasus.

Stage 1. For the lower part from the Baksan to the ruins of the northern hut see Route 6, Stage 2. From the ruins follow the path, which goes to the Donguzorun Pass (Route 6). Where it starts to rise to the pass turn to the right, north, and head for the right bank moraine of the glacier in the northern corner of the upper cirque. Follow a discernible path on its crest, and on gaining its upper end rope up and go on to the glacier. Cross it in a western-northerly direction and climb to the saddle (snow of 20°), aiming at its left side and keeping to the rocks on your left which border the snow slope. 2½ hours from the ruins. From the wide snow saddle an array of shapely peaks of the Dolra Range is seen to the south and to the east is the impressive triangle of the West face of Nakra Peak (4,277m) with Donguzorun Peak behind it.

There may be a bergschrund straight under the saddle, so descend (roped up) a short snow slope of 25-30° in a slanting traverse, down and to the right. When on the glacier (Bezymyaniy) go north along the right side of the upper basin, leave an ice-fall to your left and immediately before another one, at the end of the glacier, turn to the right and come to the right bank moraine. There is a campsite there [in the pocket behind the moraine (3,100m)] and a path going down. 2 hours from the saddle. In one more hour the path will bring you to a war memorial on the floor of the head of the Nenskra Valley (2,700m) with a campsite nearby. From there follow the path over the screes and rubble of the Nenskra's left bank, cross by stepping stones the stream flowing from under the Bezymyaniy glacier and in 1 hour you reach the place where the river is squeezed between an old moraine on the left and the mountainside on the right. (An avalanche snow bridge which holds till late in the season can be used to get to the right bank with a path on it leading to the Chiperkarachai Pass.) Lower down the floor of the valley levels and screes give way to alpine meadows. For half an hour the path goes over the river, (on the left bank) through moraine hills, then descends to meadows with clear streams and good campsites. Total time is 6½-7 hours.

Right opposite, on Nenskra's right bank, on a green slope between two streams, the zig-zags of a path, heading west to the Chiperkarachai Pass (Route 6) are visible. 500-600m down the left bank, above birch brushwood, on the left bank of a side stream there is another path climbing to the Bassa Pass (Route 6). It diverges from the main one in the valley at the mouth of the steam and the place is marked with a cairn. (If walking down the main path, you come to big blocks scattered on the floor and above them black rock with many thin waterfalls, it means you have passed the cairn and have to return.)

1½km down the valley there is a bridge to a former kosh site on the right bank, but the main path goes on by the left one, through low birch and beech bushes. From the bridge it is 38km to Chubery Village, the first one with some chance for transport. The bridge is a very dubious affair, it depends entirely on the water-level in the river, but 2km upstream, opposite the path to the Chiperkarachai pass there is an avalanche snow bridge, surviving usually till late August. 10km down from the wooden bridge there is another one - to the path on the left bank of the Dalar River. 6km down from the Dalar's mouth a bridge takes the path to the right bank but soon it returns back to the left one. The first village (a very small one) where a road begins, practicable for vehicles, is on the left bank, 14km from the Dalar's mouth.

There are no accommodation and rescue services in the valley and the first post office is as far down as Khaishi, 10km from Chubery. Some foodstuffs (bread, cheese, meat) can be bought at koshes and villages.

ROUTE 10: From the Baksan through the Azau Gorge, via the Chiperazau Pass (1A, 3,260m) to the Nenskra Valley. *(See maps 1, 9 & 12)*

An easy 2 days' walk, which does not demand any climbing experience and equipment. Rather a large but almost level glacier, without crevasses, on the northern side of the pass and screes with patches of snow on the southern one. The views from the pass are not spectacular but the Azau gorge offers very interesting volcanic scenery. And Mt Elbrus is always there, seen almost from every high point of the route.

Stage 1. From the lower station of the Elbrus cableway the "gates" of the Azau gorge are seen to the west. Follow the path on the left bank of the Azau

River going through moraine debris and in places very close to the black overhanging wall to the right. Watch for rock fall there, especially when it rains. The gorge itself is not too long - 400-500m. Then the valley widens and the path turns gradually to the right to reach in 1½ hours the snout of the Greater Azau glacier, covered by moraine. To get to its easy part the path climbs (along its left side) rather steep eroded slopes adjacent to the body of the glacier. Keep on the alert for stone fall. Cross the glacier, finding the way among moraine hills, slightly gaining height and aiming at the right edge of the steep-looking rocks on the glacier's right bank. The path to the campsite runs to the left, above them. 500-600m higher up on the right a huge ice-fall begins, rising to the Khotyutau snowfield, at the foot of Mt Elbrus. The path climbs the high right moraine of the glacier to reach a large and very popular (so, much littered) campsite, called the Sandy Hotel, which is behind the moraine, on the left bank of the Azau stream, running from the head of the valley. There is another campsite right under the Chiperazau glacier which can offer a better position for the next day. To get there follow the path on the left bank for 30-40 minutes and cross the stream to its right bank under the snout of the glacier. 3½-4 hours from the cablecar station.

Stage 2. From the campsite go south and climb gentle scree and snow leading to the glacier. The wide rocky saddle with the small pyramid of a war memorial is seen from afar on the south-west. The glacier is safe, without any crevasses, so there is no need for rope. In mist keep to the ridge stretching from Chiperazau Peak (west of the saddle) north-east and go along it to the pass. There are many memorial tablets there to Soviet troops who were trying to capture the pass in the autumn of 1942. Mt Elbrus stands in all its majesty on the north and the upper reaches of the Nenskra Valley opens out on the south. 2-2½ hours from the campsite.

From the saddle the path makes a descending traverse to the middle of the scree ridge, forming the left side of the upper cirque under the pass and from there runs down a steep slope straight to the floor of the valley covered by spring avalanches snow. 1½ hours. Walk over that snow to the right bank moraine of the Bezymyaniy glacier. There is a war memorial at the lower end of the moraine and a campsite near it. 30-40 minutes. Total time is 4½-5 hours. For the way down the Nenskra Valley see Route 9.

ROUTE 11: From the Head of the Baksan to the Upper Reaches of the Ullukam Valley via the Azau Pass (1A, 3,260m, between Chiperazau (3,840m) and Azau (3,688m) Peaks, at the Head of the Azau Gorge). *(See maps 1, 9 & 12)*

The Azau Pass is considered to be easier than the Khotyutau (1B, Route 17), connecting the same valleys but on the whole the walk through the Azau Gorge is more strenuous and circuitous. Technically the snow descent on the western side of the Azau Pass (100m, 25-30°) may be more difficult for the moderate walker than the crossing of the broken lower part of the Greater Azau glacier on the eastern side of the route via the Khotyutau Pass. That part does look serious but in fact it is fairly innocent. All the crevasses can be jumped over easily. Still, for those not keen on long glacier travel the route via the Azau Pass remains the only one from Baksan to Ullukam. And besides, the Azau Gorge with its high overhanging wall made of black volcanic hexahedral pillars and the huge icefall of the Greater Azau glacier, forcing its way through a narrow rock gate, is well worth seeing. The route takes 2 days and together with the Khotyutau Pass can make an easy 3 days' walk rich in views of Mt Elbrus, including stunning close-ups from the Khotyutau snowfield. The route is rather popular with Soviet walkers and most of them make it without any equipment: not for the sake of the idea of "clean" walking, they just cannot get it. Nonetheless, the authors have never heard of any accidents there. In theory a rope may be needed on the western side, so take it if you can use it, especially if there are some novices in your team.

For **Stage 1,** from the head of the Baksan to the Sandy Hotel campsite see Route 10.

Stage 2. Take the path on the left bank of the Azau stream flowing from the small glacier seen on the west above the step of glacial slabs. (There is a similar looking hanging upper basin to north-west, higher than that of the Azau Pass. Do not mistake it for the right one.) Follow the stream and in 2 hours it will bring you under the step. Turn right and climb screes and snow patches to the ridge bordering the small glacier on the north. The gully between the ridge and the glacier, turning to the left, leads eventually to the upper field of the latter, with the pass in sight, 200m away, to the south-west on the ridge bristling with rock spires. $3^{1}/_{2}$ hours from the Sandy Hotel. There may be one or two narrow crevasses, so keep to the ridge on your right. Anyway, the pass is so popular that normally there is a track in the snow, and if you are there early enough, that is before 10.00am, the danger is purely nominal. 3¹⁄₂-4 hours from the Sandy Hotel.

Descend, traversing to the right, a snow slope (100m, 25-30°) to the upper scree and snow cirque. Find a path there and walk straight down, skirting a glacier, to the floor of the valley with plenty of good sites for tents (2,700m). 1¹⁄₂ hours from the saddle. Follow the path on the right bank of the Ulluozen stream (the first left tributary of the Ullukam River) which in 1¹⁄₂ hours brings you to a kosh at the confluence of the two, on the left bank of the latter. Grassy campsite. Total time is 6¹⁄₂-7 hours.

If you are going to the Khotyutau Pass take the path winding in long and steep sweeps on the left side of the Ullukam Gorge. If you are going down, cross the Ullukam River by a footbridge to its right bank and walk down over meadows (swampy in places) to a small summer farm village called Voroshilov Kosh (2,200m). 40 minutes. The long, spacious and green Ullukam Valley opens out to the north-west. The first village, Khurzuk, is 23km downstream on a rough track. The Kosh is rather busy, so there is a chance to get a lift with a truck.

ROUTE 12: From the Sandy Hotel Campsite to the Khotyutau Snowfield via the Ekho Voyny (Echo of War) Pass (1A, 3,350m, on the Ridge going East from Azau Peak and forming the Right Side of the Rock Gates of the Greater Azau Glacier's Ice-fall). *(See maps 1, 9 & 12)*

The route is just a clever shortcut from the Azau Gorge to the Khotyutau Pass (Route 17) and may be very helpful when crossing the Khotyutau snowfield from the pass to the middle cableway station in poor visibility. Instead of nerve and brain racking attempts at route-finding in mist on the vast field, just turn to the right immediately after the saddle and walk in a wide loop, first south, then south-east, and north-east in the end, along the low, eroded ridge, bordering the southern part of the field. Do not lose much height, and in 1¹⁄₂ hours you inevitably come to the saddle of the Ekho Voyny Pass, which is level with the snow of the field (and there will be a tiny tarn under it). Descend from the saddle to the south-east by snow (30°, 50m), then take a path on the left bank of a stream in a steep gully. On reaching a grassy terrace with many outcrops of glacier smoothed rocks and quiet brooks (30-40 minutes from the saddle) turn to the right, cross the stream and descend south-east over the same mixed terrain.

Leave to your left some rock bluffs which are closer to the right bank moraine of the Greater Azau glacier and to the right there will be fairly

*steep grass slopes. When on the path going along the left bank of the Azau
stream turn to the left and in 10 minutes it brings you to the Sandy Hotel
campsite. 1¹/₂ hours from the saddle. Time from the Khotyutau Pass is 3
hours.*

Stage 1. Going in the opposite direction, walk from the campsite for 15-20
minutes, turn to the right and go up grass slopes, avoiding the steeper ones
on the left. The pass is 500-600m to the left of a minor rock peak which is
directly above the ice-fall of the Greater Azau glacier. The peak is clearly
seen from everywhere, so it is rather difficult to miss the pass. From the
green terrace with streams and outcrops turn left into the steep gully with
a stream and a path on its left bank, leading to the saddle. 2¹/₂-3 hours from
the Sandy Hotel.

**ROUTE 13: From the Baksan to the Head of the Malka Valley
(North of Mt Elbrus), via the Syltran (1A, 3,050m, at the Head of the
Syltransu Valley), Kyrtykaush (1A, 3,242m, on the North-East Ridge
of Islamchat Peak (3,680m) and North Karakaya (0 Grade, 2,880m,
on the North Ridge of Karakaya Peak 3,350m).** *(See map 10)*

*This easy trekking route is a variation of part of the Elbrus circuit. It is the
crown of all the walks in the Elbrus Area, excelling them many times in the
unbelievable scenery of the fantastic world of a gigantic extinct volcano.
The four variations are routes to the head of the Malka Valley from the
Baksan, with the rest of the circuit common to all of them: the Balkbashi
Pass, north-west of Mt Elbrus, and Khotyutau Pass to south. The route has
another considerable attraction of its own: the highest (2,950m) and
largest (30sq.km) lake in the Elbrus area, Syltrankel, set grandly in an
amphitheatre of snowy mountains. The trek takes 4 days; no climbing
equipment is needed.*

*Besides being a part of Elbrus circuit the route, linked with other
routes, or their parts, can make small circuits from Baksan to Baksan.*

Stage 1. Two side valleys, Syltransu and Kyrtyk, joins the Baksan at upper
Baksan Village, 23km downstream from the town of Terskol and 17km
upstream from the town of Tyrnyauz. There is a roadbridge to the left bank
of the Baksan River, where, at the foot of the left mountainside the village
is situated. At its western end the long sweeps of a rough track going into

73

the Syltransu Valley begin. Take that track, turning soon into a path, climbing in pine woods over a canyon, on the right bank of the river. It takes two hours to get to the tree line. There is a kosh on the meadow of the left bank and a good campsite on the right one. The wide bridle path ends here. Follow a narrow footpath on the right bank, to reach in 1 ½ hours a high step across the valley. The path rises steeply to its top, from where the head of the valley is seen with another rock step ahead. Syltrankel lake is higher up, behind it. To get there climb a scree slope either on the right or left side of the step. The sight of the large lake with ice-floes and high peaks around is a good reward for 6 hours' walk. There is enough place for tents on the northern bank.

Stage 2. The wide saddle of the Syltran Pass is seen to north-west. A scree of 25° leads to it and the ascent takes 1 hour. The pass is an excellent vantage point, and a small peak (3,539m) to the right with easy scree slope, leading to it, is even better. The views from there encompass Mt Elbrus, its eastern ridges and all the Kyrtyk Valley.

A 30 minutes sliding descent by a loose scree of 30° brings you to a path on the left bank of the Mukal stream in the short, hanging Mukal Valley. Follow the path descending a step overgrown with grass and bushes, then shortly before the Mukal stream meets its left-hand valley neighbour, Mkyara, cross the former by stepping stones to the right bank and follow the Mkyara's right bank to its confluence with the Subashi (2,500m) which form the Kyrtyk River. 1 ½ hours from the pass. 1km down the Kyrtyk River there is a bridge which takes you to the left bank with a rough road on it. Follow the road 1km down to the mouth of the Ulluusenchi Stream, coming from the left. There is a kosh there, on its left bank. 4 hours from the lake.

Go to the north on the road, climbing a grass slope on the right bank of the Ulluusenchi River. 1 hour. Higher up (40 minutes walk) the river takes a large left tributary - the Guitcheusenchi stream, and the road turns right, going up its right bank. The walk on a path along the gently inclined Ulluusenchi Valley to the upper screes takes 2 hours, the valley turning gradually to north-west, then to west.

Follow the path, crossing the river to its left bank and climbing old moraine hills to the wide saddle of the pass seen to the north-west. The head of the valley with Islamchat Peak (3,680m) rising over it is in view on the west. The saddle is flat and large enough for many tents, there is water source and an inevitable war memorial. There is a view north-east to the vast green pastures of the upper reaches of the Islamchat Valley, and further to North Karakaya Peak (3,350m) with the low saddle of the next pass of the route, North Karakaya, on its northern ridge. Total time is 6 hours.

Stage 3. In 1 1/2 hours the path, going over the scree and grass terraces, takes you to the confluence of the two streams forming the Islamchat River, crosses the left one and goes close to the river in the narrow valley. Watch the left mountainside for the path climbing to the North Karakaya Pass over grassy slopes. It takes 20 minutes to get from the confluence to the point where it branches off. It rises north, meets a stream, turns west following its gully, then turns north again, crosses a grassy spur and from there heads for the saddle. 2-2 1/2 hours from the Islamachat River. In good weather the enormous white mass of Mt Elbrus spreading its glaciers like paws into the black and red fields of volcanic rock and debris and the enchanting green bowl of the head of the Malka River is an unforgettable sight.

The path descends along the left bank of the stream, flowing into the Karakayasu River, then crosses it, turns to the right, passes above a long rock step and meets in the end, near a small farm, the track coming from the Beresun Pass, which is on the same ridge as the North Karakaya but 4km further to north. The track takes you to a suitable campsite (there are plenty of them) on the bank of the Karakayasu River (a right tributary of the Malka River). 2,400m, 2 hours from the North Karakaya Pass, total time is 6-6 1/2 hours.

This particular part of the upper reaches of the Malka River is well known in the North Caucasus for its warm (22°C) Narzan springs, called the Djilisu springs: powerful fountains welling into deep basins, specially made for taking baths which are believed to have good curative properties. Many ailing people come here in summer, pitch tents or use old hovels and stay for weeks, some for the whole season, during which the place is very busy. This does not in the least mean it is easy to get there from the nearest towns of Tyrnyauz (44km by a rough track) and Kislovodsk (a regular bus service to the Dolina Narzanov tourist base - 37km and 43km more of a track again). It should be noted that because of numerous farms and koshes along the Malka Valley the traffic there is fairly busy.

ROUTE 14: From the Head of the Malka Valley to the Baksan via the Irikchat Pass (1B, 3,643m, on the East Ridge of Chatkara Peak (3,898m). *(See map 10)*

The route involves much glacier travel, unroped though, and the northern side of the pass can be of some difficulty for a novice - snow of 25°, 100m long. Late in the season two or three crevasses may show on the lower part of the slope but it does not create route-finding or safety problems. Crampons may be useful when tackling that slope. The route takes 3 days. Mind that on some maps the Malka River at its source may have the name of Birdjalysu or Djilisu.

Stage 1: To get to Djilisu springs (see Route 13, Stage 4) from the campsite on the right bank of the Karakayasu River take the track coming from the Beresun Pass and follow it west, over bridges, to the left bank of the Malka River, to the place where its left tributary, the Kyzylsu River, forms a spectacular waterfall called Sultan. There are two ways to the campsite under the Irikchat Pass, on black screes near the Birdjalychiran glacier. The first one is a path on the right bank of the Malka River and the other one is along the path on the crest of an old lateral moraine, high over the river bed.

The second variant is much more scenic with the only disadvantage of being "dry", without any drinking water. Head due south, ascending the grass slopes of the right bank of the Malka River and take one of many narrow shepherds' paths which keep this direction. In 2 hours you come to an old moraine, which is a distinct border between the pastures and the area of jumbled, multicoloured volcanic rocks. Turn to the right and follow the path on its crest, over the Malka River. The lunar landscape of an extinct volcano unrolls around you, the higher you walk: green valleys between black basalt walls, red and yellow cliffs of crazy shapes. To the south-west is Mt Elbrus, ever present, enticing and menacing, and, looking back across the valley, green foothills go away into the blue haze of the faraway plains. In another 2 hours you come to vast fields of small black screes. There are many barely discernible paths here. Walk south in the direction of an isolated rock pyramid (Kalitsky Peak) jutting out right in the centre of a sweeping ice-field. There are many cosy small valleys and dry stream-beds for camping but with the next day in mind find a site closer to the Birdjalychiran glacier on black screes (there will be a glacier tarn to the left). 6 hours from the springs.

Stage 2. The largest snowfield in the Caucasus, Djikauguenkez, is indeed as long in any direction as its name. It takes $2^{1}/_{2}$-3 hours to cross it from the campsite to the foot of the Irickchat Pass. The field is flat, without any crevasses and the only danger (very real in the afternoon) is "snow swamps", that is layers of water under the snow. The only way to avoid this is to start early (6.00am). Head due south, go on to the glacier, leave Kalitsky Peak to your right and make for a gap on the low rock ridge

Mt Elbrus and Irikchat Valley from helicopter

descending to the east from the East summit of Mt Elbrus and barring the way to the south (Achkeryakol lava flow). To the left of the gap a yellowish low rock hill with a level upper crest is seen. There are two ways to the Irikchat Pass: either to the left of the hill, straight up a snow slope of 25°, or to its right up a gentle glacier of 15° with some crevasses (roping up is obligatory there) and then to the left on to the top of the hill. 3-3¹/₂ hours from the campsite.

There is a clear path on the small screes of the flat hill's top. It slants to the left, above the ice-fall of the Irikchat glacier on the other, southern side of the ridge and meets the path, zigzagging down from the left saddle. Further down it follows the left bank of the Irikchat River in the narrow valley to reach in 1¹/₂-2 hours small, grassy patches among big blocks of an old moraine. Camping. Total time is 5-5¹/₂ hours.

Stage 3. All the way down the Irikchat Valley to the Baksan the path is on the left bank. Steadily the green valley with sheep scattered on its sides broadens and turns to south-east. There is a steep grassy descent at the confluence of the Irik and Irikchat Rivers, which the path zigzags down. A good view opens out of the short Irik Valley with its graceful embankment-like long moraine and Mt Elbrus over its head. Soon after the confluence a grand view of the Main Range is afforded to south-east, across the far-away Baksan Valley. It stretches from west to east, displaying its host of summits, many of which are over 4,000m. Mt Ushba's two inimitable fangs (4,695m, 4,710m) catch the eye instantly. For an hour the path runs through the pleasant shade of the pine forest, then climbs against eroded bluffs. There is a Narzan spring there, 50m below. It is 30-40 minutes to get to Elbrus Village with its ugly cement blocks of flats. Cross the river, coming from a canyon, by a footbridge and walk to the bus station on the road in the Baksan Valley. Total time is 5 hours.

ROUTE 15: From the Baksan through the Kyrtyk Valley to the Ulluusenchi River, the Left Tributary of the Kyrtyk River. *(See map 10)*

The route is a day's valley walk, just a variation for the Route 13.

Take a rough road, going north on the left bank of the Kyrtyk River, which is far down in a narrow gorge. In 2-2½ hours you come to the first large left tributary, the Zugulla River. The valley expands and turns gradually west. The road goes over the river to avoid swampy meadows. In 1½ hours the valley gets narrow again and the road comes down to the river. There is a kosh on the right bank and a bridge to it. The yellow spur of Ullukaya Rock (2,856m), standing on the left bank and jutting out close to the river is noticeable from afar (another 1½ hours to reach it). There are the caves of prehistoric man inside the rock and some of them are accessible. The upper part of the Kyrtyk Valley spreads out west with the white cone of Mt Elbrus ahead. In 40-50 minutes you come to the mouth of Ulluusenchi River. Total time is 5½-6 hours.

For the next two stages to the head of the Malka River see Route 13, Stages 3 and 4.

ROUTE 16: From the Head of the Malka Valley to the Village of Khurzuk (the West Caucasus) via the Balkbashi Pass (1A, 3,690m). *(See map 9)*

A pure trekking route with a bridle path all the way, part of Elbrus circuit.

Takes 3 days. The feature of the route is two river wadings, not dangerous but cold.

Stage 1. From Djilisu mineral springs (see Route 14, Stage 1) which are on the left bank of the Malka River, at the point where it takes its left tributary, the Kyzylsu River with a 20m high waterfal, cross the Kyzylsu by a bridge and take a path climbing steeply north-west up the left side of the Kyzylsu's canyon. Soon it meets a jeep track, going west along the left bank. In 40 minutes you pass a kosh to the right and in 1 hour more there are another two koshes, on both banks. Wade the river to the right one. In the morning it is not a big problem, just a 3-4 metres wide shallow stream, though fast and cold. Once on the other side head for a rough track going up rather a steep grassy incline in the westerly direction. Making for the track keep as far away as possible from the kosh - shepherds' dogs do not like strangers!

The Irakhitsyrt plateau (2,700-3,000m) over which the track goes to the west is quite a rare feature for the High Caucasus and a 3 hours walk over this immense airy roof offers superb views of Mt Elbrus. The Balkbashi Pass is clearly seen to the south-west, to the right of the border line separating the snowfields of Mt Elbrus from the screes of the long ridge stretching north and forming the edge of the "bowl" of the Malka Valley's head. In one more hour you come down again to the Kyzylsu River, flowing from the south-west there. There is a good campsite, shortly before the river, in a small grassy valley to the left of the track. 6 hours from the Djilisu springs.

Stage 2. In the morning wade the river (or find convenient stepping stones) to the left bank and make a slanting ascent of the old left-side moraine of the Ulluchiran glacier. On its crest turn to the left and follow the path going south-south-west through the screes of the mountainside, high above the glacier. Leave to your right a vast scree cirque. The view south shows the immense northern glaciers and snow fields of Mt Elbrus and the West Summit's ice-falls and rock buttresses. It takes 3 hours to reach the Balkbashi Pass, including a short scree ascent of 25° under the saddle. The pass brings into view a large part of the West Caucasus.

The path descends along a wide grassy ridge with some outcrops of decayed rock and with two minor valleys to the right and left. Lower down the path may be rather vague, so keep to the right, cross the stream running down the right valley and follow a path on the right side of the Bityuktube (Bityuktyubekol) Valley, to reach (2-2$^{1}/_{2}$ hours from the pass) a campsite on the right bank of the river. There is a spring of warm Narzan on the left bank and a kosh a short way downstream, on the right one.

Mt Elbrus from the Bityuktyube Valley

Stage 3. Follow down a jeep road on the right bank of the Bityuktyube River, past the kosh. Soon the river disappears in a deep gorge on the left. The V-shaped valley is lovely and looking back, for a long time you will have a sight of Mt Elbrus towering over the green wide cup of the valley. Further down it is wooded, with an abundance of berries and flowers. It takes 5-5½ hours to get to the age-old Karachai settlement - Khurzuk. There is a good campsite short of the village, on a meadow, 500m above the road.

ROUTE 17: From Khurzuk Village to the Baksan via the Khotyutau Pass (1B, 3,546m, on the Ridge connecting Mt Elbrus with the Main Range). *(See maps 1 & 9)*

The route which takes 2 days can be a part of the Elbrus circuit. The shortest, very popular and scenic way from the West Caucasus to the Baksan Valley, involves much glacier travelling. The main and only difficulty is on the eastern side of the pass - the crossing of the broken section of the Greater Azau glacier, where there are no real crevasses but simply glacial moats filled with snow. The route-finding can take some time but is always practicable. A rope should be taken, more for psychological purposes than for belaying. In bad weather (often early in the season) there may arise a real problem - how to find the way from the pass to that section. For the solution see Route 12. The village of Khurzuk, unspoiled by modern civilization, with its 12th-century watch-tower makes an interesting part of the route.

For the description of this route in the opposite direction, from the Baksan Valley to the head of the Ullukam Valley, see the Mt Elbrus Chapter, the ascent from the west, Stage 1. It only gives the eastern side, but the western one does not present a single difficulty in navigation.

Stage 1. Take the jeep road up the Ullukam Valley. After the first 9 level kilometres the road comes to a big left tributary valley in the south, Uzunkol, narrow and wooded. The mountainsides of the Ullukam Valley close in, the road goes deep into the pine forest and rises steeply up. The river can be heard far down in the canyon. The two walls of the latter at one point come so close to each other, that a big stone was enough to join them, thus making a natural bridge. Beyond the canyon the valley widens again and the road levels out. In 6 hours it brings you, through farms and over pastures, to a large even meadow with a small farm-hamlet, called Voroshilovsky Kosh, at the junction of three valleys - Ullukam, Ulluozen and East Kichkinekol. The residents of the hamlet are so used to travellers that a tiny woollen bazaar gathers very quickly. Go east along the path on the right bank of the Ullukam River, cross it by a bridge (there is a kosh at the confluence of the Ullukam and Ulluozen Rivers on the right bank of the latter) and camp on a meadow, among low shrubs, under the canyon, seen north-east, out of which the Ullukam River breaks forth. An insignificant white summit, seen in the same direction is Mt Elbrus.

Stage 2. Take the path which zigzags to the right of the canyon, rising to the hanging upper valley. It takes 2 hours to reach the first stream flowing into the Ullukam River from the right (looking up). There is a good place for camping on the right side of the stream (and two or three herds of black, menacing looking yaks). To north, at the head of the valley, the sheer red walls of Kyukyurtlyu Peak rise to 4,634m (an eye-catching sight at sunset) and it is merely a spur of merely the West Shoulder (4,900m) of Mt Elbrus! Cross the stream, turn to the right and follow the path on its right bank, leading to the wide saddle of the pass, seen to the east-south-south. The path goes over screes and boulders and disappears among large blocks under the saddle. $1^{1}/_{2}$ hours from the turn. A striking view of the South Face of Mt Elbrus is afforded from the pass - immense snowfields with ice-falls and low black ridges between them.

The Khotyutau snowfield, on the eastern side, lies flush with the saddle. Do not go south-east, in the direction of the lower part of the Greater Azau glacier, or you will have to cross the convex crevassed part of the snowfield near the saddle. Instead, from the pass descend to the left, into a snow depression and follow it until it brings you on to the open glacier. It takes 1 hour to cross the snowfield and to get to the narrow medial moraine, going south-east, right into the rock "gates" of the Greater Azau's huge ice-fall. Cross the moraine to the left (there are cairns on big blocks there) and then cross the glacier in an east to northerly direction, between two ice-falls. The best way to do it is as follows: go at right angles to the medial moraine, between two large crevasses, to the central lengthwise depression of the glacier, then turn to the right and follow it for 150-200m, before turning to the left and crossing the rough ice terrain to the left bank. 1 hour. There is a path there going in the general direction south-east over black screes, past a large glacial lake, skirting the snout of a glacier. It turns to the right and follows a dusty ridge to the second station of the Elbrus cableway called Stary Krugozor. Beware! If the path is lost, do not go to the right (south) in search of it: the abrupt walls of the Azau gorge fall there! Keep to the left, to the glaciers, until you see the cables of the cableway. The last section of the path is almost under them, a little to the right. 1 $^1/_2$ hours. The last cabin goes down at 3.00pm, but on foot it is only 30-40 minutes by the tractor road to the first station on the Azau Glade. And from there it is 3km of a metalled road to the town of Terskol, in the Baksan Valley. Total time is 7 hours.

ROUTE 18: From the Baksan to the Head of the Malka River through the Kyrtyk Valley via the Djikaukenguez Pass (N, 1B, 3,520m, in the North-Eastern Ridge of Chatkara Peak 3,898m). *(See map 10)*

A fairly easy 3 days' route, consisting mainly of a long valley walk and glacier travel: can be part of the Elbrus circuit. Involves the traversing of the largest ice-field in the Caucasus, the namesake of the pass, Djikaukenguez, with the technical part of the route on the western side of the pass - 100-120m of snow, 30°. The ice-field is flat, without crevasses and does not demand roping up, but in late August a bergschrund may appear on the western side of the pass and make a rope a very practical thing. All the way the route is dominated by Mt Elbrus and the crossing of the volcanic desert of its northern slopes is an unforgettable experience.

For **Stage 1** see Route 15, Stage 1.

Stage 2. From the campsite by the mouth of the Ulluusenchi follow the road on the Kyrtyk's left bank to the confluence of the Subashi and Mkyara Rivers (forming Kyrtyk). 1½ hours. Remain on the road on the left bank of Subashi and in 1 hour's time take a path branching off to the left to gain the top of the rock step of the valley, where its head opens out to the south-west with Chatkara Peak right ahead. On its northern ridge the saddle of the Djikauguenkez Pass can be seen. Further north there are another two saddles. In 1½ hours one more rock step across the valley is reached. Cross the river to the right bank and ascend a scree slope leading to the upper cirque. When there, walk west over gently inclined screes to the foot of Chatkara Peak and find a suitable campsite there. 5-5½ hours from the previous one.

Stage 3. Early start. Go to north-west by scree and snow slopes of 25° at the foot of Chatkara Peak to gain soon a featureless snowy depression going to the saddle of the pass, low, covered with scree. 1-1½ hours. Mt Elbrus and the white sea of the Djikauguenkez snowfield are the view from there. Bearing in mind the eventual bergschrund down there under the saddle, make a descending traverse to the right. The steepness, 30° at first, slackens 100m lower down. Once on the snowfield, head first a little north of west for Kalitsky Peak at the far end of the field. On nearing the central moraine, stretching from south to north, turn to the right and walk north, along the moraine leading to the snout of the Birdjalychiran glacier.

The flat field is notorious for its "snow swamps", layers of water under the snow. If you find yourselves there late in the day it may be quicker to make a long loop than to cut across the lowest central part. Keep to the moraine and come to the vast terrain of black volcanic screes. 2-2½ hours from the pass. Walk north over this until the head of the Malka River opens out on the left (one of its sources, to be exact, which is given a couple of other names on different maps - Birdjalysu and Djilisu). There is a path on its right bank but the other one, on the crest of the old right side moraine, far up above the valley, is much more interesting for its views and with many lovely spots for camping. The moraine makes a wide loop, turning to the right and where it comes to its end the path veers to the left into a minor grassy valley. The number of shepherds' paths there may be confusing, but keep walking north along the stream in the valley and inevitably you will come to a rough track, going in the same direction. Soon it turns to the left and brings you again to the Malka River, with warm Narzan springs, called Djilisu, on its left bank. For details see Route 13. 2½-3 hours from the snout of the glacier. Total time is 6-7 hours.

Chegem and Bezengi Valleys

Going from west to east, the second major northern valley, next to Baksan, is the Chegem which has many attractions along its length, the main one being the upper reaches of the Garaauzsu River, the right source of the Chegem River. On the west the valley is bordered by the Adyrsu range with the Kilar Pass (Route 1), leading to the Baksan Valley; on the south by the Main Range with the Tviber Pass (Route 22) leading to Upper Svanetia and on the east by the Kargashil range with the Rakit Pass (Route 23) to the Bezengi Valley.

There is a regular bus service along the valley between Nalchik and Bulungu (2½-hour bus drive, 4 runs a day), the last village in the upper reaches with a post office (telegraph and telephone). (Another one is 6km downstream in Verkhny Chegem Village.) A jeep road goes 6km up from Bulungu and divides at the confluence of the Garaauzsu and Bashilauzsu Rivers. The left track runs up the former, to the Chegem tourist base (2,200m), the right one leads through the latter, to the Bashil tourist base (2,050m), both are 13km from Bulungu. The accommodation is very basic: wooden summer cabins with a common toilet and shower. You can get to the bases by a chance truck, or try to hire one at Bulungu or Verkhniy Chegem. The Chegem base can probably claim to have around it the most spectacular high mountain scenery in the whole Central Caucasus, with the Main Range rising here to a height of 4,614m at majestic Tikhtengen Peak.

In its midstream, 55km from Nalchik, the Chegem River cuts through the Skalisty Range in an impressive canyon 5km long and at one particular place just 20m wide, with overhanging walls 300-400m high. The long exquisite veils of the Chegem waterfalls draw many visitors to the area. Above Verkhny Chegem Village, there is a group of sepulchres of 15-17th centuries giving the place a really ancient and somewhat weird look. Quite close to it, on the left bank of the Djilisu River (flowing into the Chegem River), there is another amazing relic - a staircase of 4-8th century cut in a sheer rock face and apparently leading nowhere!

The upper reaches of the Garaauzsu and Bashilauzsu Rivers are the territory of the Kabardino-Balkaria national nature reserve. The border and a guards' cordon is 6km up from Bulungu at their confluence. Unfortunately you cannot "book" a permit for travelling there but have to present yourself in person at the office in the town of Sovetskoye in the Cherek Valley (1 hour drive from Nalchik). And it is highly likely that the authority will seize an opportunity and charge for the slip of paper in hard currency.

Practically speaking a rescue service does not exist in the valley. There is a nominal head of "checking and rescue service" at each base but he is so undermanned and under-equipped, that any operation demanding both will inevitably take a lot of time.

Another northern valley next to the Chegem is the Bezengi. Its river, Cherek Bezengi, together with Cherek Balkar, which is further east, forms the Cherek River, almost equal in its length and volume to the Baksan and Chegem. The valley, arid, only lightly wooded in its upper parts, is gorge-narrow for 20km down from Bezengi Village. The 9km of chaotic moraines from the Bezengi glacier at its head, form a long and austere way to the most dramatic alpine scenery in the whole Caucasus. As a headwall it has one of the three Caucasian wonders - the Bezengi Wall, a monumental mountain barrier 12km long without any considerable depressions and rising above the glacier for nearly 2km. (The other two wonders are Mt Elbrus and Mt Ushba.) The largest (36.2sq.km) and longest (17.6km) glacier is there, and five out of seven summits over 5,000m are concentrated in the area.

The only easy route connecting the valley with its western neighbour, Chegem, is via the Rakit and Koru Passes (Route 23). All the other passes on the Kargashil Range, separating the valleys, demand good climbing skills and equipment. The second and the last, relatively easy way out of the area is to Upper Svanetia, over two high passes, across the vast upper fields of three large glaciers (Route 25). But just to visit the place and climb one or two vantage points near the Wall is well worth time and effort (Route 26).

There is a regular bus service between Nalchik and Bezengi Village, the last one up in the valley. But it is rather erratic, so, if you have come to Nalchik in the morning, the best thing to do is to take any bus going via the town of Babughent (1½-hour drive) at the confluence of the two Chereks and from there get a lift with some truck to Bezengi Village (25km). And there always remains a possibility of hiring a taxi at Nalchik. One thing to remember: the traffic is fairly scanty, so, when going from the mountains back to Nalchik try to get to Bezengi Village before lunchtime, otherwise you risk being stuck there and having to camp beside the road.

There is a rough track, 18km long, going from the village up the treeless left side of the valley to the Bezengi mountaineering base, which is on the right side, behind the high old moraine, near the snout of the Bezengi glacier. For many years it was listed among "the international mountaineering bases", therefore accommodation and rescue service are quite good there.

There are two huts in the area. The lowest one is the Misseskosh hut, a simple cabin, sleeping 10-12 persons, on the right bank of the Bezengi glacier, between the moraine and mountainside, 4km from the mountaineering base. The old path connecting them, high above the glacier, has been badly eroded during the last decade and fallen into disuse. A new path breaks to the right immediately after the bridge leading to the base, and goes on the right bank of the river, then along the right side of the glacier, close to the steep moraine slopes. These are rather dangerous in heavy rain, so, going up in rainy weather, turn right as early as practicable to the centre of the glacier, covered by moraine hills. The hut is not visible from anywhere on the glacier but after $1^{1}/_{2}$ hours' walk on the path you come to a section of broken ice right ahead where normally climbers turn right to the centre of the glacier. To the left a steep narrow gully, cut by water in a slope of packed earth, with a large boulder in its middle, is seen. A discernible path leads into it, giving 15-20 minutes climb to the hut. The cabin is placed high over the dark-grey chaotic moraines of the glacier, on a large alpine meadow (2,500m). A small climbers' cemetery adds to its aloofness and solitude. It is much more difficult to find the hut when going down. Walking along the centre, keep an eye on the right side and, having passed on your right the last minor ice-fall, find an easy way to the side moraine. That has to be the place described above.

The way to the Djangi Hut (3,100m), which is at the foot of Dykhtau Peak (5,200m), is detailed in the Route 26 description.

This area is a domain of the reserve as well. But to get a permit you will not have to make a long special trip to Sovetskoye, for fortunately the town is just 6km from Babughent, down the Cherek Valley.

ROUTE 19: From the Bashil Tourist Base in the Bashilauzsu Valley, to the Lekzyr Glacier, over the Main Range, via the Bashilauz Pass (2A, 3,490m, between Sarykol (4,088m) and Karakaya (3,806m) Peaks). *(See maps 12, 13 & 14)*

The pass is the easiest one between these areas and the route may be interesting for those who love glacial scenery (the upper basins of the

Lekzyr glacier offer much of this) and need some reasonable technical difficulty to get a satisfying sense of achievement. The most demanding part is on the northern side of the saddle - 130-150m of a snow ascent, 40-45°, without any bergschrunds underneath. The full set of equipment is needed. The northern part of the route is on the territory of the nature reserve. When on the Lekzyr glacier there are two variants to take: either to turn west and find the path from the Mestiysky Pass (Route 2) leading to Mestia (two days the whole route), or to turn south-east and cross the Bashil Pass (Route 20) to the Tviber glacier and from there to the Bezengi area, 4 days.

Stage 1. At the southern skirts of the Bashil base take an old track on the right bank of the Bashilauzsu River. In 30 minutes it brings you to a stream, which has cut a deep gully in the mountainside on the left. Lower down it ramifies and can be easily crossed. Further up ignore a bridge to the left bank and follow the track, which soon narrows into a path. In 30 minutes the latter comes to a rock step across the valley with a cluster of pine trees on top of it. The river roars in a canyon and the path climbs above it through alpine meadows. In 1 hour it comes to the moraines of the right flank of the valley with many tent sites there (2,200m).

From the campsite go west through moraine hills, come on to the Bashil glacier and cross it in the same direction, aiming at the stream which issues from the North and West Bashil glaciers and comes to the body of the main Bashil glacier at right angles. Climb along the left bank of the stream, cross it where practicable and go west, leaving to the left the snout of the West Bashil glacier seen above a band of rocks. There is a tarn in the corner between the left moraine of the West Bashil and the right one of the North Bashil glaciers with a good campsite on its banks (3,100m). 6 hours from the base.

Stage 2. Go south-west and come on to the surface of the West Bashil glacier, almost flat in its middle part. Keep to its left side, avoiding the central crevassed section. Right ahead, to the south-west, a deep depression on the Main Range is seen with a big rock in the middle. From the campsite to the foot of the saddle, which is on the right side of the rock is 2 hours' walk. 1 more hour to climb the scree and snow slope, 130-150m, 40-45°. The saddle brings into view the vast upper fields of the Lekzyr glacier and the north walls of the Svetgar range.

Descend screes to a small tarn under the saddle. From there make a traverse to the left to reach the eastern saddle which was seen from the West Bashil glacier to the left of the big rock in the middle of the deep depression.

And from that saddle make a slanting traverse to the right (scree again) to a snow gully, leading down to the glacier. Keep to its right side, leave an ice-fall to your left and soon you reach the upper basin of the East Branch of the Lekzyr Glacier. 1 hour from the pass. To join the path going from the Mestiysky Pass, turn to the right, west, and walk to the corner of the big right side moraine, where it changes its direction from south to west. There is a campsite on the moraine, right at the corner. (For the way to Mestia see Route 2.)

ROUTE 20: From the Upper Basin of the Lekzyr Glacier to the Tviber Glacier via the Bashil Pass (1B, 3,460m, between Bashil (4,148m) and Tot (4,000m) Peaks). *(See maps 13 & 14)*

There is a lot of roped up glacier walking on the route but no really steep slopes (there is one, 100m, 25-30°) and the views of the Main Range from the pass are excellent: all the ridge bordering the Lekzyr on the north with a dozen peaks over 4,000m. Linked with the Mestiysky, Bashilauz, Lychat, Tviber, Semi and Upper Tsanner Passes, the Bashil Pass can make a central part of many exciting long distance walks in this heavily glaciated, austere and spectacular section of the Central Caucasus. The first crossing was done in 1888 by A.Mummery, so it is a classic Caucasian Pass. It takes one day and the full set of equipment. The northern part of the route is on the territory of the nature reserve.

Stage 1. An early start is a must for any long glacier walk and this is exactly what this route is. The eastern branch of the Lekzyr Glacier has in its turn three branches, taking their source in the snowfields of the Main Range. All of them have ice-falls, separated from each other by short ridges. The way from the upper Mestiysky campsite (at the corner of the right side moraine under the south face of Ullutau Peak [see Route 2]) to the Bashil Pass is a semi-circle at the foot of those ice-falls. Thus the huge crevasses in the central part of the plateau are left to your right. From the last ridge make a left hand loop to the east in the direction of the graceful pyramid of Bashil Peak (4,148m), then south-east and in the end almost south, to the wide and low saddle of the pass. 2 hours.

Having taken in all the views from this relatively low but strategically placed vantage point, descend south-east to the almost flat upper plateau. Turn steadily south and in 30-40 minutes there will be a snow descent of 25-30° to the lower field of the West Laskhedar Glacier. Go south, to the right side moraine, bordering an ice-fall, and descend a path on the moraine to reach the Dzynal Glacier. $2^{1}/_{2}$ hours from the saddle. At a pinch you can camp at the upper end of the left side moraine (1 hour from the saddle) and come down by that side as well but there are very steep grass slopes down there, dangerous when wet. So the right variant is preferable. Once on the Dzynal glacier (fairly rough terrain, partly open and dry, partly moraine covered), head for the left side moraine of the short body of the Tviber glacier. At the point where the moraine makes a sharp turn south-south-east there are several sandy tent sites (a little up to the east, on the northern side of the moraine). 3 hours from the Pass. For the way down see Route 22. $1^{1}/_{2}$-2 hours along the left bank of the glacier a comfortable campsite is reached, near the confluence of the Tviber and Kitlod Rivers.

ROUTE 21: From the Bashil Tourist Base in the Bashilauzsu Valley over the Main Range via the Lychat Pass (2A, 3,500m, between Bodorku (4,180m) and Lychat (3,900m) Peaks) to the Campsite on the South Side, between the Lychat and Dzynal Glaciers, called the Lychatsky Campsite. *(See maps 13 & 14)*

A moderate route by Soviet high level walkers' standards and, as a matter of fact, the easiest and shortest way between the base and the cluster of glaciers forming the eastern branch of the Tviber glacier. The technical part of the route is on the northern side of the pass. Short snow ascents up to 30°, and a bergschrund under the saddle, normally with good bridges. The south side is a steep scree and loose rock gully, 50m, and some snow of 25° leading to the glacier. All the rest is glacier travelling (with a reasonable number of crevasses) and scree walking. Bearing in mind crevasses and the bergschrund, the best time is the first half of the season. Full set of equipment. The route takes 2 days, with plenty of time on the second day to descend much lower than the Lychatsky campsite, if you go down to Upper Svanetia (Jabeshi Village, Route 22). If you return to the northern side of the Main Range via the Tviber Pass (Route 22) you should camp at the Lychatsky campsite. The northern part of the route is on the territory of the nature reserve.

Stage 1. For the way from the Bashil base to a campsite at 2,200m on the right side moraine of the Bashil glacier, see Route 19. From there take a path which climbs to the crest of the right moraine of the Bashil glacier and follow it. There will be a tiny turbid lake on the left and a large ravine, cut in the moraine by water, which you leave to your right, passing above it. Beyond the ravine the path traverses south-west to west, by screes and gentle glacial slabs, the valley's right flank. The rock bluffs hanging over the huge lower ice-fall are left to your right. At some spots the path is ill-defined but there is a chain of cairns linking its traceable sections and leading to the upper Bashil campsite (2,650m) at the lower end of the ridge running down from the south and bordering the glacier on the east. $3^{1}/2$ hours. The lower ice-fall is far down and the flat ice plateau between that and the upper one, almost level with the campsite, is to the right.

Stage 2. Rope up and walk on to the plateau, turn left (south), along the lower slopes of the bordering ridge. Where it begins to curve south-east continue to walk south, across the glacier, leaving the steep and heavily crevassed fields of snow-capped Bodorku Peak to your left and the short rock ridge, going north from Laskhedar Peak (which is 700-800m to the north-west from Lychat Peak on the Main Range) to your right.

Sometimes late in the season the right edge of the glacier under the bordering ridge turns into a rugged ice terrain and is impracticable for walkers. In this case on reaching that difficult spot, turn to the right (west) and skirt it at its foot. After that turn again south. From the campsite it is 2 hours to reach the foot of the snow ascent under the pass and another $1^{1}/2$ hours to mount its three consecutive rises (25-30°) with a few very impressive crevasses between them. The saddle itself is a long snow ridge with many rock spires sticking out of it and a bergschrund underneath bridged by snow. Take a minor saddle, the nearest to Lychat Peak. $3^{1}/2$ hours from the campsite.

Descent to the Lychat Glacier takes 40-50 minutes. First it is a scree and loose rock gully (45-50°) and after it divides (bear to the right there) - scree and snow lower slopes of Lychat Peak. When in the gully make sure there is no one beneath you: it is inevitable you will drop stones on them. The Lychatsky campsite (3,150m) is at the right end (looking down) of the long and high band of glacial slabs, dividing the Lychat and Dzynal Glaciers, near the lower end of the short south ridge of Lychat Peak. For the way down to Jabeshi Village see Route 22.

ROUTE 22: From the Chegem Tourist Base in the Garaauzsu Valley over the Main Range to the Town of Mestia via the Tviber Pass (1B, 3580m between Bodorku (4,180m) and Kulaktau (4,060m) Peaks). *(See maps 13 & 14)*

From time immemorial the pass, the easiest one in the whole area of the upper reaches of both the Chegem and Cherek Bezengi Rivers, was used by local people for driving cattle across the Main Range. And for many years there existed a trekking route over the pass, run by a State Tourist Organisation. There are two huts-refuges on both the northern and southern sides of the Pass, now derelict. The route does not involve any climbing, but there is much walking on dry glaciers and moraines. The eastern side of the pass is snowfields of 15-20°, the western one is a scree descent, 100-120m, 35°. Early in the morning it may be frozen, so there is no need to be in haste to get to the pass. Rope may be useful if you are late and have to cross the glaciers in the afternoon (it was never used by trek groups) but there is no need for ice-axe and crampons. The route enjoys really fine alpine scenery, especially at the head of the Garaauzsu Valley, with the dominating north walls of Tikhtengen Peak (4,614m). The northern part of the route is the territory of the nature reserve.

Stage 1. From the Chegem base take a tractor road on the right bank of the Garaauzsu River, cross by bridges two torrents, the Tyutyurgu and Shaurtu, and follow a path going south-west along the right bank of the Kulak River (or still Garaauzsu on some maps). The path climbs old moraines, overgrown with low, twisted and bent birches, comes to the end-moraines of the eastern tongue of the Kulak glacier (separated from the western one by a rock hill (3,000m) called Karatyube). Further up, the path disappears on large screes. Going south-west, cross the moraines, then the body of a dry glacier, descending from the left, and head for Karatyube hill. The hut is at its foot, and the side of a moraine, 50-70m high, leads to it from the glacier. 3-3¹/₂ hours. The building is in decay, with heaps of litter around, but there is much better option for camping. Two campsites are available higher up: on top of the hill and at the upper end of the high moraine seen to the left, with a path rising to the site. 30-40 minutes. Total time is 3¹/₂-4 hours.

Stage 2. Walk south-west over the Kulak glacier, dry here, along its longitudinal moraines. The glacier curves west and the upper basin opens out. The pass is to the north-west, in the right (looking up) corner of the cirque, to the right of a minor rock peak standing on the ridge which connects Kulaktau and Bodorku Peaks. Undulating snow of 15-25° leads to the saddle. Making for it, leave a moderate ice-fall to your left. In poor visibility a good guiding line is the colour of the rock under your feet. If you are on the right way it should be black, but if you try to deviate too much to the right on the slopes of Bodorku Peak, then it will change for yellowish limestone. 4 hours from the campsite to the pass.

The descent looks unpleasant. It is rather a steep scree slope (frozen in the morning) of 35°, 100-120m. Once down in the upper basin of the Lychat Glacier, go in a wide loop keeping close to the ridge which walls the basin. There are almost no crevasses there and if the snow is firm enough a rope is not needed. Head for the right bank moraine of the glacier. Where it comes to a high rock step barring the flow of the glacier (it goes down in a steep ice-fall far to the left) there are plenty of sites for tents. Lychatsky campsite (3,150m). 2 hours from the pass.

Stage 3. Follow south one of the paths falling down steep screes and glacial slabs and leading on to the Dzynal Glacier, dry there. Keep this direction until you reach the central longitudinal moraine. From there walk along it south-west making for the point where the left bank moraine changes its direction from south-west by west to south and becomes the moraine of the Tviber Glacier. Half a kilometre before the turn some sites for camping can be found. Turn south with the moraine and follow it to a comfortable grassy campsite on the left bank of the Tviber River, near its confluence with the Kitlod River (2,400m). 5 hours from the previous campsite.

Stage 4. In the morning you face the task of crossing the Tviber River. There are two options: the first one, rather exciting, is to use the remnants of the suspension bridge downstream from the campsite. Technically it is possible but belaying may be advisable, not to mention your boots and trousers getting wet through because of the cables being too low above the water. The second one is an avalanche snow bridge 300m upstream from the campsite.

The path on the right bank leads to a gorge called The Gates of Georgia and goes for 50-60m on a one metre wide ledge on the right wall of the gorge. A green V-shaped valley which opens out to south is the Tviber Valley. The path plunges into high and lush southern vegetation and, good and wide, runs down to the village of Jabeshi, all the way on the right bank (past the deserted southern hut-refuge). Nonetheless there are two or three unpleasant passages, 15-20m wide - across steep eroded earth slopes, demanding careful moving. 4 hours to the village. (A regular bus or (more likely) a passing truck to Mestia (1-1$\frac{1}{2}$ hours).)

ROUTE 23: From the Chegem Tourist Base in the Garaauzsu Valley to the Bezengi Mountaineering Base in the Bezengi Valley over the Kargashil Range, via the Koru Pass (1A, 3,650m, at the Head of the Charaksu Valley) and the Rakit Pass (1B, 3,500m, on the North Ridge of Kargashil Peak (3,900m). *(See map 14)*

The second pass is the only one available for the modest walker on the Kargashil Range, separating the Chegem and Bezengi Valleys, and very scenic at that. Two giants of the Bezengi area, Dykhtau (5,204m) and Koshtantau (5,150m) peaks and a part of the Bezengi Wall are seen from the saddle. The route takes 2 days and its hardest bit is the western side of the Rakit Pass - 70-80m of scree and snow of 25-30°. Well defined paths can be found in the valleys only, so the navigating demands some experience in mountain walking. The route is on the territory of the nature reserve.

Stage 1. Leave the base so as to be on the glacier early. Take the road down the valley and walk 2km to a large level meadow, with the Charaksu River beyond it, flowing into the Garaauzsu from the right. There is a high grassy old moraine with sparse pine trees, which comes down to the meadow from the Charaksu Valley (on its left bank). Climb to its crest, follow it up, then, without losing height, traverse to the left, to the river's bed. Where the valley's floor begins to level out cross the river by stepping stones and walk up over some grass terraces to a steep large scree which is the end moraine of the North-Koru Glacier.

At this point the valley changes its direction from south-east to south. Climb the moraine south, go on to the glacier, almost flat and without crevasses and keep walking, first still to south, then turning gradually to south-east, aiming at the saddle which is visible in the left (looking up) corner of the upper cirque. The saddle is a long and wide ridge of shale rock, level with the snow of the glacier. 6-6¹/₂ hours from the road. The Koru Pass brings you a view of half the Kargashil Range, with the highest Peak Djorashty-Kurshogan (4,280m) to the south. To get better views you can ascend the easy Koru Peak (3,710m) to the south-west, 40-50 minutes.

Descend small screes to south-east, bearing slightly to the right, to reach (in 20-25 minutes) a meadow with a stream and the ruins of a kosh (3,200m). Camp on the meadow.

Stage 2. Follow the path going down north-east over gentle grass and scree terrain and leave to your right the huge end-moraine of the northern branch of the South Bulungu Glacier. In 40 minutes you come to the confluence of the two streams coming from the North and South Bulungu Glaciers and forming the Bulungu River (2,900m, a campsite). From there go east and climb the western grass and scree slope, leading to a saddle seen on the left (looking up) side of a minor peak. The latter rises on the West Ridge of Kargashil Peak (1km from it), at the point where the ridge turns sharply to north. So, the way is over the northern part, close to the minor peak, then along the western one to the Rakit Pass, which is north-east of Kargashil Peak. The first saddle (3,300m, 2 hours from the confluence) brings you into sight of the Rakit Pass, seen to the east. Walk there without losing much height across the upper cirque, over screes and a glacier covered with snow. The last rise is 70-80m, 30°. 4 hours from the campsite. Over the vast Bezengi Valley with its grey extensive glacier far down, the mass of Dykhtau Peak (5,204m) dominates the view south and part of the Bezengi Wall is visible to its right. For a better view there is an easy scramble (40-50 minutes) to the top of Kargahil Peak (3,910m), south-west of the saddle.

There is a broken rock in the middle of the saddle. Start to descend from the right side of the rock into a scree gully and come to a wide cirque. Find the stream whose source is in the lower part of the cirque and follow its bed. There are four short waterfalls along its course which have to be bypassed. The first one is skirted on the left by a well-defined goat path; the second on the right, by descending into a short grassy ravine, which leads again to the stream; the third on the left, and the last one on the right, by climbing on to the ridge and rounding a protruding rock on it. Further down descend fairly steep grass slopes to the road in the valley (2,000m). 2¹/₂-3 hours from the saddle. One more hour to the Bezengi mountaineering base on the right bank, behind the right side old moraine. Total time is 7¹/₂-8 hours.

ROUTE 24: From the Chegem Tourist Base via the Zeleniy Pass (1A, 3,600m, at the Head of the Ullukurchkhu Valley) and back to the Base. *(See map 14)*

An interesting 2 days' circuit from the Chegem base with a pass, which is an excellent vantage point. The route is a pure trekking walk without any technical spots but the path is not everywhere as good as it should be on a trek. All the route is on the territory of the nature reserve.

Stage 1. Behind the two-storey building of the base take a path going south-east, on the right bank of the Ullukurchkhu River. After a short level section it rises steeply into the gorge, through tumbled rocks and bushes, then leaves the canyon far down to the right and in 1½ hours brings you to a flat green terrace, with a superb view back of the north face of Tikhtengen Peak (4,614m). Follow the path, rather faint in places, to another grassy ascent leading to another terrace. 1½ hours. There the path goes down to the river and leads to the third ascent and the third, swampy, terrace, higher up, barred by an old terminal moraine. The valley curves east here. Climb the gully between the right mountainside and the moraine to reach the fourth (and last) terrace, covered with moraine rubble. 1 hour. The West Koru Glacier leading to the pass (not seen yet) opens south-east. The clear saddle straight ahead (east) is a pass to Bulungu Valley. Camp on the terrace (3,400m). Total time is 4-4½ hours.

Stage 2. Go by the crest of the right side moraine of the West Koru Glacier and, having passed the snout, move on to the surface (snow of 20°). Leave to your right a deep crater with a small lake in it and head for the wide low saddle seen in the south. 1½-2 hours. The views from the pass are among the best in the area, so an easy scramble of the peak on the left is well worth 1 hour's time.

Come down into a wide scree gully, which turns gradually from south to south-west. In 40 minutes it brings you to a place on the floor of the valley, known as the Upper Tyutyurgu campsite (3,200m). Take a path, going from there north-west by west, along a deep stream bed (looking more like a canyon) and dropping down a steep scree of 35° on the right bank of the stream. Further down the path eases and gets vague on blocks and boulders but the direction is the same. In 40-50 minutes you come to the lower Tyutyurgu campsite on an old grassy moraine (2,900m).

The path runs down from the moraine to the floor of the valley, to reach in 40 minutes its mouth-step, which is a 250-300m grassy slant of 30-35° on the right side of the canyon of the Tyutyurgu River. 40-50 minutes after the mouth-step the path turns north and goes for half a kilometre in a pocket between the right side moraine of the Shaurtu Glacier and the mountainside. Then there follows a short ascent and a much longer descent to the pebbly floor of the Shaurtu Valley, where the path joins the other one going along the Kulak River. 1½ hours to the base. Total time is 6-6½ hours.

ROUTE 25: From the Town of Mestia to the Bezengi Mountaineering Base over the Main Range via the Semi and Upper Tsanner Passes (the first one is 2A, 3,850m, on the Nashkodra Range, close to Tikhtengen Peak; the second - 2A, 3,990m, on the Main Range, on the South-West Ridge of Ortokara Peak (4,250m)). *(See maps 13, 14 & 15)*

This 5 days' route is the only easy walk in the close vicinity of the Bezengi Wall. Two high snow passes and the upper basins of three large glaciers are crossed for almost two full days of glacier travelling in the highest and wildest part of the Caucasus. The only technical problem is 5-6m of steep (40-45°) snow on the eastern side of the Upper Tsanner Pass, with a bergschrund underneath late in the season. So, if you are not ready for this do not plan the route for August. You will need a full set of equipment, and rope is a must. The northern part of the route is in the territory of the nature reserve.

Stage 1. Take a bus or get a lift from Mestia to Jabeshi Village 1-1½ hours. The Tviber Valley comes to the village from the north. Cross the Mulkhra River to its right bank by a bridge and take the path on the right bank of the Tviber River. In 5-5½ hours it will bring you to the derelict hut-refuge at the tree line. To be in a better position for the next day walk for a further 1-1½ hours to get to the campsite at the confluence of the Tviber and Kitlod Rivers, on the left bank of the former, 300-400m up from the remnants of the suspension bridge (see Route 22).

Stage 2. Follow the path on the right bank of the Kitlod River to the snout of the Kitlod Glacier, come on to it (it is covered with black schist there) and walk up, keeping closer to the right bank. There are two big ice-falls higher up. Half-way between the snout and the first ice-fall (there are glacier smoothed bluffs, jutting out of the moraine screes of the right bank and bordering the ice-fall) turn to the left 300-400m below the bluffs and take the path along a stream coming down to the glacier at right angles. The path rises steeply up its bed, turns to the right and leads to a campsite on top of the bluffs. From there follow a path over moraine rubble along the right bank and come out to the level part of the glacier between the ice-falls. And again half-way, immediately before the difficult crevassed area begins under the upper ice-fall, turn to the left and follow the path up a steep ravine in the left-hand mountainside. The path goes to the right, above the glacier, through the vast picturesque fields of black schist and comes to numerous tent sites on the bluffs over the second ice-fall, the Upper Kitlod campsite (3,300m). 5½-6 hours from the previous campsite, 7-8 hours from the southern hut-refuge.

Stage 3. Early start. Head north-east to the Main Range. The way to the Semi Pass is a wide loop to north-east, east and south-east, along the Main Range. Even in poor visibility the route-finding is not a big problem. The glacier is crevassed but not too heavily. A short snow ascent of 25° leads to the pass, which is under the towering spurs of Tikhtengen Peak, at the very beginning of the Nashkodra Range. A breathtaking view of the Bezengi Wall's rear is afforded from the saddle with the graceful snow pyramids of Gestola (4,860m) and Tetnuld (4,974m) Peaks. Mt Elbrus and Mt Ushba are seen to the west and the high snow saddle of the Upper Tsanner Pass is straight ahead to the east, with a sea of snowfields between the two passes.

Descend north-east the snow of 25°. Once on the upper basin of the Tsanner Glacier turn gradually east and walk along the Main Range to a rock spur jutting out into the basin at its middle. 4½-5 hours from the

The Bezengi Wall from Barankosh

campsite. If you do not plan to make both the Semi and Tsanner Passes in one day, camp here on snow or use two or three sites on the small scree at the foot of the spur. But if you do want to make it, bear in mind that besides being a very long day's walk (up to 10 hours), the condition of the snow on the crevassed glacier beyond the Upper Tsanner Pass will be very bad in the afternoon, which turns simple glacier travelling into a very unpleasant, even nerve racking experience.

Stage 4. Early start. Walk east along the Main Range, not too far from it, across the upper snowfields of the Tsanner Glacier to the low saddle of the Upper Tsanner Pass under Ortokara Peak. An undulating snow slope of 20-25° leads to the pass. The eastern side looks steep. It is a short (5-6m) snow pitch of 40-45°, with an eventual bergschrund underneath which, late in the season, can be a problem. If it is filled, then the problem is purely psychological, because the slope under it curves lower down into a gently inclined basin. The reward for being ready to tackle this toy-pitch is a Himalayan-like view of the Bezengi Wall's front and the enormous bulk of Dykhtau Peak (5,204m), soaring up right opposite, across the valley.

Dykhtau Peak from the Kel Pass

The central part of the Ortokara Glacier on the eastern side of the pass is heavily crevassed. So, going down, make once again a loop under the ridge walling the basin - to the north-east, east, and finally south-east. Before the glacier falls steeply to the south-east turn to the left on to a saddle on the ridge of red scree and decayed rock, bordering the glacier on the east. It is the Kel Pass (3,600m). 5 hours from the campsite on the Tsanner Glacier. You can camp here and relish the views from this high viewpoint, or 40-50 minutes of fast and exhilarating striding down the red schist will take you to a large green meadow with a tarn (and the white Wall mirrored in it). It lies between the mountainside and the left bank moraine of the Bezengi Glacier, at a place called Barankosh. A nice quiet place to spend a rest-day. Total time is 5½-6 hours.

It takes 3½-4 hours to get to the Bezengi mountaineering base. Take a path climbing to the crest of the moraine and then where practicable come down to the glacier and walk along its centre through the moraine hills. Lower down keep closer to the right side and watch out for a minor ice-fall (about two thirds of the glacier's length from the Barankosh). Skirt its lower end to the right bank and find a path going up a steep gully in the moraine side (with a large boulder in the middle). The path leads to the lower one of the two huts in the Bezengi area ("Misseskosh"). If you do not need it follow the path going down under the steep eroded moraine sides. When it rains this way may be dangerous through landslides and then it is safer to walk more to the left, over the glacier.

On nearing the snout bear to the right and join the path. Where it forks, one branch going down along the river, the other rising to the moraine's crest, take the second one which leads to the base.

ROUTE 26: Bezymyanny and Sella Peaks. *(See map 14)*

You can spend two very interesting days walking to the Jangi Hut (3,300m) at the foot of the Bezengi Wall and climbing a couple of good vantage points. The first one is Bezymyanny Peak (4,050m) on the south-west ridge of Dykhtau Peak, right opposite the highest part of the Wall, and the second one, Sella Peak (4,370m), named after Vittorio Sella, stands in the centre of the upper basin of the Bezengi Glacier's eastern branch and views both of Dykhtau and the Wall are afforded from there.

From Barankosh mount the moraine, then where practicable come down to the glacier and head for the corner of the right side moraine, which changes its direction there from north-west to north-east. Near the corner

Bezengi Valley, the Bezengi Wall

find a way through a rough glacier terrain, climb the scree of the moraine side and follow the path on its crest. 4-4¹/₂ hours from Barankosh to the hut.

Bezymyanny Peak. The hut stands at the lower end of the ridge running north to the peak. Walk the screes, snow patches and rock bands along the eastern side of the ridge. On reaching the upper cirque, with a glacier on the right and Dykhtau's rock walls towering above it, turn to the left and climb west up a steep scree and broken rock slope leading to a saddle on the ridge. From there turn to the right and scramble to the top. 3-3¹/₂ hours.

Sella Peak. From the hut go to the south-east, cross the northern ramification of the Bezengi Glacier's eastern branch, round the lower end of Sella's south-west ridge and climb its eastern scree slopes to the north-east. Once on the ridge turn to the right.

The scramble to the summit is easy and exciting, first along the gently inclined wide ridge, with an almost sheer ice drop on the left, then some broken rocks and, under the summit, 3-4 metres of snow, 50°. 4-4¹/₂ hours from the hut.

It takes 5¹/₂-6 hours to walk from the hut back to the mountaineering base.

100

West Caucasus: Gvandra

The easternmost part of the West Caucasus is a stretch of the Main Range more than 40km long from the ridge connecting the latter with Mt Elbrus in the east to the Daut range in the west. The mountains are considerably smaller in scale than in the Central Caucasus but the vegetation is more abundant and lush and, granite being the main rock here, most streams and rivers are enticingly clear. Many valleys either up or downstream can boast exquisite scenery.

The highest point is Gvandra Peak (3,984m), hence the nickname of the area, "Gvandra", by which it is known among Russian walkers and climbers who, using this name, usually mean the northern slopes of the Main Range.

The southern slopes are much steeper and more often than not the valleys there are narrow gorges, covered by high grass and tenacious, dense shrubs. Lower down there are tall and light beech forests. This steepness and vegetation is ever ready to obliterate even such vague paths that exist in the upper valleys. So walks across the Main Range and long travelling on the southern side can only be recommended to highly experienced mountain walkers. However, the long ridges branching off from the Main Range to the north offer quite a scope for easy passes with good paths, and the navigating here is always within the capability of the modest walker.

There are two major valleys in the area: Ullukam (30km long) on the east and Uchkulan (20km) on the west (closed for private cars). Their rivers (bearing the same names) merge together and form the Kuban River, one of the biggest in the North Caucasus. For many centuries the valleys served the Karachais as pastures and because of this, for two thirds of their lower length they are treeless and not very interesting for the views.

In terms of transport and accommodation facilities the area does not come near to what it can offer in terms of natural beauty. All the roads are mere jeep tracks, and the only decent accommodation (twin rooms specially refurbished for hard currency clients) is at the Uzunkol climbing base, strategically and agreeably placed in the pine forest of the Uzunkol Valley. This is right at the centre of the area, in the proximity of the finest peaks with the hardest granite walls. The Uzunkol River is a left tributary of Ullukam and its mouth is 8km upstream from Khurzuk Village with another 7km from there to the base. There are two small tourist bases in Kertmely Glade, at the confluence of the Nakhar and Gondarai Rivers (forming Uchkulan) which belong to some obscure local organizations. In theory accommodation (rather ascetic) is possible there but demands negotiations and waiting, and in the end it may turn out that nobody is interested even in dollars, not to mention roubles.

Two large villages, the only ones in the area, both with post offices and food shops, are age old "ouls" (the stress is on "u"), Khurzuk and Uchkulan near the confluence of the Ullukam and Uchkulan Rivers. There is a regular bus service (3-4 runs a day) between the villages and the town of Karachaevsk, 45km down the Kuban Valley, which for 30km is a narrow, densely wooded gorge without any settlements. Right at the lower end of the gorge, on the outskirts of Karachaevsk, the Russians built a fortress at the beginning of the 19th century to block the way down for Karachai guerilllas. Another historic place is where the Khudes River flows into the Kuban. In 1828 Russian troops, having made a long journey from Kislovodsk military settlement and down the Khudes Valley, descended on Karachai fighters and routed them. That battle fixed the fate of the land which has been since then a part of Russia.

The only way to get straight from Mineralny Vody Airport to the villages is in a hired truck, bus or simply by taxi. The latter makes the easiest and quickest approach, even though pretty expensive. It takes 4½-5 hours. Or you can get to Karachaevsk by a regular service bus from Mineralny Vody Airport and from Nevinnomysk Railway Station (3½-4 hours).

The Gvandra area is considered to be a sort of Karachai ethnic sanctuary: the place where this people originated. In contrast to most other regions of the Caucasus, this particular area, thanks to the 30km long canyon, was well guarded against any big migration waves or nomad raids for a very long time. There have been many archaeological finds at the ancient settlement which were discovered in the vicinity of Uchkulan Village, proving that the Koban people lived there undisturbed from the 5th century BC till the 10th century AD, when the Alans arrived. In 1396 the savage Timur's raid followed. His hordes combed the Ullukam Valley up to the foot of Mt Elbrus. A stone watch-tower of the 12th century in Khurzuk is witness of that cruel and irresistible human lava flow. The village is an interesting place to visit. Some corners have survived the tide of modern civilization and look almost exactly as they were two or three centuries ago.

Six routes across the Main Range and two over northern branches are included in this chapter. Together with the routes connecting the area with the neighbouring ones they cover all the valleys accessible to the moderate walker.

ROUTE 27: From the Chiryukol Valley to the Nenskra Valley through the Talychkhan Valley via the Talychkhan Pass (1B, 3,250m, between Talychkhan (3,670m) and Chiryukolak (3,516m) Peaks). *(See map 1)*

The route takes 2 days, goes in remote and unfrequented side valleys and demands navigating rather than technical skills. There is a snow slope on the northern side of the pass, 150m, 30-35°, so the full set of equipment is advised. On the south side is an excellent sight of the hundred metres high waterfall of the Manchkhap River. There are fairly good paths on both sides and the glaciers are easy to cross.

Stage 1. There is a comfortable campsite in the pine grove at the junction of the Talychkhan and Chungurdjar streams, on the left bank of the Chiryukol River which they form. From the camp walk up, cross Chiryukol by a foot-bridge and take the path on the Talychkhan's right bank. In 1 hour the tree-line is reached and the narrow upper valley opens out, stretching ahead and gradually turning to the right, south. A further 2 hours walk brings you to a barricade of huge blocks, covering the valley's right side. That natural bridge takes the path over the river to the left bank only to return after 100m. The Main Range opens south rising above a long flat meadowland. South too Chiryukolak Peak dotted with numerous small hanging glaciers stands at the head of the valley. The pass and the East Talychkhan Glacier under it are to the left (south-east), hidden from view by a moraine adjacent to the left-hand mountainside.

A comfortable campsite on a mossy ground among dwarf birches is at the upper end of a short moraine which begins at the base of Chiryukolak Peak and descends north, to a step of glacial slabs, separating the bodies of the East and West Talychkhan Glaciers. The ice-fall of the latter is seen south-west above another band of glacial slabs. The streams outflowing from both the glaciers meet under the lower end of the short moraine, a few hundred metres beyond the flat meadowland. Cross the eastern one and climb through the band of easy slabs to the moraine and further to the campsite on its top. 4 hours from the Chiryukol River.

Stage 2. The East Talychkhan Glacier is seen to the east from the campsite, with the rounded, massive summit of Talychkhan Peak to the left of Chiryukolak Peak. There are three depressions on the ridge connecting them. The pass is the leftmost, closest to Talychkhan Peak. Go on to the glacier and cross it to the south-east. Leave the ice-fall to your right, traversing the snow and scree lower slopes of Talychkhan Peak, above the glacier. Then return to it again and climb the snow slope leading to the saddle, 150m, 30-35°. 2½-3 hours from the campsite. A view of fine peaks on the west is afforded from the pass. Down in the south only a small gently inclined glacier is visible, but south-east, across the gap of the Nenskra Valley, Shtavler Peak with its white head (3,995m) rises stately, and the peaks of the Dolra range are in the far background.

Descend a short loose scree slope to the glacier and, walking down, keep to its left side, closer to Talychkhan's base. Leave the steep glacial slabs to your right and make a slanting traverse of the screes at the base, heading for the red rocks of Talychkhan's rock spur. Use the scree immediately before that for coming down to the floor of the Manchkhap Valley. It runs to the east. A barely traceable path goes down the left grassy bank to reach in 1 hour thick brushwood, where it disappears. Lower down the river plunges in a 100m high waterfall, so leave the bushes leading to the canyon to your right and climb 100m up on to the grassy ridge, which is to your left. From there descend a long grass slope to the Nenskra River. 3½-4 hours from the pass. Total time is 6-7 hours. The mighty waterfall is in clear view from the river. The path down the valley is on the left bank. To get there walk 2½km upstream and find a bridge. If it is swept away, use an avalanche snow-bridge higher up which normally holds till late August.

ROUTE 28: From the Uzunkol Mountaineering Base to the Nenskra Valley via the Myrdy-Dalar Pass (1B, 3,100m, under the south-west wall of Kyrpych Peak (3,800m) and through the Dalar Valley. *(See map 2)*

The route takes 2 days and gives a taste of walking in a typical southern valley, steep and densely vegetated. There is some walking over reasonably crevassed glaciers and the hardest section is on the descent, 150-180m of snow, 30°. A short snow rise of 20-25° is on the north side of the saddle. The full set of equipment is needed.

Stage 1. For the way from the Uzunkol base to the Myrdy Campsite at the head of the Myrdy Valley see Route 34. Reverse its last descending part. 3-3$\frac{1}{2}$ hours from the base.

Stage 2. The usual early start at 5.00-5.30am. From the campsite climb south among glacial slabs, using the path where it is clear. The lower dry part of the Myrdy Glacier is rather crevassed but the route-finding does not present any serious difficulty. Its central part is almost flat, with the pass seen to the south - a wide saddle under the abrupt rock wall of Kyrpych Peak. The snow ascent leading to it is up to 25°. 3 hours from the campsite.

There is a large snow plateau on the south side of the saddle. Cross it in a south-east direction to reach a snow descent of 30°, 170-200m long, leading to the upper basin of the South Dalar Glacier. Further down keep closer to the base of Kyrpych Peak. On reaching the heavily crevassed part of the glacier turn to the left and make a slanting traverse of glacial slabs and screes, leaving to your right the snout plunging into the large Dalar Lake and providing it with beautiful green icebergs. 2 hours from the pass.

[Should that long snow descent of 30° turn into ice late in the season, take the following way instead. From the saddle go in a south-westerly direction to reach in 20 minutes a depression, which is a pass in the Moguashirkha Range, running south from the Myrdy Pass and separating the Saken and Dalar upper valleys. Descend from that pass on to the South Dalar Glacier and cross it to its left side.]

The Dalar River outflowing from the lake rushes steeply down the valley for the first kilometre. To cover that distance through screes and broken rocks along the steep left bank will take a lot of energy. There is a kosh at its end, where a side stream comes from the left and a path begins. The latter is very tricky, through high grass, boulders and birch thickets. It takes 2 exhausting hours to thread one's way (crawling sometimes) through all the obstacles to get to the stream coming down from the Zamok Glacier, on the left. The path grows a little better but nonetheless it takes another 2$\frac{1}{2}$ hours to reach the Nenskra Valley (on the left bank all the way). Time from Dalar Lake is 6$\frac{1}{2}$ hours (for mere 7km!) and total time is 9$\frac{1}{2}$ hours. At a pinch it is possible to find some tiny, uncomfortable sites on the way down or camp near the kosh up in the valley, but the whole place is covered with muck. For the details about the Nenskra Valley see Route 9.

ROUTE 29: From the Uzunkol Mountaineering Base to the Saken Valley via the Myrdy-Saken Pass (1B, 3,100m, under the South-West Wall of Kyrpych Peak (3,800m). *(See map 2)*

The route is not much more difficult than that to the Dalar Valley, going over the same pass (Route 28), but it promises a rather exciting descent into the Saken Valley which demands not so much climbing skills as steady nerves, or the habit of walking close to a precipice. Another attraction of this route is a gorgeous beech forest and thickets of ferns so tall that you can easily get lost in them. The route takes 2 days. The full set of equipment is needed.

Stage 1. For this and the first part of Stage 2, as far as the Myrdy Pass see Route 28.

Stage 2. From the pass walk over the snow plateau due south, aiming at a truncated pyramid which stands over the Dalar-Saken Pass. The pass brings into view both of the valleys. Go to Saken by easy snow. Soon you come to an edge of rocks plunging down almost vertically. Turn to the right and head for a glacier, descending steeply from the ridge of the Main Range half a kilometre ahead to the north-west. Follow a rock shelf covered with scree which leads there, clinging to a steep rock face and 2-3 metres wide at its narrowest parts. As a matter of fact the slant is easy, like a Dolomite via ferrata. What follows, a steep scree slope of big, unstable blocks by the left side of the glacier, is more risky and exhausting. It takes half an hour to get through this and come to a level sand and gravel terrace, with many streams and rivulets running from the snout of the glacier, giving birth to the Saken River. 1¹/₂-2 hours from the pass. At the end of the terrace the river reaches a waterfall. Leave that step of glacial slabs to your right, cross a left side tributary by an avalanche snow bridge and pick up a path on the left bank in the narrow Saken Valley. It takes 1¹/₂ hours to get to a kosh at the tree-line and some minutes more to reach a clearing, good for camping. Another 2 hours through wild southern vegetation take you to a foot-bridge to the right bank, with a Narzan spring and some cottages around it (a sort of local spa). Here a jeep track takes over and leads to Saken Village which is reached in 1¹/₂ hours. A further hour's walk brings you to Omarishara Village on the caravan way over the Klukhor Pass (on the Main Range) called The Military-Sukhumi Road. Total time is 8-8¹/₂ hours.

ROUTE 30: From Uchkulan Village to Omarishara Village in Georgia via the Gondaray Pass (1A, 2,940m, between Gondaray and Ispanskoy Kompartii Peaks), through the Gondaray Valley on the North and Gvandra Valley on the South. *(See map 2)*

The route takes 3-4 days. Local shepherds and hunters have used the route from time immemorial without any equipment, but to be on the safe side take the full set, for there is a glacier and a snow ascent on the northern side of the pass.

For **Stage 1** see Route 34.

Half of **Stage 2** coincides with that of Route 34 as well, from the Kertmeli Glade to the confluence of the Gondaray and Indrukoy Rivers.

There are solid bridges over both rivers and paths on both banks of the Gondaray. Take the one on the left side of the narrow treeless valley. In 40-50 minutes the path brings you to the wide and flat gravel floor of the valley with the river ramifying there. Straight ahead (south-west) a glacier is seen over moraines but the way to the Gondaray Pass is to the south-east, to the left of a rock ridge running from the Main Range due north and dividing the head of the valley into two cirques. At the end of the valley's gravel floor a path climbs up along the right bank of a stream outflowing from the Gondaray Glacier (hidden from view so far) and coming down through a band of glacier smoothed rocks. Then the path turns to the left, skirts the band and reaches another terrace with another band of rocks above it and with the glacier, in full view to the south-east now, over the band. Camp here on the grass. 3 hours from the confluence, $6^{1}/_{2}$-7 hours from the Kertmely Glade.

Stage 3. Skirt the glacial slabs to their left, using the scree under a small hanging glacier seen east on the slope of Gondaray Peak. Soon the whole jagged ridge connecting Gondaray and Ispanskoy Kompartii Peaks opens out to the south. The pass is the lowest narrow saddle, with a rock to its left split by a vertical chimney. Walk south, cross the Gondaray Glacier and climb a short snow ascent of 20-25°, leading to the saddle. 3 hours from the campsite. In the distance south-east, over the low ridge between the Gvandra and Saken Valleys, high Moguashirkha Peak (3,847m) shines its snows.

To get to the Gvandra River do not descend straight down the steep gully under the saddle. Instead make a traverse east without losing height, scrambling across numerous gullies and keeping alert to cairns marking the way. When a long scree slope with a large snow patch descending to the river is reached, use that for coming down to the right bank. $2^{1/2}$-3 hours from the pass. Lower down there is a kosh on the left bank reached by a snow-bridge where it is reasonable to camp.

A path begins at the kosh and it is $3^{1/2}$-4 hours walk to the village of Omarishara. The path works its way through awkward large screes covered with high ferns. $3^{1/2}$km lower down the river is dammed by jumbled rocks with a snow-bridge taking the path to the right bank, into the beech forest. After another $1^{1/2}$km the path descends to reach a kosh on pastures near the river, with a bridge leading to a tiny settlement on the left bank. From there it climbs and falls for 7km to come to a deserted cottage by the river, and after another $3^{1/2}$km comes to a bridge and goes to the right bank for the last run of $1^{1/2}$km to Omarishara Village. Total time is $8^{1/2}$-10 hours.

ROUTE 31: From the Gondaray Valley to the Klych Valley via the Klych Pass (1B, 3,230m, in the South-East Ridge of South Nakhar Peak (3,882m). *(See map 2)*

The route is an interesting alternative to the route over the Gondaray Pass with its long walk down the Gvandra Valley (Route 30). It is much shorter and, because the Klych Pass is considerably higher, it is a very good vantage point, with views encompassing much of the West Caucasus, including Mt Elbrus. The descent to the well trodden path from the Klukhor Pass (Route 36) takes a little more than an hour and from there you can either walk down 6km to the South Refuge, or return to the north via the Nakhar (Route 32) or Klukhor (Route 36) Passes. Full set of equipment.

Stage 1. From the flat gravel part of the Gondaray Valley (see Route 30, Stage 2) a glacier is seen south-west, over moraine hills. Follow a path going there through rhododendrons and boulders on the Gondaray's left bank and rising to an old step of glacial slabs to come to a level terrace. $1^{1/2}$ hours. Camp there.

Stage 2. Early start. Cross a rather big stream by stepping stones and follow the path climbing to the crest of the left side moraine of the West Gondaray Glacier (the one which was seen to south-west the previous day). There is a site at the upper end of the moraine and a lot of rusty iron and dug-outs, the flotsam of the Second World War. Go on to the glacier and walking up keep to its left bank to avoid the crevassed centre. The way from the glacier to the pass is not obvious. Ignore the serrated, forbidding Main Range to the south and south-west and look north-west towards the loose rocks and screes of the lower slopes of South Nakhar Peak, the southernmost and highest in the long Nakhar Range. Head for a narrow strip of snow leading to the upper north-west snow cirque under the peak. The depression nearest to the latter appears to be the pass but it is a false one. The correct one is a narrow gap separated from the other by a flat vertical slab. 50-60m of broken rocks lead to the saddle from the snow of the cirque. $3^{1}/2$-4 hours from the campsite. In good weather the fine views of the Gvandra and Dombay areas will keep you on the pass longer than usual, and there is no need to be in haste - the descent would not take more than $1^{1}/2$ or 2 hours at the most.

Go down to a minor easy glacier, keeping again to the base of South Nakhar Peak, pass a small rocky terrace with more dug-outs and make a slanting traverse to the west of a large scree. In 1-$1^{1}/2$ hours you meet a good path running down from the Nakhar Pass.

ROUTE 32: From the Village of Uchkulan to the South Refuge of the Klukhor Pass (Route 36) in the Klych Valley, through the Nakhar Valley via the Nakhar Pass (1A, 2,885m, on the Ridge running to the West from South Nakhar Peak). *(See maps 2 & 3)*

A true trekking route with a relatively low pass and solid paths on both sides of the Main Range. It is a very popular way from the North Caucasus to Georgia and therefore the mountain seclusion is questionable on the route, especially on the south side, where it coincides with the Military Sukhumi Road. The route takes 3 days, and no climbing equipment is needed.

For **Stage 1** see Route 34.

Stage 2. From the Kertmeli Glade walk along a forest track on the left bank of the Nakhar River. Soon a path takes over, rises steeply above the gorge, then descends again to the river and maintains a level course through woods and clearings. For the next 8km it is a pleasant and not too strenuous valley walk. On reaching a bridge cross the river to a kosh on the right bank. A little west of south the Main Range opens out, low and not very impressive. The Nakhar Pass is to the left of a snow saddle in the centre and hidden from view as yet. 3km from the kosh (8 from the Kertmely Glade) the valley gets narrow and the path winds up through screes fanning from the base of the mountainside and overgrown with rhododendrons. Further up the valley is barred by a spur jutting out from its left side. Over that there is a flat marshy terrace and higher up over a step of glacial slabs another one, with many tent sites on it. Camp there. 6-7 hours from the Kertmely Glade.

Stage 3. In a south-easterly direction, over a band of glacier smoothed rocks, two snow cirques divided by a rounded rock hill can be seen. The eastern one leads to the pass which is not seen as yet. The path ascends the rock band to reach in 1 hour Nakhar Lake, lying among screes under a small glacier. If the latter is stripped of snow (in late August) leave it to your left and climb easy rocks bordering it on the west. An hour from the lake the pass is reached. A bird's eye view of the long, wooded Klych Valley is afforded from there and the clear hairpin bends of the Military Sukhumi Road are seen down and to the right.

The path zig-zags down a scree and grass slope, making a wide loop, south-east, south, and south-west, crossing numerous streams running from the left. Here again much war flotsam reminds walkers about the grim fight in the winter mountains during November and December of 1942. Having gained a big stream, choose between two options: either to jump to the left bank over a narrow canyon, or walk 10-15 minutes upstream and wade it, where it ribbons. From there the path runs down the left bank. Shortly before the mouth step of the valley, from which the stream drops in a 200m high waterfall, the path veers to the left and runs through bushes to the Military Sukhumi Road. $2^{1}/_{2}$ hours from the pass. Total time is $4^{1}/_{2}$ hours. Another 2 hours are needed to get to the South Refuge of the Klukhor Pass (Route 36).

ROUTE 33: From the Uzunkol Base to the Chiryukol Valley via the South Dolomity Pass (1A, 3,350m, on the Ridge separating the Uzunkol and Chiryukol Valleys). *(See maps 1 & 2)*

Under good and stable weather it is quite possible to make this easy route, with good paths, in one day, if you are fit enough. But if in no haste break it into two stages and camp under the pass to be on the saddle early in the morning. The dramatic view of the Kichkinekol cirque, the best in the Gvandra area, with the granite towers of Trapetsiya (3,780m), Dalar (3,979m), Dvoynyashki (3,900m) and Filtr (3,760m) Peaks is well worth a spare day. No climbing equipment is needed.

Stage 1. From the base take the path on the Uzunkol's right bank. It turns into the Kichkinekol Valley following the right bank again. In 1 hour the tree-line is reached. The valley, flat, swampy and rock strewn stretches far ahead, with the eye-catching sight of the Kichkinekol cirque. Where the valley changes its direction from south-east to south (2km from the junction, 40-50 minutes) the path comes to a kosh and a fairly big side stream, rushing in to it from the left, broken into many branches. Follow a path rising steeply along its right bank. $1^{1}/_{2}$ hours from the kosh a level grassy terrace with many tent sites is reached. Keep walking on the path which goes through screes and brings you in another hour to Dolomity Lake, tranquil and blue, with the surface reflecting red dolomite rocks encompassing the place. Camp there. $3^{1}/_{2}$-4 hours from the base.

Stage 2. The wide saddle of the pass, with a steep, jagged ridge to its left and a minor peak to its right, is seen to the south-east. There will be no glacier walking this day, so no need for an early start. It takes 1 hour to reach the pass.

From the saddle cross a snow-field, find the upper end of a long and steep gully, leave it to your left and scramble down by the easier broken rocks and scree slopes of the minor peak. It takes two tiring hours to descend to the flat sand and gravel basin, through which meanders, shallow and slow, the Chungurdjar River outflowing from under the snout of its namesake glacier. 2 hours from the pass.

Once there turn to the left along the river, come to the next grassy terrace and find a path beginning on it. It winds down a steep rock band and after that cuts along the left side of the valley, through rhododendrons and low, twisted birches. There is a campsite in a pine grove where the Chungurdjar and Talychkhan Rivers meet forming the Chiryukol, on the left bank of the latter (1,900m). There remains 6km to the Ullukam Valley, by good path and track, through forest and meadowland with koshes on them, with many charming campsites, vast fields of blackberries and raspberries (all the way on the left bank). It is a further 13km to the village of Khurzuk, by a jeep track on the right bank of Ullukam. For the way up the valley see Route 17.

ROUTE 34: From the Village of Uchkulan to the Uzunkol Mountaineering Base in the Uzunkol Valley via the Ak-Tyube Pass (1B, 3,350m, on the Ridge dividing the Ullukam and Uchkulan Valleys, right under the highest Summit of the Area Gvandra Peak (3,980m)). *(See map 2)*

A very scenic route through the highest part of the area, near the long icy north face of Gvandra Peak. The difficult spot is on the eastern side of the pass - 60-80m of snow, 30°. There is glacier travelling on both sides and though simple the full set of equipment should be taken. The route is 3 days long.

Stage 1. There are many koshes up in the mountains, so you stand rather a good chance of getting a lift with a truck going up the valley. If you are not lucky in this (by Murphy's Law, a truck normally catches up with you on the road only when it cannot make any difference), shoulder your rucksacks and take the track, leaving the village and going on the Uchkulan's left bank in the wide and bare valley enlivened only by birch groves and barberies. After 10km the road crosses the river by a bridge and after 7km on the right bank comes again to the left one. The incline gets steeper and the river roars through its narrow rocky bed. 3km, 40 minutes walk remain to the Kertmely glade, with many comfortable tent sites there. 6-7 hours from the village.

Stage 2. Walk 15-20 minutes along the road on the left bank, then cross the Nakhar River by a bridge to the right bank and take a track on the left bank of the Gondaray River, going through the sparse woods. 40-50 minutes walk brings you to a clearing with a foot-bridge to a kosh on the right bank. The narrow, wooded valley of Djalpakol comes from the east here to join the Gondaray Valley. Keep to the left bank and in 40 minutes the track brings you to a rock step across the valley and a bridge over the gorge worked out in the step by the river. Follow a track on the right bank to reach in 1 hour the inflow of the Indryukoy River from the right.

A cosy campsite is on the Indryukoy's right bank in a grove of fir-trees. The sight of the high peaks of the Main Range to the south-west makes walking more agreeable and less tiring. A forest track climbs up the right bank of the Indryukoy River and comes to an end on a clearing shortly before the tree-line. A path takes over and leads past a kosh to the junction of the Ak-Tyube and West Kichkinekol streams. The hanging Ak-Tyube Valley is seen to the east. There is a foot-bridge to the left bank of the Ak-

Tyube stream and a campsite there, in a pine grove, 2½ hours from the Gondaray Valley.

There are steep paths on both banks of Ak-Tyube, rising to the upper valley, with a kosh there and a foot-bridge over the stream. 1 hour. To the south-east the dazzling white north face of Gvandra Peak, 2½km long and rising slightly less than 1km over the glacier, dominates the scene. The Ak-Tyube Glacier, girdled below by a band of glacial slabs, opens higher and to the left of the Gvandra Glacier which is under the face. It takes another hour to follow a path over the alpine meadows and lower screes of the left-hand valley side to a campsite under the right bank moraine of the Ak-Tyube Glacier. 7-7½ hours from the Kertmely Glade.

Stage 3. A cairned path along the moraine and over some slabs brings you to the glacier, gently sloping, with a few narrow crevasses. Roping up would be a prudent decision. Head south-east for a minor rock pyramid. There is a wide snow saddle to its left but the pass is on the other side and will show later, with Gvandra's north-east snow ridge descending to it. From the saddle (2 hours after setting out) the flat plateau of the Myrdy Glacier is seen far below, with the sheer granite wall of squat, gloomy Kyrpych Peak (3,800m) at its far end, right opposite, and the graceful tower of Dalar (3,979m) behind it, to the left.

Make a slanting descent to the left, on to the glacier (60-80m, 30°) and head for the left side moraine to find a path there. After the moraine the path goes slightly to the left, rounding a band of glacial slabs. Lower down, on the shelf of a grassy slope there is a large campsite (Myrdy Campsite, 2,900m) from which the path winds through a maze of big blocks and comes to the flat swampy floor of the Myrdy Valley. 2 hours from the pass. For almost an hour the scene is not changing, with only numerous crossings of the left side-streams to enliven the walking. On reaching a kosh at the tree-line, cross the river by way of a foot-bridge to the right bank, then in 15-20 minutes return to the left one and a further 40 minutes walk will bring you to a bridge again, over the Uzunkol River this time, which is formed by the Myrdy and Kichkinekol Rivers. The mountaineering base is on the right bank in the pine forest. 4 hours from the pass. Total time is 6-6½ hours. In good weather a very agreeable camping site, a little below the junction, on the Uzunkol's left bank can be a good alternative to the base.

ROUTE 35: From the Village of Uchkulan to Ullukel Lake, one of the largest in the West Caucasus, at the Head of the Kichkinekol Valley (its river is a left tributary of the Uchkulan). *(See map 4)*

A nice walk to a deep and beautiful mountain lake (with trout!). The walk itself, up and down the Kichkinekol Valley only takes 7-8 hours, but try to get a lift at least as far as the mouth of the Karasu River, which meets the Uchkulan valley 10km upstream from the village of Uchkulan. Should a lift be unavailable, the only alternative to a 12-13 hours walk is to take with you tents and sleeping bags and camp near the lakes (there are smaller ones besides Ullukel).

Near the mouth of the Karasu River the road goes over a bridge to the Uchkulan's right bank. Follow an old track on the left one. In 20-30 minutes you come to the mouth of the Kichkinekol River, a wooded gorge with a path winding steeply through the pine forest on the left bank. In 2½-3 hours a kosh at the tree-line is reached and a big side stream from the left is crossed by stepping stones. From there it takes a little more than an hour to climb steep screes to reach two small, shallow tarns. Another two are across the river, on the right bank. Leaving to its left a high waterfall, the path leads to the main lake, which is reached in 40-50 minutes. A wide choice of grassy sites on the north and east shores and a dramatic view of the reddish rocks of Ryndjy-aghe Peak (3,730m) to the west are a good reward for the dull walk in the Uchkulan Valley. 5-5½ hours from the mouth of the Kichkinekol River and 2-2½ hours back. Total time for the return walk from Uchkulan Village is 12-13 hours.

West Caucasus: Teberda-Dombay

What was said about the beauty and attractions of the Gvandra area applies fully to the Teberda-Dombay, further west, with some superlatives added. It is the sort of place where thoughtless atheism is easily undermined by a doubt that all this could be made just by Nature playing dice - so creatively measured and balanced are all the elements of that beauty. Hardly any other part of the Caucasus can boast so gracefully shaped granite pyramids and towers with small, lace-like glaciers hanging over green, lavishly wooded valleys, crystal clear streams and more than a hundred tarns, enlivening scree cirques with the reflected sky and snow. Thanks to the National Reserve status accorded in 1936 (and with very strict regulations), much of the beauty is left unspoiled by the recreation industry, and looks now almost the same as it did when it was first discovered and marvelled at by some educated Russians at the end of the last century. Nonetheless, the area is a fairly well developed recreation and mountain sports centre, the second one in the Caucasus after the Baksan Valley. That means metalled roads coming very close to the Main Range at two points, hut-refuges, two mountaineering bases with Rescue Service and big hotels.

The first terminal point is the Dombay Glade (1,850m), the junction of three valleys, wooded and beautiful. The Amanauz, Alibek and Dombay-Ulghen, are encircled tightly by the Main Range and two northern branches, which leave a narrow gorge between their arms for the Amanauz River to run north and meet the Gonachkhir coming from the right to form the Teberda River. It is a place of unrivalled beauty but, alas, the most crowded one of the area - an inevitable price for the convenience of a good road and hotels. If you do not like this, walk in the Teberda's side-valleys, any of which can promise the purity of untouched nature, seclusion and quiet. And rather likely - a meeting with chamois or a glimpse of the Caucasian bear.

Two seven-storey hotels, *Dombay* and *Gorniye Vershiny,* Dombay mountaineering base and the head of Rescue Service are there at the junction. The second climbing base, Alibek, is 6km upstream, in the charming Alibek Valley. As at the Uzunkol climbing base in Gvandra, there are a number of specially refurbished rooms there for hard currency clients. The forest road goes on the left bank of the Alibek River and is connected with the main metalled road on the Amanauz' right bank by two bridges over the Dombay-Ulghen and Amanauz. There is also a hut-refuge (neglected, without panes) at the head of the Alibek Valley, near the snout of the Alibek Glacier (1-1½ hours walk from the base).

The Dombay mountaineering base is on the left bank of the Amanauz. The Glade can boast two cableways, neither of much use to walkers as time savers for approaches. A cable-car connects the *Gorniye Vershiny Hotel* (on the Amanauz' left bank) with the upper station at 2,520m on the spur of Mussaachitara Peak (3,012m); a chair-lift goes from the lower station on the right banks of Amanauz and Dombay-Ulghen for 2½km almost without gaining height along the road in the Dombay-Ulghen Valley, at the second station it turns to the left and runs straight up to Point 2,520m. The chair-lift level section could be used by those going to the Ptysh or Chuchkhur Passes, but, taking into account queuing and waiting, there would be only a very slight gain of time. During the summer of 1992 both sections of the chair-lift operated on Saturdays and Sundays only, and the cable-car was at a standstill. There is a post office with telephone service (at the *Dombay Hotel*) and a food shop on the Glade. The farthest point you can get on the phone is Moscow. Note that there is no access to the Dombay Glade for private cars.

The second tourist centre in the area is the small town of Teberda (1,300m) 23km downstream, with three tourist bases named Klukhori, Teberda and Azghek (and a much larger number of sanatoria). There is a post office, food shops, a nature museum and a sort of zoo, keeping some species of the rich local fauna. The office of the Nature Reserve is there as well: the place to get a permit for walking within its boundaries. Owing to the curative properties of the local climate, the town, buried in the tall pine forest, is considered to be a health resort. And no wonder. It has richly ozoned air, only 16 days a year without sun and 90 with no cloud, the rest - sunny with some cloud, and neither severe frosts nor oppressive summer heat typical of the foot-hills to the north.

The second longest valley of the area is Gonachkhir, Teberda's right tributary, with a good road all along its length coming to the hut-refuge at the foot of the Klukhor Pass (30km from Teberda town). The pass is age-old, strikingly picturesque on both sides, and a time-honoured caravan way over the Main Range, from the North Caucasus to the Black Sea. It was already well known to the ancient Greek colonies on the Black Sea's northern coast. Besides the usual trading items of wool, honey, leather and weapons, a slave trade was very active and it was going on till the middle of the 19th century.

In the first half of the 19th century the Teberda Valley was deserted, after a disastrous plague epidemic, and it was only in the late sixties that people settled there again. In the eighties the Russian Government considered quite seriously the idea of building a railway from the town of Nevinnomyssk in the north to Georgia's capital Tbilisi, through the Caucasus, with a tunnel under the Klukhor Pass. Shortly before World War I the project came very close to being carried out, because that meant the possibility of a quick transfer of troops to the Turkish border. Nevertheless it was never realized in full. A cart-track built in 1863-1896 from the town of Cherkessk to Sukhumi and called the Military Sukhumi Road has remained a horse and foot path because of inescapable snow and stone avalanches. Among the three ancient ways over the Main Range (the other two are the Mamisonski and Krestoviy Passes on the east) this one undoubtedly stands out for its rich scenery and wilderness.

The Teberda-Dombay area proper is the upper reaches of the Teberda River (a left tributary of the Kuban), about 30km along the Main Range, with the Kyshkadjer and Teberda ranges as the eastern and western boundaries. However, the northern valleys of Daut on the east and Aksaut with Marukh on the west are included in this chapter for convenience. There is not much to be said about the three valleys, none of which can boast good roads and hotels, not to mention cableways. None of them have any permanent habitations, and two villages in the middle of the Daut and Aksaut Valleys, Daut and Krasniy Karachai, serve only as summer residences for shepherds and farmers. There is also a summer settlement of geologists at the head of Aksaut, with a road going to it from down the valley. All the three have farms and koshes along their length and paths connecting them. The farthest point in the Daut Valley you can get to by a regular service bus from the towns of Cherkessk and Karachaevsk is the road between Karachaevsk and Khurzuk Village, which crosses the Daut River 25km downstream from Daut Village. In the Aksaut it is Khasaut-Grechesky Village (a post office) connected with the summer village of Krasniy Karachai (43km) and the geologists base at the head of the valley (another 23km) by rather a rough road. Thanks to the base and road, there is a relatively good chance of getting a lift there, though private cars are not allowed in either the Daut or Aksaut Valleys. The next one, the Marukh Valley, is the worst in terms of approach. The bus terminus, Marukh Village (a post office) is more than 50km from the head of the valley, with only a rough jeep track leading to the upper koshes. Taking all this into consideration and keeping in mind the Teberda Valley, it would not look a good idea to choose one of the three as an approach valley.

There is a regular bus service, several runs a day, between the town of Teberda and the capital of Karachai-Circassia, Cherkessk (100km), Mineralny Vody Airport (213km) and Nevinnomyssk Railway Station (166km). There are two buses a day from Mineralny Vody Airport to the towns of Cherkessk (113km) and Karachaevsk (168km). There is a separate bus service between Teberda and the Dombay Glade (20km).

The whole stretch of the Main Range from the Klukhor to Marukh Passes, about 50km, is so jagged and steep that, besides these two, only three more passes across it are included here, making just five out of 30. The former two are easy, the latter three are relatively easy - 1B-2A. In return, the vast area of the northern ranges, long and high, is a very good playground for the moderate walker.

ROUTE 36: From the Gonachkhir Valley over the Main Range to the Klych Valley via the Klukhor Pass (0 Grade, 2,782m, at the Head of the Gonachkhir Valley). *(See map 3)*

A gem among Caucasian treks with the only and inevitable disadvantage of being too popular. On the northern side the Gonachkhir Valley, spacious, with graceful rock peaks encircling its head, is among the most scenic in the West Caucasus and on the southern side many waterfalls, deep canyons and age old ruins are in store for the traveller. The pass itself is enriched with a large tarn, turquoise, with milkish tint, 500m long and 35m deep. For many years the route was used as a trek run by an All-Union organization. There are fairly basic but large hut-refuges on both sides, the northern one (2,000m) being 6km from the pass and the southern (1,250m) - 16km (with all the road's curves). So, the best direction for the crossing is from north to south, to make those long 16km on the descent. There is a caravan path all the way and the route takes a day - a rather long one though, 8-10 hours.

Stage 1. There are no navigation problems on the route. Starting from the several cabins of the Northern hut-refuge, you can use either the path which cuts the bends of the Military Sukhumi Road, or the road itself (seen from anywhere), which demands more time but presents an agreeable contrast to the steep path which is awkward when wet (up to 40° at places). From the Refuge the path runs in a south-easterly direction along the right bank of the North Klukhor River and soon reaches a war memorial, with the lower Klukhor waterfall in view ahead. The steepest part of the path is there

118

and above that it joins the Road. The upper waterfall of the river draining Klukhor Lake is 300m from the latter. The path crosses the river and comes to a large snow patch. A track in the snow takes over and leads to the saddle. $4^{1}/2$-5 hours from the Refuge.

From the pass the road goes to the right and descends in long sweeps. The path runs straight down through steep screes, along the left bank of the Klych River. In 2-$2^{1}/2$ hours the low grassy saddle of the Nakhar Pass (Route 32) on the Main Range opens to the left. The stream with a waterfall coming down from the pass is crossed by way of an avalanche snow bridge. After this the valley turns at right angles and runs south-west. All the way the road is on the left bank, at places right under rock cliffs with minor waterfalls streaming on to it. 3-$3^{1}/2$ hours along the road the Southern hut-refuge is reached on the right bank, among giant fir-trees. Total time is 9-10 hours.

The organized trek over the pass is not in operation nowadays, so there is no traffic in the lower stretch of the Klych Valley between the Refuge and Omarishara Village. For chance of a lift, or to catch a regular service bus, you have to walk down 12km more, to the village. The walk is not without its own pleasures, through tall, clear deciduous forest, past the impressive Klych Fall (7km downstream) and the remnants of the Klych border fortress of 13-14th centuries, which marked the border line of the medieval Abkhazian state. For the lovers of old ruins there is another fortress (10-11th century) in the village of Omarishara, at its eastern edge.

And the way to Sukhumi down the fantastic Kodori Gorge on a road clinging to the sheer wall of a canyon is sure to remain an everlasting memory.

ROUTE 37: From the Dombay Glade to the Chkhalta Valley via the Ptysh Pass (1B, 3,000m, on the East Ridge of Ptysh Peak (3,685m) on the Main Range). *(See map 3)*

The second easiest way over the Main Range of the Teberda-Dombay area after the Klukhor Pass, though far from being a mere caravan way. A very typical Dombay Pass, with a fairly easy northern side and a steep southern one somewhat tricky for navigating. There are no technical problems except for some crevasses on the North Ptysh Glacier and a rock ledge on the south side of the saddle where continual care is required, but the descent into the South Ptysh Valley is a really ankle-twisting affair - because of steep grass slopes there. Bird's eye views of deep gorges are a reward for this. The route takes 3 days and the full set of equipment is needed.

Stage 1. A good path goes along the right bank of the Dombay-Ulghen River, first by the cables of the chair-lift, then through birch groves and meadows, to reach in 2 hours the foot-bridge across the Chuchkhur River coming down from its hanging valley on the left. The hairpin bends of the path to the Chuchkhur Pass (Route 38) are clearly seen on the left side of the waterfall. Turn to the right on the bridge and follow the path for another 2 hours to the campsite above the snout of the North Ptysh Glacier where its right bank moraine abuts against the mountainside (2,300m). On the south the deep and wide saddle of the pass is in view, with the north-east ridge of Ptysh Peak rising to the right like the back of a pangolin. The curves of the mountain are so clean and spectacular, that it is well worth the 4 hours walk just to see it.

Stage 2. Make an early start to have enough spare time for descending the south side. Rope up and cross the crevassed glacier to the saddle. 3 hours. A very good view from there of Dombay-Ulghen Peak (4,047m), the highest in the West Caucasus. The canyon of the South Ptysh River is far below. Numerous waterfalls stream into the canyon from the South Ptysh Glacier, the northern part of which is under the saddle. Descend to the glacier by an inclined ledge on the steep rock slope and follow its left bank moraine (with some tent sites at its upper end). Where convenient descend from the moraine and make a long traverse to the left, across many glacial slabs, screes and streams, to reach in $1^{1}/_{2}$ hours a steep alpine meadow with tall grass and, lower down, brushwood and jutting rock steps. Continue making a gently inclined slanting traverse in the same direction. There is no way straight down, because of the canyon to the right. There are some woods above its lower end. Go through these, and descend to the river to pick up a vague path on the same left bank. In 15-20 minutes it brings you to the mouth of a stream flowing into the South Ptysh from the north. There is a kosh there on a meadow and many good tent sites. $4^{1}/_{2}$-5 hours from the pass; total time is $8^{1}/_{2}$-9 hours.

Stage 3. Cross the South Ptysh before the confluence by way of a foot-bridge and follow a path on the right side of the valley over the river. In 30 minutes it descends to it again. There must be a shepherd's foot-bridge here to the left bank. In case it has been swept away, find a snow bridge which holds often till late July. If it does not exist wade the river where it is divided into two arms by an island. For several kilometres the floor of the valley is covered with rock debris and rotten tree trunks overgrown with vegetation - the result of the earthquake of 1963. An exhausting path goes along the steep left bank, climbing and falling, working its way through all the obstacles. In an hour it rises to a beech forest, then in 40 minutes comes to the upper part of Ptysh Village and another 20 minutes bring you to its lower part, where the South Ptysh flows into the Chkhalta River. From here there remain 6km down by a jeep track to the village of Chkhalta on the Military Sukhumi Road with rather a busy traffic during summer. Total time is 4-4¹/₂ hours.

ROUTE 38: From the Dombay Glade to the Gonachkhir Valley via the Chuchkhur Pass (0 Grade, 2,717m, on the North Ridge of Maly Dombay-Ulghen Peak). *(See map 3)*

A very useful, easy and quick way from the Glade to the head of the Gonachkhir Valley (to the Klukhor and Kiche-Murudju Passes. Routes 36, 45) with the dramatic views of the north faces of the highest peaks of the area - Dombay-Ulghen (4,046m) and Bu-Ulghen (3,917m). The route takes one day.

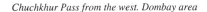

Chuchkhur Pass from the west. Dombay area

For the way to the path, branching off to the Chuchkhur Pass in the Dombay-Ulghen Valley see Route 37. Turn to the left on this path, zig-zagging up the right bank of the Chuchkhur River. On attaining its hanging valley the path levels out and runs east over alpine meadows strewn with boulders and higher up through old screes. 3½-4 hours from the Glade to the pass. On the descent the path runs along the left bank of a tributary stream flowing into the Bu-Ulghen River. The views of the upper cirques on the south are eye-catching all the way from the pass to the river, and the short valley itself is exceptionally beautiful. The path meets a forest track on the left bank of the river. On reaching the Gonachkhir River the track crosses it by a bridge and joins the metalled road in the valley. 2-2½ hours from the pass, 5½-6 hours total time.

ROUTE 39: From the Dombay Glade to the Geological Base in the Aksaut Valley via the Alibek Pass (1A, 3,165m, at the Head of the Alibek Valley). *(See map 5)*

An easy trekking route with paths all the way, without any need for special equipment. It runs parallel to the Main Range, thus affording excellent views of its high peaks; Belalakaya (3,861m, the Caucasian Matterhorn), Erzog (3,863m), Djalovchat (3,880m), Aksaut (3,910m). The route is the shortest way between the Glade and the head of the Aksaut Valley.

Stage 1. Find a path at the western edge of the Alibek climbing base in the Alibek Valley and follow it. 25-30 minutes after setting off the path divides. Take the right-hand one which climbs a steep grass slope, winding in long sweeps and then turns to the left to reach a stream, running from the cirque under the Alibek Pass. There it climbs up along its left bank gaining a grassy terrace then another, rocky one with many tent sites. Camp there. 3½-4 hours from the base.

Stage 2. The wide saddle of the pass is seen to the north-west, to the right of a solitary rock spire. The path goes over old moraine screes (with some patches of snow) to reach in 1½ hours the saddle. The pass brings you a superb view of the giant horse-shoe of the Dombay Glade, walled by an array of the highest summits of the West Caucasus. To the north-west there stands the impressive black pyramid of Karakaya Peak (3,892m).

Descend about ½km west across a gentle snowfield, then pick up a path seen on the old moraine to the right which will lead to a tarn at its lower end.

The path follows the stream draining the tarn and falls into a long hollow, strewn with large blocks and with many tent sites. 2 hours from the saddle. The place is called the Green Hotel. Continuing down, the path crosses alpine meadows then descends steeply to the tree-line and comes into sight of a large glacier to the south. It is the longest one in the West Caucasus, Djalovchat, 5km long. The river Djalovchat is far down in a deep canyon to the left. At one point the path comes very close to the latter.

Further down it is steep again and can be lost in high grass and rhododendrons. If so, keep to the right, away from the canyon and go on descending. Where the Djalovchat flows into the Aksaut there is a promontory and a good campsite under fir-trees. 4-4½ hours from the pass. It is still 1-1½ hours walk down a path along the right bank of Aksaut to the geological base. The path is rather uncomfortable, rising and falling, climbing over boulders and tree trunks to avoid the river which runs at places right under the mountainside. There is a bridge over the Kti-Teberda River which flows into the Aksaut shortly before the base. It is easy to find a campsite around the latter. Total time is 7-7½ hours.

There is shorter, but less picturesque way from the Green Hotel. Going down, look out for a path branching off to the right. It traverses the spur of Kti-Teberda Peak and joins a jeep track in the Kti-Teberda Valley, leading to the base. 4-4½ hours from the pass.

ROUTE 40: From the Geological Base in the Aksaut Valley to the Upper Reaches of the Chkhalta Valley via the Aksaut West Pass (1B, 3,150m, at the Upper Basin of the West Aksaut Glacier, on the Main Range). *(See maps 5 & 10)*

This route is rather demanding, not so much in real climbing skills as in the psychological readiness to tackle short pitches of easy but steep scrambling and long snow slopes of 30-35°. The ability to feel confident without the guiding line of a path, with only a sketch-map and description is essential. The route crosses the wildest part of the West Caucasus and its southern side is the improbable cleft of the Chkhalta Valley, running for more than 30km between the Main Range and the green Chkhalta Range, parallel to the former. The snowy tops soar 3,000m above the green floor of the valley. Uncountable streams cascade down the walls in clouds of spray, crowned with rainbows.

A unique feature of this long and narrow southern valley is a jeep road with good bridges all along its length, made by geologists for their own purposes and connecting it, via the Adanghe Pass (2,300m) with another long valley on the west, Bzyb. The only problem is to reach the road, having got over the Main Range. More often than not it is not easy or straightforward. This route is no exception. Once in the valley you can walk either up (6-7 hours) to the Adanghe Pass, (Route 44) leading into the head of the Bzyb Valley, with a number of routes there over the Main Range to the Arkhyz area, or down to Chkhalta Village (regular bus service) on the Military Sukhumi Road, 37km.

The best time for this walk is the first half of the season, when all the slopes on the ridges are snow, not ice. It takes 2 days, with the full set of equipment.

Stage 1. From the geological base, which is half a kilometre below the mouth of Kti-Teberda River, follow the road on the right bank of the Aksaut. The road rises to the left, into the Kti-Teberda Valley. Cross the Kti-Teberda by a bridge and take a rough path, climbing and falling on the same right bank of the Aksaut. The ramified river, meandering on the flat gravel valley floor can be far enough from its bank to leave this part of the bed dry and good for walking. If so, take this opportunity and head for a wooded promontory, visible to the south. The promontory with its tall fir-trees is a nice place for camping.

From the promontory the path rises to a foot-bridge over the Djalovchat River, the next right tributary, rushing out of its canyon, and descends again to the valley floor which narrows. The path winds through birch brushwood, away from the river and comes to the tree-line. 2-2$\frac{1}{2}$ hours from the base. In another hour the snout of the Aksaut Glacier is reached, a clean ice slant. The way to the pass is over the Aksaut West Glacier, seen on the west in a narrow gorge. The stream running from there joins the Aksaut River near the snout of the Aksaut Glacier.

Use the latter as a bridge across the Aksaut River, descend to the right bank of the stream and walk along it, through screes and jumbled rocks to the snout of the Aksaut West Glacier. Go west, over its dry surface and where the glacier curves south find a campsite on the left-side moraine. 6-6$\frac{1}{2}$ hours from the base. The huge dark bulks of the rock peaks around the confined valley create a somewhat oppressive atmosphere.

Stage 2. The wide snow saddle of the pass and the way to it are clearly seen to the south. To avoid the crevassed right side and centre of the upper basin, keep to the left bank without coming too close to it. 2$\frac{1}{2}$-3 hours to the pass. The flat rocky saddle is a convenient place for camping. South-west, under

Mt Ushba and the peaks of the Bezengi area from the slopes of Mt Elbrus
Mt Elbrus from the Adyrsu valley

Ptysh pass and Ptysh peak from the north
Klukhor lake under the Klukhor pass

the saddle, lies the heavily crevassed Karach Glacier. The line of descent is not obvious, so do not try to go down in poor visibility. In such a case the only answer is to wait on the pass for a break in the clouds. From the saddle go, without descending, south-east along the Main Range, innocent there, come to the easy snow ridge branching off south-west from the Main Range, and follow it for 500-600m. On reaching a steep snow slope on the right side (200-250m, 30-35°) go down past the crevassed glacier, which is to your right, to moderately steep glacial slabs. Find a way down among them and come to a scree cirque where several streams meet to form the Karach River. Descend by its right bank past its short canyon with a waterfall. Below the fall a traceable shepherd path can be found, running to a kosh where the Karach River flows into the South Marukh River. 4-4¹/₂ hours from the pass, 6¹/₂-7 hours total time. A good path on the South Marukh's left bank leads to the road on the left bank of the Chkhalta River. 1¹/₂ hours.

ROUTE 41: From the Geological Base in the Aksaut Valley to the Marukh Valley via the Khalega Pass (0 Grade, 3,000m, on the Mysty-bashi Range) and from the Marukh Valley to the Chkhalta Valley via the Marukh Pass (1A, 2,746m, on the Main Range). *(See map 5)*

For many centuries the second of these passes was a trade way connecting the northern coast of the Black Sea with the Alan state in the North Caucasus. It went through the Marukh Valley on the north and Chkhalta on the south. The route is easy, with good paths all the way, but not without its own thrills, such as a path cut in a rock slope above the river and the probable wading of the Aksaut River. The main charm is the Chkhalta Valley (see Route 40) but both the northern valleys, spacious, wooded (especially Aksaut) and wild, without busy tourist traffic, are very good to visit. The route takes 2 or 3 days and no climbing equipment is necessary.

Stage 1. The Khalega Pass is at the head of the Khalega River which flows into the Aksaut from the left, 2¹/₂km downstream from the mouth of the Kti-Teberda River and 2km from the geological base, where there should be a bridge over Aksaut. If it is swept away walk down 1km on the road and find the place where the river ramifies and its arms are shallow, even if fast and cold. The crossing should be made in the morning before the snow on the glaciers starts to thaw and raise the water level. After heavy rains (which are not infrequent in this part of the Caucasus) the wading can be too dangerous, in which case the only alternative is to walk down 8km to the bridge and to return to the Khalega's mouth by a path on the left bank. (If you go up from Krasny Karachay Village there are no river crossings. Then it is simply a valley walk, 13km on the road and 8km on the path, all the way on the left bank.)

After crossing on the left bank of the Khalega River the path rises past a kosh to three consecutive terraces, and it takes 4-4½ hours to reach the last rocky one with a large tarn and a war memorial on it. The broad depression of the pass is visible to the west with a clear path going to it. The dugouts, rusty shells and cartridge-cases are reminders of the bitter fight between the well-equipped and trained German "Edelweiß" division and Soviet infantry in August, 1942. The graceful and daunting black pyramids of Karakaya (3,896m) and Marukh rise on the south. In about an hour you come to the saddle. The views from there are not too spectacular but pleasing, with the gentle green Ujum Range to the west across the valley. The deep depression of the next pass, Marukh, can be seen to the south-west.

On the descent do not miss a path branching off to the left from the main one running down on the right bank of a stream, which flows into the Marukh River. The left branch goes west, south-west and south, traversing the spur, which stretches north-west and borders the North Marukh Glacier. Eventually the path comes to the right bank moraine of the glacier, to a campsite in a pocket. 1½ hours from the pass.

[The first stage has to be broken into two if you have to walk those 8+8km down to the bridge and then upstream to the mouth of the Khalega River along the Aksaut Valley. In which case camp by the kosh on the first terrace in the Khalega Valley.]

Stage 2. The Marukh Pass with the tiny white pyramid of a war memorial is visible to the south. Cross the glacier, dry there, in this direction, a little to east, heading for a snow ascent on the eastern side of a band of glacial slabs walling the head of the valley. A path is seen from that ascent, climbing up among broken slabs to the wide and flat saddle, with the inevitable war remnants on it. 2½ hours from the campsite.

The path falls steeply to the South Marukh Glacier, easily inclined, with a few narrow crevasses. Cross it to the south-west, past an ice-fall on the left. The path shows again on the right side moraine and runs down on the right bank of the South Marukh River. The first ½km it clings to the wall of a canyon. After this it descends to a meadow. In 2 hours time it brings you to a bank of big blocks. Having passed that, find an avalanche snow bridge and cross the river to the left bank. The path continues there through tall grass and soon comes into sight of the mighty Azyrt waterfall. There is a kosh at the tree-line, where the Karach River flows into the South Marukh and the next one at the confluence of the South Marukh and Adanghe Rivers forming the Chkhalta. $2^{1}/2$-3 hours from the snow bridge. Total time is $7^{1}/2$-8 hours. About the Chkhalta Valley see Route 40.

ROUTE 42: From the Head of the Aksaut Valley to that of the Marukh Valley via the Karakaya-Marukh Pass (1B, 3,200m, on the North Ridge of Karakaya Peak 3,892m, the Mysty-Bashi Range). *(See map 5)*

An interesting alternative to the caravan way over the Khalega Pass, a little shorter (if you go to the Marukh Pass) but more difficult and sterner in scenery. One of the most impressive peaks of the area, black, forbidding and shapely Karakaya, is passed close by. The route is for those unwilling to carry their crampons and ice-axe without ever using them! The pass is crossed in one day. On both sides the snow slopes are rather steep (up to 35°) but not too long - 80-100m. The full set of equipment is required.

Stage 1. The way to the pass begins on the left side of the Aksaut Valley, right opposite the mouth of the Kti-Teberda River. The hairpin bends of the path going to the pass are seen on a big old grassy alluvial cone. To get there, if you are on the right bank, you have to cross the Aksaut River by a bridge at the geological base, which is about 500m downstream from the mouth. Should the bridge be swept away, the quickest means of crossing is to wade the river about 1km downstream from the base, where it ramifies. At the end of a sunny or rainy day it may be found impracticable. Then wait for the next morning and try again, or, better, go down on the road 8km to the solid bridge. (See Route 41.)

Take the path on the cone which rises over the tree-line, turns south and goes almost level above the valley for a distance of a little more than 1km to attain the Karakaya stream (with a kosh on its bank) outflowing from a very long snowfield. Go up west along the stream. From the snowfield there opens out on the west the black rock ridge with the two notches of the pass, and to its left the ridge, ragged and steep, rises to the top of Karakaya. A small glacier is seen under the peak. The snow runs up to both the saddles, growing steeper under them (30-35°). The total time of the ascent from the

127

Aksaut is 5¹⁄₂-6 hours.

To the east the pass brings you views of an array of the Dombay's Peaks including the "Matterhorn of the Caucasus" - Belalakaya Peak - in the centre. The views west are limited. Below the saddle lies the North Marukh Glacier more than 3km long. Descend steep snow (80-100m, 30-35°) and come on to the crevassed glacier. Walk (roped up) north-west, to the right side moraine and find a campsite behind it. 1¹⁄₂-2 hours from the pass, 7-8 hours total time.

[For the way from the campsite to the Marukh Pass see Route 41. To descend into the valley you can either go down along the moraine's right bank on the good path making for the Marukh Pass, or 500-600m short of that is the path from the right, from the Khalega Pass (Route 41). Or, cross the glacier to the west and join the valley-path on the left bank.]

ROUTE 43: From the Head of the Aksaut Valley to the Chkhalta Valley via the Khamurza Pass (2A, 3,300m, on the Main Range, between Maly Djalovchat and Maly Aksaut Peaks). *(See map 5)*

The hardest and highest pass at the head of the longest glacier of the area (5km) with austere Alpine landscapes on the northern side contrasting sharply with the southern one, steep and lavishly vegetated. Basic climbing skills are necessary for the crossing and the full set of equipment. The difficulties are steep snow slopes (30°), one of them 250-300m long and a short pitch of rock scrambling. The route takes 3 days. If the Khamurza Pass is linked to the Alibek Pass, then it is 2 days.

Stage 1. The Djalovchat River outflowing from its namesake glacier runs, before it joins the Aksaut River, in a deep canyon. The only way to get to the glacier from down-valley is as follows: from the promontory with tall fir-trees at the mouth of the Djalovchat River walk up the path going along the river to the Alibek Pass and come to the Green Hotel (for this section see Route 39 Stage 2 and reverse it). 4-5 hours. From there take an ill-defined path running south and climbing the spur which stretches north-west between the Green Hotel and Djalovchat Glacier. The path rises 80-100m, comes to the crest, then makes a descending traverse to the left through awkward loose scree to reach the glacier's flat surface. Walk about 1¹⁄₂km south, then turn to the left and climb to a campsite above the band of glacial slabs, under the Sunakhet Glacier. 1¹⁄₂-2 hours from the Green Hotel, 6-7 hours total time.

Stage 2. The views from the campsite encompass the upper fields of the Djalovchat Glacier. Directly west is Aksaut Peak (3,910m) with its steep rock faces. To its left is the dark triangle of Maly Aksaut and the rock trident of Maly Djalovchat Peak ("maly" = "lower"). The Khamurza Pass is in sight between the two, closer to Maly Aksaut. Descend to the flat glacier over an old scree slope and walk in a south-westerly direction, making for a band of glacial slabs to the left of Maly Aksaut and below it.

Above the band lies the hanging Khamurza Glacier. To get to the slabs go to below the steep strip of ice, descending among the slabs to the upper basin of the Djalovchat Glacier, near the rock slopes of Maly Djalovchat Peak. On approaching the band be on the look-out for chunks of ice falling occasionally from the Khamurza Glacier. The strip of ice is 250-300m long and 30° steep, and normally has a sufficient layer of snow, but to be on the safe side, if you are not prepared for long bouts of front-pointing, do not plan this route for August.

On reaching the crevassed Khamurza glacier and going to the pass, keep to the slopes of Maly Aksaut. There is no need to attack the 60-70° snow slope (with a bergschrund below) leading to the saddle. 60-80m short of it turn to the right, climb over the marginal crevasse, find a kind of path on the rocks of Maly Aksaut and scramble to the saddle. The bergschrund is one more argument against postponing this walk till late in the season. It may be very wide by then and may demand complicated manoeuvres with ropes to negotiate it. The path is made by climbers from the Dombay Glade who regularly visit all the summits of Djalovchat's upper basin and used to camp on the saddles. Right on the pass there are several sites. About 5 hours from the campsite.

A breathtaking sight of the Chkhalta River more than 1½km below awaits you at the saddle. There are two options to choose between in descent: in fact there is no straightforward descent line to the river, so steep is the southern side. No doubt a way can be found in the end, if you persist, but the process is certain to take many hours with a highly likely and utterly uncomfortable forced bivouac somewhere midway as a result. The other option isn't quick either but is controlled all the way. Go west under the Main Range, cross the south spur of Aksaut Peak and take a shepherd path there running into the Chkhalta Valley, or find a campsite. It is about 7 hours from the Khamurza Pass, plus 5 hours to climb to it, which makes a total of about 12 hours. If you do not want this day to be so long, camp either on the pass or on the southern side under it. In the latter case you will have in all probability to construct sites for your tents on a rough and inclined terrain. Camping on the pass, water or snow can be obtained on the glacier.

Stage 3. Descend into a scree and loose rock gully under the saddle, leaving it at the earliest possibility (there is a danger of stone fall from Maly Aksaut Peak) and make a slanting traverse to the right, to the screes. Lower down rough alpine meadows level out. The strip of meadows under the Main Range is the edge of one long drop cut by steep narrow gullies. Once there, walk along the strip heading for the saddle on the south spur of Aksaut Peak to the west. On reaching the South-East Aksaut Glacier (under the peak, 1½-2 hours from the pass) skirt its snout, turning gradually to the right, and climb to the saddle along the scree and snow hollow between the rock slopes of Aksaut and the body of the glacier. The height gained is 100-120m. From the saddle (3½-4 hours from the pass) descend steep snow (30-35°, 70-80m) with a bergschrund below. Descend to the South-West Aksaut Glacier and walk to its right-side moraine. From there go down to a rocky terrace, then to the tree-line. Lower down, by a cattle enclosure under fir-trees, find a path (1½-2 hours from the spur) which brings you in 2-2½ hours to a road on the left bank of the Chkhalta River and a bridge across it. Upstream from the bridge the road is on the left bank, downstream - on the right one (and no path on the left bank!). About the Chkhalta Valley see Route 40.

ROUTE 44: From the Chkhalta Valley to the Bzyb Valley via the Adanghe Pass (0 Grade, 2,300m). *(See maps 6 & 16)*

An age old way connecting the two southern valleys, with a low pass and a jeep road. Both the valleys stretch parallel to the Main Range on the south side of the Dombay and Arkhyz areas, so the pass is a key-point for those travelling there. It is 5-6 hours walk from the confluence of the South Marukh and Adanghe Rivers to the pass (9km) and 3-3½ hours more (12km) from the pass to a long and circuitous path branching off to the Naur Pass on the Main Range (Route 57).

Stage 1. Cross the South Marukh River by a bridge and walk through the forest on the easily inclined road along the left bank of the Adanghe River. In 2 hours (5km) you come to the lower end of the ridge separating the Adanghe River flowing from the west and the Gherighele coming from the north-west. The road and a path, cutting its bends, rise along the crest of the ridge. In 2½-3 hours the tree-line is reached and in 1 hour more the pass itself, with the panoramas of both valleys.

On the descent follow the road which crosses two tributary valleys, the

Pardgali and Satkharo (with numerous mineral springs in their upper
reaches) and comes to a geological base (2,150m) on an alpine meadow of
the right mountainside of the Shkhabztsa Valley. A fine view across the
Bzyb Valley of the Bzyb range and jagged Khimsa Peak (3,150m) is
afforded from there. A path on the western edge of the base leads west over
meadows, down into the forest and comes to a large clearing on the Bzyb's
right bank, opposite the mouth of its left tributary, Psykva. (Note that,
going upstream to the Adanghe Pass, you will have at this point to choose
between the well-trodden path breaking away to the left, to the geological
base, and the poor not much frequented path, following the Bzyb's right
bank up to the pass.)

From the clearing follow the path down and in an hour or so, walking
through fir and beech forest with fields of strawberries, you come to the
mouth of another left tributary, the Ubush River, with high rock walls
towering over it. There is a bridge across Bzyb there, a nice campsite and
a kosh (on the right bank). The good path from the Naur Pass (Route 57)
descending the right mountainside comes to the kosh.

Stage 2. From this point to Pskhu Village, the first one down the Bzyb
Valley, is 30km. With two passes (2,050m and 2,055m) to be crossed it
means more than 45km in real walking distance. Besides, the village of
Pskhu is not a regular bus service terminus. (The place is so isolated, that
the Bolsheviks discovered and put it under control no earlier than 1930!)
It is still a long (about 40km) and circuitous way from there in a chance
vehicle over another pass (Anchkho, 2,000m) to Ritsa Lake where you can
take a bus to Sukhumi (137km) or Adler (147km) airports. Evidently, this
is not the most convenient way to get out of the mountains after a walk, even
though some parts of the route are of stunning beauty.

Two quicker and easier ways back to civilization from the head of the
Bzyb Valley (which is 112km long) are either over some pass on the Main
Range to Arkhyz Village or over the Adanghe Pass and down the Chkhalta
Valley to the Military Sukhumi Road. Should an accident happen in this
remote spot, the place to go for help is the geological base in the Shkhabztsa
Valley. There they have a radio station and a helipad.

Nonetheless, for those who insist, the description of the way to Pskhu
Village is as follows. From the bridge opposite the mouth of the Ubush
River take either upper or lower path on the Bzyb's right bank. The first one
goes way up over the river, the second, very close to it. In high water take
the upper one. They meet on the left bank of South Psysh River near its
mouth (1$^{1}/_{2}$ hours). Cross it by way of a foot-bridge and take the path rising

to the Gvashtkhva Pass - not easy to find because the number of them is confusing. The correct one is well trodden, and its general direction is a little north of west. It leaves the Bzyb River on the left, far down in a canyon. In short, at any fork always take a left branch if it is wide and steep. In 2-2½ hours it brings you to the tree-line, in another hour reaches a grassy ridge with koshes on a meadow (2,200m), turns to the left and descends along the crest of the ridge to the Gvashtkhva Pass (2,050m). The descent to the Gribza River along its left tributary-stream takes 2 hours. Total time is 7-8 hours. The valley is a meadowland, good for camping. The path to the next pass, Chamashkha, begins on the right bank near the kosh at the confluence of the source-streams forming the river, 2½km upstream. It climbs west in the beech forest and in 2-2½ hours brings you to the pass, with a bird's-eye view of the huge, green Pskhu hollow, and to the north-west the way to civilization, the Agurispta Valley, 15km long, and the Anchkho Pass at its head. The Chamashkha Pass is a flat plateau, with a cone of Bzybskaya Peak (2,660m) on the left. There remain 18km to the village of Pskhu on a rough track - through a settlement of geologists on the right bank of the Baul River, then on its left bank. Total time is 7-8 hours.

ROUTE 45: From the Gonachkhir Valley to the Nakhar Valley via the Kitche-Murudju Pass (1A, 3,150m, at the Head of the Kitche-Murudju Valley). *(See maps 2 & 3)*

Partly the route goes through the Teberda National Reserve, clean, unspoiled, and with charming views. There are chamois coming to sniff at your drying socks (literally!) and evidence of the bear's thrillingly close presence: you are quite likely to see the animal. The route is easy enough to do it without any climbing equipment. 2 days.

Stage 1. The path into the Kitche-Murudju Valley breaks away from the road in the Gonachkhir Valley shortly before the bridge (over the former). It goes on the right bank through the pine forest, zig-zagging up the mouth-step of the hanging valley, to reach the tree-line in 1 hour. In 40-50 minutes more you come to the bend in the valley which turns from north-east to south-east. What follows after the bend is several flat swampy terraces separated from each other by old moraines. On gaining the second terrace two twin snow saddles with a rock between them come into view in the south-east. The left one is the Kitche-Murudju Pass. Follow the path for another 1½ hours and short of a band of glacial slabs to the south-east, barring the way to the Kitche-Murudju Glacier, find on the level terrace a suitable campsite. 3-3½ hours from the road.

Stage 2. Head for a hanging glacier in the north-east and climb a scree slope, leaving the rock band to your right. There is sandy ground above the slope with a war memorial and some remnants of a crashed plane. There turn south-east and walk over glacial slabs and screes to the glacier and gently inclined snow leading to the left saddle. 2 hours from the campsite. From the pass fine views of three sharp Nahkhar Peaks to the east and of many summits of the Dombay to the west can be seen.

Descend a short scree slope to the Chauluchat Glacier, small and inoffensive. Keep to its left side to avoid a band of steep slabs right ahead. Come to a small tarn under the glacier and follow down the left bank of the stream draining it, to reach a flat terrace strewn with big blocks, where several streams meet to form the Chauluchat River. Go down its left bank through dense and high rhododendrons, trying to follow the path, rather vague there. The caravan path along the Nakhar River is on its right bank and to get there you have to cross the river by stepping stones where practicable. 4-4½ hours from the saddle. Total time is 6-6½ hours.

ROUTE 46: From the Daut Valley to the Nakhar Valley via the Uzlovoy Pass (1B, 3,100m, on the East Ridge of Daut Peak (3,748m). *(See maps 2 & 3)*

The route takes 3 days for approach, crossing and descending. There is no climbing, just some easy rock scrambling. On the northern side lies a fairly large glacier for this area under the north wall of Daut Peak and some slopes, up to 30°, normally screes, but early in the season awkward snow. So, the full set of equipment should be taken. There are paths on both the banks of the Daut River but you can never be sure about flimsy bridges made by shepherds. Often they are swept away by high water.

Stage 1. The valley walk on the right bank from Daut Village to the last right tributary side stream, 1km from the snout of the Daut Glacier, is 20km long and takes 7-8 hours. Camp there on a meadow.

Stage 2. Walk along the river to the snout, get on the glacier and head for the right side of the ice-fall, blocking the way to the upper basin. Climb a scree gully (snow early in the season) on the right side slope, bordering the ice-fall and come to the basin. To the south rises the low pyramid of Daut Peak. On its east ridge you can see three consecutive minor rock peaks: one is right under the mountain itself, the next one is to the left and a little in the distance, and the last one is seen to the south-east to east. The depression to the left of this last is the Uzlovoy Pass. The other two depressions are also passes to the Nakhar Valley but, with the heavily crevassed approaches leading to them, they are much more difficult. The snow under the Uzlovoy is not steep and without yawning bergschrunds. 4¹/₂-5 hours from the campsite.

From the pass traverse 70-80m south-east the broken, loose rocks of the minor peak, which was seen from the glacier to the right of the saddle. Having skirted the peak you find yourself on its ridge running south-east. Descend from the ridge to the south by scree and snow to a rocky terrace. From there descend a long and fairly steep grassy slant, with jutting rocks, to an alpine meadow: a meeting place for numerous streams and a good campsite. 1-1¹/₂ hours from the pass. Total time is 5¹/₂-6 hours. It is still 3¹/₂-4 hours descent to the Nakhar Valley, so if you are tired and in no haste, camp there.

Stage 3. The stream from the South Daut Glacier, running through the meadow, falls into a canyon cut in the band of steep rocks bordering the meadow on the east. There is an indistinct shepherd's path, which begins on the left bank, above the canyon and goes down rather steeply. Once in the Nakhar Valley, turn to the left (as you go down) and in 40 minutes you reach a track and a foot-bridge to the right bank, with a path on it. 3¹/₂-4 hours.

ROUTE 47: From the Town of Teberda to the Daut Valley via the Epchik Pass (0 Grade, 3,000m at the Head of the Epchiksu Valley) and from there to the Village of Uchkulan via the Karachaiaush (0 Grade, 2,500m, on the Daut Range between Daut and Uchkulan Villages). *(See map 4)*

A pure trekking walk, taking 3 days, all the way on good paths, with out any snow (except in early June), varied and interesting for its views, with numerous koshes and farms along the way and the excellent morning view of Mt Elbrus from the Epchik Pass.

Stage 1. Find a path beginning north of the tourist base (on the right bank of the Teberda River, 1km downstream from the car bridge). It goes north along a narrow artificial water channel, skirting the base of Kelbashi Peak (2,810m), reaches the Djemagat River and comes to a bridge. 1^1/2 hours. Cross the river and take a road in the forest on the right bank. Soon it goes over to the left one, then back again and remains there, leading to a two storey tourist hut-refuge at the junction of the Epchiksu and Goralykol Rivers. 3 hours from Teberda. There the road ends. Cross the Epchiksu by a bridge and take a good path through the forest on the left bank, far from the river. Soon the path comes down to the bank and eventually crosses by way of a footbridge. Returning to the left bank it leaves behind the last pine grove and climbs alpine meadows to reach a fine campsite on a flat grassy shelf, by a small tarn. 4 hours from the hut-refuge, 7 hours total time.

Stage 2. It takes 1 hour to walk to the pass in the sight of the huge, white, rosy-tinted Mt Elbrus towering over the minor ranges to the east. The path rising to the next pass, Karachaiaush, is clearly seen on the western slopes of the Daut Range.

On the descent take either the left or right branch of the path dividing under the saddle; they meet again lower down anyway. It zig-zags down screes and in 1 hour comes to alpine meadows on the left bank of the Kendelesu Stream and follows it all the way down to the Daut Valley, with deserted Daut Village. Total time is 4-4^1/2 hours. The village, built early in the 18th century, is a sort of ethnographic memorial of the old Karachai life.

If you are short of time and not tired, you can get to Uchkulan Village on the same day. It is a further 6^1/2-7 hours walk, 4-4^1/2 hours up to the Karachaiaush Pass and 2-2^1/2 hours down. Otherwise, camp in the agreeable wooded valley, with sharp rock peaks in view to the south.

Stage 3. To find the path climbing to the Karachaiaush Pass go along the road a short way downstream and come by a bridge to the right bank. The wide well-trodden path begins behind a small farm. A long haul to the pass takes 4-4^1/2 hours. Uchkulan Village with all the roads and bridges in the valley is visible from the saddle.

ROUTE 48: From the Town of Teberda to the Daut Valley via the Kyshkadjer Pass (1A, 3,200m, on the North Ridge of Kyshkadjer Peak (3,825m). *(See map 4)*

The route trades the Epchik Pass for another one on the same Kyshkadjer

Range, a little further south. It is higher and more demanding in terms of fitness and navigating experience, but not much more difficult technically. Being off the beaten track it goes through wilder upper valleys and affords charming sights of tarns framed in green meadows and rocks. It takes nearly the same time as Epchik and no special equipment is needed.

Stage 1. For the way to the confluence of the Epchik and Goralykol Rivers see Route 47. From there, instead of turning to the left into the Epchiksu Valley, keep on going south-east to east and pick up a poor path winding in the pine forest on the steep right bank of the Kyshkadjer River, flowing into the Goralykol River 300m up from the confluence. In 3 hours the path brings you to the tree-line, where the valley levels out. Cross the river to the left bank by stepping stones. In one hour more you come to a wide meadow with big blocks strewn all over it. Head for the left edge of an old moraine stretching across the valley and climb a large scree leading to the terrace where Greater Kyshkadjer lake lies. On the south rises the high triangle of Kyshkadjer Peak and the low saddle of the pass is seen south-east on its north ridge. Camp by the lake. 5 hours from the confluence. Total time from Teberda is 8-8^1/$_2$ hours.

Stage 2. Leave the lake to your left and climb an unstable scree slope (30°) leading to the saddle. 2 hours. Descend much gentler scree to a cirque with snow patches where the Kichkinesu River begins. Follow its left bank which is a succession of grassy terraces. At the tree-line (there is a kosh there) the river falls into a canyon and from the kosh the path zig-zags down in the pine forest. On the floor of the valley it meets a jeep track on the left bank of the Daut River. Turn to the left and follow the track to Daut Village. 30 minutes. Total time is 6-6^1/$_2$ hours.

ROUTE 49: From the Town of Teberda to the Head of the Daut Valley over the Kyshkadjer Range via the Nazly-Ryndjy Pass (1B, 3,350m, on the North-East Ridge of Nazalykol Peak (3,600m). *(See map 4)*

The walk takes 3 days, with the last stage of only 3-4 hours, and is easy enough for the moderate walker. Its difficult spot is a snow gully, 70-80m, 30-35°, on the western side of the pass. The full set of equipment should be taken. The rest of the route is a lot of screes, some of them very unpleasant - big unstable blocks - and small safe glaciers. The upper valleys do not see much tourist traffic, so the paths are not too good there. This demands a certain amount of experience in mountain navigation. The Nazlykol Valley belongs to the Teberda Nature Reserve.

Stage 1. For the beginning see Route 47, Stage 1. Instead of crossing the Djemagat River walk along the path upstream and when the Nazlykol River is reached (1^1/2 hours from Teberda), turn to the right and follow a steep path on its wooded left bank. In 2-2^1/2 hours it brings you to a clearing, passes over the river, with a hut-refuge there on the right bank, and in another 1^1/2 hours comes to the tree-line. The head of the valley comes into sight. The pass and the upper basin of the Nazlykol Glacier under it are hidden from view by a high and precipitous rock spur jutting into the valley. The snout of the glacier is seen to the right of the spur, but to get there you would have to negotiate the moraine hills of big unstable blocks. It is safer to round the spur to its left, even though it means tackling a snow gully.

Meanwhile, follow the right bank, skirt a swampy meadow, and cross the river by the natural bridge of rocks damming it. Ascend to a terrace, where the river is wide and quiet, and climb a grassy moraine to find the next terrace, with a tarn on it. Camp there. 1 hour from the tree-line. Total time is 6^1/2-7 hours.

Stage 2. Head for the snow gully (30-35°. 70-80m) in the glacial slabs which is in clear view to the left of the spur, mount it (preferably using the steps made in the soft evening snow overnight) and come on to the vast gently inclined upper basin. The pass is a wide saddle seen to the south-east and decorated with rocks of curious shapes. The steep ridge of Nazalykol Peak descends to it from the right. 3^1/2-4 hours from the campsite.

Descend steep scree to a snowy hollow, veer to the right and come on to a narrow strip of the Ryndjy Glacier under the south-east ridge of Nazalykol Peak. Over its end moraines descend to the upper, smaller, Ryndjy Lake, leave it to your right and come down to the next grassy terrace. Camp there. 2^1/2-3 hours from the pass. Total time is 6-7 hours.

Stage 3. The choice of the left or right bank of the Ryndjy stream to descend along depends on where you go once in the Daut Valley. If you take Route 46, over the Uzlovoy Pass to the Nakhar Valley, go down by the right one, but if you want to get to Daut Village (18km) take the left bank, with a fairly good path beginning near the lower (larger) Ryndjy Lake. There is a path on the right bank as well, but ill-defined in many places. It takes 3-3^1/2 hours to reach the Daut River. Late in the season when all the avalanche snow bridges over it have thawed, the only way to get to the right bank is to walk 2¹/₂km upstream to the snout of the Daut Glacier.

ROUTE 50: From the Town of Teberda to the Aksaut Valley via the Baduk Pass (0 Grade, 3,004m, on the Teverda Range, at the Head of the Baduk Valley) and the Aruchat Pass (1A, 3,000m, at the Head of the Bolshaya Marka Valley). *(See maps 5 & 7)*

A lovely trekking walk, varied in views, with a lot of tarns, alpine meadows and screes as the main terrain and without any snow (except in early June, of course). It takes 3 days and no special equipment is needed. From the Aksaut you can walk to the Marukh Valley over the Khalega of Karakaya-Marukh Passes (Routes 41, 42) and cross the Main Range by the Marukh Pass (Route 41).

Stage 1. From the town of Teberda walk on the forest track along the left bank of the Teberda River to the mouth of Khadjibey River, flowing into Teberda 6km upstream from the town. Or you can take a bus by the good road on the right bank. Get off at the suspension-bridge and pass over to a glade on the Khadjibey's left bank, with a guards' cordon on it. Pick up a path near the cordon, which runs in the forest, far from the river. In 50 minutes it comes to a bridge. Cross it and follow a way-marked path branching off into the hanging Baduk Valley on the right.

One hour from the bridge the tree-line is reached. Soon the river vanishes from sight, running under a natural rock dam, which holds a small tarn. The path runs past a second tarn, crosses the river by a natural rock bridge to the left bank and comes to the third and largest tarn, with many tent sites around. 3 hours from the cordon. The path goes on through brushwood and tall grass and climbs steeply to a wide flat terrace with big blocks strewn over it and a tiny tarn. Camp there. 4-4¹/₂ hours from the cordon.

Stage 2. The head wall of the valley and the Baduk Glacier are seen to the south-west, but the Baduk Pass is on the north-west and is hidden from view by the three successive steps of the valley: a grassy one, one with many rock outcrops and the third and last - a rock cirque with the uppermost tarn. 3-4 hours from the campsite. The pass opens out on the north-west, above the grass, scree and loose rock slopes leading to it. It is attained in 1 hour. The saddle is a curious transverse rocky corridor on the ridge. A very good view back to the east shows the summits of the Dombay and Daut. On the west stretches the green, smooth ridge separating the Bolshaya Marka Valley (its flat upper part is seen under the pass) from the Aksaut, and to the south-west a hanging glacier is in sight above a step of glacial slabs.

Descend a scree slope (with snow patches in the first half of the season) to Marka Lake on the flat, marshy valley floor. Over a length of 2km it remains horizontal, then a rock step, 200m high, is reached. The path climbs down the step to the left of the falling stream. [To descend the valley cross the stream by big stepping-stones at this point and follow the right bank. Soon the stream meets another one, coming from the left. $1^{1}/_{2}$-2 hours from the pass. It is 15km downstream from this confluence to the summer farm village of Krasny Karachai in the Aksaut Valley and 9km to the point where the path joins another one, well beaten, going along the Malaya Marka River].

The way to the Aruchat Pass, however, is up the left source of the Bolshaya Marka River. Coming down the right source from Marka Lake do not cross the stepping stones under the rock step, but follow the left bank and, on reaching the confluence, walk up the right bank of the left source over low rock steps and grass. In 1 hour a green terrace is attained, walled by a step of glacial slabs covered with moraine rubble. Above the step the Aruchat Pass is visible to the west as a depression on the ridge running north from the west shoulder of an unnamed peak, 3,602m. The peak itself with a distinctive rock spire is seen to the left and the pass is right at the junction of the jagged and smooth parts of the ridge. $2^{1}/_{2}$-3 hours from the Baduk Pass. Total time is 7-8 hours.

(There is a much shorter way from the Baduk Pass to the green terrace, but practicable only in good visibility. From the flat upper part of the valley under the pass make a traverse to the left of a smooth spur separating the two sources of the river and come down to the terrace. It will take $1^{1}/_{2}$-2 hours.)

Stage 3. Mount the step of glacial slabs, find a path rising steeply to the saddle, a narrow gap on the rocky ridge. $1^{1}/_{2}$-2 hours from the terrace. The grassy head of the Aruchat Valley with a kosh at the tree-line is in view to the west. Descend steep scree and snow leading to the upper cirque and from the kosh follow the path on the right bank of the river. In the Aksaut Valley the path meets the road on the Aksaut's right bank, at the point 7km from the geological base and 15km from Krasny Karachai. 3-4 hours from the pass, 5-6 hours total time.

ROUTE 51: From the Town of Teberda to the Arkhyz Village over the Passes: Mukhu (0 Grade, 2,764m, on the Teberda Range), Kyzylaush (0 Grade, 2,900m, on the Mysty Range) and Ozerny (0 Grade, 2,500m, on the Morg-Syrty Range). *(See maps 7 & 8)*

A trekking route with rather busy tourist traffic. Its line is parallel to the Main Range, 15-25km away from it. The route goes over the grassy northern ranges with soft picturesque scenery (with views of high peaks to the south). There are many farms, koshes and some hut-refuges, good paths and, in July, August and September, no snow. Teberda and Arkhyz are the termini of regular bus service lines connecting them with the main airport of the North Caucasus, Mineralny Vody. Being a couple of dozen kilometres away from the Main Range, even the high points of the route usually enjoy good weather when further south all is cloudy and rainy around the snowy ranges. The route takes 4 days. The last part of the route, the western side of the Ozerny Pass, lies in the territory of the Arkhyz Branch of the Teberda Nature Reserve, so a permit has to be obtained at the office in Teberda.

Stage 1. In the northern part of the town the main road crosses the Mukhu River flowing into the Teberda River from the left. Take a forest track on the right bank of the Mukhu. In 20-25 minutes, having passed the cottage of a guards' cordon, get over to the left bank, treeless. A strip of forest remains on the right bank over a stretch of 5km. A long 2 hours haul brings you to a meadow where the Azghek River flows into the Mukhu. The head of the Azghek Valley seen to the south is walled by the impressive rock face of Azghek Peak (3,322m). The track runs past a farm on the meadow to another farm, reached in 40-50 minutes, and through a meadowland studded with age-old boulders to yet another farm (40 minutes). 4-4½ hours from Teberda. The wide saddle of the Mukhu Pass opens on the west, but it will take 2½-3 hours to get there. Camp somewhere in the vicinity of the third farm.

Stage 2. A path takes over from the track and rises to the pass over alpine meadows. Before the final ascent the Mukhu River turns south-west. Good views of high rock and snow peaks on the south (Malaya Marka 3,750m, Khadjibey 3,740m) and east (Kyshkadjer 3,810m) are afforded from the saddle. On the west the ridge separating the Aksaut and Bolshaya Marka Valleys and, beyond it, the Mysty Range with the low depression of the next pass, Kyzylaush, are clearly seen. The Malaya Marka River starting from under its namesake peak runs north almost parallel to the ridge and turns west under the pass. Follow the path, going down through scree and coming to a kosh. Cross the river by a foot-bridge and take a path on the grassy, level left bank. Soon it plunges into the pine forest, with the river on the right roaring in its steep bed, and comes to the Bolshaya Marka River. 1-1$\frac{1}{2}$ from the pass. Cross the Malaya Marka by way of a foot-bridge, walk half a kilometre down along the river's right bank to a kosh in a meadow, and find a bridge to the left bank, with a wide path there. In 1$\frac{1}{2}$-2 hours, having crossed the river several times, you come to Krasny Karachai Village in the Aksaut Valley. Total time is 5$\frac{1}{2}$-6$\frac{1}{2}$ hours. A good alternative to camping near the village is to spend an hour or so walking up the road in the Aksaut Valley and find a nice campsite in a birch grove.

Stage 3. Walk on the road up the Aksaut's left bank for 9 easy, agreeable kilometres through groves and clearings, past koshes to a farm which is at the mouth of a left-hand tributary, Kyzylaush stream. 2$\frac{1}{2}$-3 hours. Take a path in a birch grove on the left bank which soon zig-zags in the forest up the mouth-step of the hanging valley. The valley levels out and a kosh at the tree-line is reached. 1 hour from the Aksaut River. Go due west on a vague path along a grassy crest on the left bank, then leave the stream, turning south, and head straight for the saddle seen to the west. 3-3$\frac{1}{2}$ hours from the Aksaut. The next pass, Ozerny, is in view north-west, between the flat summit of Morg-Syrty Peak (3,140m) and sharp Karabek Peak (2,980m). On the east the far away profile of Mt Elbrus looms above the previous pass, Mukhu.

Descend the steep path leading through alpine meadows to a kosh, which is, as ever, at the tree-line, on the right bank of the stream. Through the forest it runs down steeply and comes to the right bank of the Marukh River, well wooded, in contrast to the left one. The valley is a pastureland with numerous koshes and farms scattered all along its length. Find a suitable campsite in the forest by the river. 1-1$\frac{1}{2}$ hours from the pass, 6-8 hours total time.

Stage 4. Walk down 2km, find a bridge and pass over the Marukh River to the left bank. Immediately at the bridge a good path breaks away north-west, making for the Ozerny Pass through pine trees. In 1$\frac{1}{2}$ hours the tree-line (with a kosh there) is attained and there follows another 1$\frac{1}{2}$ hours on the path, steadily rising over dull meadowland used extensively as pastures.

An unusual (for this part of the Caucasus) sight awaits travellers on the Ozerny Pass (3-3$\frac{1}{2}$ hours from the Marukh River). A green undulating plateau stretches north from the summit of Morg-Syrty Peak, and is almost level with the pass. The deep wooded hollow of the Bolshoy Zelenchuk Valley is seen on the north.

The way down is not obvious: follow the stream with the only problem of choosing the better bank. The path leading to Arkhyz Village crosses westward the meadow on the western side, passes over the source of the Livnevy River (its valley runs to north-west), goes past a post marking the Reserve's border and up the low grassy dividing ridge between the Livnevy and Rapachai Rivers. On reaching the latter, the path goes a short distance along its right bank, then comes by a foot-bridge to the left one and, keeping the same westward direction, starts numerous ups and downs across soft grassy ridges with streams between them.

In 2-2$^{1/2}$ hours the level grass of the last ridge is attained and the steep descent begins on the right bank of the Revunok stream, flowing into the Bolshoi Zelenchuk River. The tiring traverse and the steep treeless descent is at last compensated for with the shade of the forest and a gently inclined path. 1 hour after the last ridge the path meets a forest track on the right bank of the Bolshoy Zelenchuk. Turn to the left, pass over the Revunok by a bridge and walk up to the village of Arkhyz. 30-40 minutes (2$^{1/2}$km). Total time is 6$^{1/2}$-7$^{1/2}$ hours.

ROUTE 52: From the Town of Teberda through the Azghek Valley over the Azghek Pass (1A-1B, 3,100m, between Khadjibey (3,740m) and Azghek (3,322m) Peaks), through the Khadjibey Valley and back to Teberda. *(See maps 5 & 7)*

An attractive 3 or 2 days' circuit through wild unfrequented valleys, past beautifully set tarns with ice floes (Khadjibey Lake, at 2,900m) and over rather a high pass, interesting to "hard walkers", which has on its northern side a snow ascent, 100m long and 25-30° steep.

Stage 1. For the way from Teberda to the mouth of the Azghek River see Route 51 Stage 1. Cross the Mukhu River by a bridge and follow a track going through the forest on the Azghek left bank. At the tree-line the track passes over to a kosh on the right bank. A path takes over and goes on along the left one, over a succession of grass and boulder terraces to end up by a kosh on a swampy meadow. 1$^{1/2}$-2 hours from the Mukhu River. Right on the south a high and steep rock spur separates the two sources of the Azghek. The way to the Azghek Pass is along the western one. Reach a grassy terrace with boulders and camp on it. 2$^{1/2}$-3 hours from the Mukhu.

Stage 2. There is another stream junction at the western end of the terrace. The left one (looking up) flows through a long hollow coming from the south-west and the other one falls down a band of glacial slabs and screes to the west. A rock spire between the lower end of the hollow and the band acts as a marker. The saddle of the pass is visible to the south-west, to the right of the characteristic truncated cone of a rock, sticking up. Walk along the left-hand stream and where its bed is covered by a long snow strip climb, to avoid it, the left grassy side in the same direction. A small glacier and a gully leading to the saddle (100-120m, 25-30°) come into view soon. 3-3½ hours from the campsite to the pass.

The view south encompasses the head of the Khadjibey Valley, one of the wildest valleys of the area. Under the abrupt, serrated ridge of Baduk Peak lies Khadjibey Lake, cold, with floating chunks of ice and dark blue even in sunny weather. It takes an hour to reach it by scree and easy rock slopes. The place is not too comfortable for camping, so, if you are not going to get to Teberda this day (7-8 hours from the lake), camp at some convenient spot lower down. A more or less clear path is to be found as far as half the length of the valley.

Stage 3. Take the left bank for descending and lower down find the path. At two places it changes the banks and meets the good path by the mouth of the Baduk River. 4-5 hours to the Teberda River, another 2½-3 hours to the town.

West Caucasus: Arkhyz

Looking at the map of the West Caucasus one is surprised to see how dramatically, by half a kilometre, fall the heights of the Main Range and the northern branches west of the low depression of the Labinsky Pass (at the head of the long Bolshaya Laba Valley) and how sparse and insignificant are the glaciers there. The part of the Main Range east of the pass is the southern border of the Arkhyz area, the last area of the classical alpine type, high and covered with ice and snow. The eastern and western borders are the Ujum and Arkasara Ranges. The highest summits are Pshysh (3,780m) and Sofiya (3,640m), with the average height of the peaks 3,400-3,500m, and of the passes 2,800-3,000m. The technical difficulty of the latter are one or one and a half grades lower than that in the neighbouring Dombay area. Since it is almost as picturesque, the Arkhyz area is more agreeable and comfortable for beginners or very modest high level walkers.

The spacious Arkhyz hollow where three broad valleys meet - Arkhyz, Psysh and Kizgych - is famous for its beauty and as a health resort, the high Abishira-Akhuba range protecting it from the northern cold fronts. There's a lot of sunshine in the vast lavishly wooded valleys, charming vistas, a choice of easy, but glaciated and scenic passes and, last but not least, a good road connecting Arkhyz Village with Mineralny Vody Airport. All this makes the area very attractive for walkers.

The main and only permanent settlement is Arkhyz (1,500m), with regular bus services to Cherkessk, capital of Karachai-Circassia (124km, several runs a day), Mineralny Vody (237km, one run) and the nearest railway station Nevinnomyssk (204km). If you miss the only bus from Mineralny Vody Airport, you can go instead to Cherkessk, Karachaevsk or to the town of Zelenchukskaya (66km) from where there are more buses to Arkhyz.

The accommodation at the village cannot be compared to that of the Dombay's hotels. There are three tourist bases (more like youth hostels than hotels), but very small, 70-100 people each. The largest one, "Arkhyz", belongs to a Karachai-Circassia Tourist Organization (there is a Rescue Service at this base, tourist, not climbing, but it is better than nothing), the other two are private centres, the property of Moscow organizations. Normally they are cram-full during summer and stray travellers are not welcome. There is also a tiny regular hotel, owned by the local forestry organisation; a very rough affair. There is a car-camping site for motor-car tourists, but note, though, that the Psysh Valley is closed for private cars.

All the valleys of the area, except Kizgych, which is a part of the Teberda Nature Reserve, have fairly good roads (not metalled of course) to their upper reaches. In the Sofiya Valley the road goes almost to the head, to the Ice Farm (a true one, under a glacier 16km from the village). Two permanent summer camps belonging to the bases (a cottage or two and a row of military tents) are situated along the road, the first one is 7km from Arkhyz, the second, 11km. In the Psysh Valley a road reaches a farm 11km from Arkhyz, only one third of the valley's length. The road in the Arkhyz Valley comes very close to the Pkhiya Pass, connecting the area with the Bolshaya Laba on the west. The cottages of a camp belonging to the "Arkhyz" base is 11km from the village. A permit for visiting the Kizgych Valley (the domain of bisons brought there in 1963) and the Dombay area (if you walk there from Arkhyz) can be obtained at the Reserve's office in the village, but the most reliable place to get it (even though more expensive) is the head office at the town of Teberda.

For those interested in the history of the East the Arkhyz area has something to offer. Because of its position on the shortest and easiest way from the North Caucasus to Byzantia (via the Sancharo Pass), and judging from many archaeological finds there, the upper reaches of the Bolshoy Zelenchuk Valley are considered to be the political and religious centre of the powerful Alan state which, by the 12th century had spread all over the North Caucasus. The main place of historical interest is the site of an ancient settlement, assumed to be the capital of the Alan state, at the village of Nijny Arkhyz (22km upstream from the town of Zelenchukskaya), on the river's right bank. If you go to Arkhyz by rented car or taxi, stop there for an hour or so. The remnants of the capital are about 3km long, with the streets oriented meridionally and with two Byzantine style cathedrals, surprisingly well preserved. There are many more ancient sites upstream, as high as the valleys of Psysh, Sofiya and Kizgych, but being badly disintegrated and overgrown they can interest only specialists.

South of the area lie the upper reaches of two long valleys, Chkhalta and Bzyb. The first one is more interesting for the views in its upper part, the second - in the middle and lower parts. The Chkhalta, with a jeep track all along the valley, eliminating any navigation problems, is a much more straightforward way to civilization than the Bzyb, with its two passes on the route to the village of Pskhu. For the details about the first valley see Route 40 for the second one - Route 44.

ROUTE 53: From the Village of Arkhyz to the Head of the Kizgych Valley and to the Head of the Marukh Valley via the Bugoychat Pass (0 Grade, 2,900m, on the Ujum Range). *(See maps 5 & 6)*

An easy trekking route through a long, unspoiled, wild valley, populated only by deer and aurochs, with a pass free from ice and snow. The disadvantages are an awkward, tiring path, often flooded and the annoying number of stream crossings. The route takes 2 days, with the first one somewhat long, but then the second one is just 3-3¹/₂.

Stage 1. On the southern edge of the village find a bridge over the Bolshoy Zelenchuk, pass over and take a forest track running south, away from the river (on its right bank). The border of the Reserve (do not forget to obtain a permit!) is marked with a fence near the bridge. The track goes between the red rocks of the western ridge of Morg-Syrty Peak and a wooded hill in the middle of the valley, past a small overgrown lake. Where the rocks jut forth into the river a path breaks away and climbs above the water. Further up the way is through agreeable birch groves and glades. In 2-2¹/₂ hours time a war memorial is reached.

The path goes on, climbing over rocks barring the way and descending to flat sections of the valley floor with numerous meandering arms of the river Kizgych, some of which have to be crossed. Do not be upset about the many crossings or the flooded path; you will have your feet wet by the evening anyway.

Soon the Main Range with its snows opens out on the south. In another 2 hours, through the forest, the path brings you to a place suitable for wading the two or three arms of the river, to a wide path on the left bank. The wading, even though uncomplicated, is not a trifling affair, the water being 80-100cm deep. The path on the left bank, running through grass 2 metres high, is very spectacular. About 1¹/₂ hours along that path a big hut is attained where it is possible to spend a night at a pinch.

Or continue along the right bank, less beaten. At the mouth of the Bugoychat stream, flowing into the Kizgych from the right, there is a foot-bridge over the river. The mouth of the Bugoychat stream is 7-7¹/₂ hours from the village. The Bugoychat Glacier and the upper snowfields open to the south. Follow up the path on its right bank. It veers to the left from the river, crosses a side-stream, goes through shrubs and a large patch of raspberry-canes and climbs, with many ups and downs, among tall, age-old fir-trees, their trunks covered with hanging lichen, to the crest of an overgrown moraine. The Bugoychat is heard at first on the right, falling through a deep wooded gorge, then the path goes steeply away from it, heading west. A sensation of wilderness and seclusion is overwhelming there. Deer, bear and aurochs are very likely to be met in this valley. Camp on a grassy low hill above the tree-line where the valley levels out. Total time is 8-9 hours.

Stage 2. The wide green valley goes east to end up under a serrated rock ridge with a deep depression in it, which is not yet the pass. It takes an hour to walk up through alpine meadows and screes under the steep rock wall on the left, to the vast terrace which brings into view a sharp rock peak with the true saddle to its left. A grassy gentle ridge leads to the pass. 1^1/$_2$-2 hours from the campsite. The Khalega and Marukh Passes (Route 41) can be seen from there, with Karakaya Peak between them. Sofiya and Chuchkhur Peaks are in view in the west.

Descend over scree and grass into the Marukh Valley, bearing slightly to the right to avoid steep rock steps. The well trodden path on the Marukh's left bank, leading to the Marukh Pass is reached in 1-1^1/$_2$ hours, 3-3^1/$_2$ hours total time.

ROUTE 54: From the Head of the Kizgych Valley to the Chkhalta Valley via the 810th Regiment Pass (1B, 3,000m, at the Head of the Bugoychat Valley). *(See maps 5 & 6)*

A route coinciding partly with the previous one but with a more difficult pass on the Main Range, leading to the South Marukh Valley. There is a crevassed glacier and some snow of 25-30° on the northern side and a steep descent, without a good path, on the southern one. 2 or 3 days; full set of equipment. As on all the routes through the Kizgych Valley a permit is a must.

Stage 1. For the way to the low grassy hill in the upper valley leading to the Bugoychat Pass see Route 53. On the hill find a poor path, breaking away to the south and take it, making a traverse up and through the dense, exhausting birch brushwood and descending gradually into the wide flat upper valley of Bugoychat under the glacier. A tarn is passed on the way. Walk up on the Bugoychat's right bank, heading for a big rock hill, smoothed out by the ancient Bugoychat Glacier, right in the middle of the valley. On its northern side dwarf birches grow and the southern one abuts against the present glacier. There is a small tarn on its top and sites for tents (2,500m). About 1 ¹/₂ hours from the low grassy hill or 9-10 hours from the Arkhyz Village. A reasonable thing to do is to break the walk by camping somewhere in the Kizgych Valley.

Stage 2. To the south-east of the rock hill stands a sharp rock pyramid encircled by the glacier on all sides except the north-west. From the campsite rope up and walk south-east, turning east and rounding the pyramid, closer to its flanks, bypassing the wide crevasses of the glacier's rise. From the pyramid head due east and make one more crevassed ascent, all the crevasses being skirted without difficulty. The pass and the way to it - a long snowfield, bordered on both sides by rock ridges - open out. There are some hidden crevasses under the snowfield which steepens below the saddle to 25-30°. The easier, more gradual option is the rocks on your left. 2 hours from the campsite.

A good view of the South Marukh Glacier between the heavy masses of Marukh and Karakaya Peaks is afforded from the flat rocky saddle. Walk east over a large snow patch to a steep rock step and descend by a stream bed. From under the step bear to the right and find a gentle, low grassy ridge leading lower down to a scree slope which takes you to the path running from the Marukh Pass. For the way to the Chkhalta River see Route 41. 4-5 hours from the pass, 6-7 hours total time.

ROUTE 55: From the Village of Arkhyz through the Kizgych Valley to the Head of the Bzyb Valley via the Kongur Pass (1B, 2,900m). *(See map 6)*

A long 3 days' walk through the finest valley of the area, rich in wildlife. The Caucasian flora is represented royally by trees considered to be the highest in the CIS: fir-trees, 700 years old and 60m high in the Kizgych-bash, the left source of the Kizgych. The right source, the Dolina Vodopadov Valley ("Waterfalls' Valley") is a marvellous place as well - a short (4km) green glen filled with the roar of innumerable waterfalls. The only technical difficulty of the pass depends on the snow conditions. When the steep small scree slope under the saddle (on the northern side) is covered with snow (30° steep, 200m long), it may actually be easier to ascend than the dry, loose, exhausting scree. Full set of equipment and a permit.

Stage 1. Camp in or by the hut on the left bank of the Kizgych (see Route

53). 5½-6 hours from the village. Or, if you have chosen the right bank to get to the junction of the Kizgych and Bugoychat Rivers, cross the Kizgych by a foot-bridge (two tree trunks) and find a place for camping there.

Stage 2. From the confluence the path goes steeply above the river through the tall forest closing in on the traveller. In an hour it runs out to a glade. The white ribbon of the Kizgych is seen far down in the gorge to the left, and ahead the river is almost hidden from view in a precipitous canyon cut through a step of the valley. The waterfall here is a sight worth the risk of trying to get closer for a good look. Its name is Chertova Melnitsa ("Devil's Mill"). Above the Mill the path goes over a meadowland and comes to the junction of the Kizgych-bash and Salyngan River (the Dolina Vodopadov Valley) flowing from the south. The place is remarkable in August for the abundance of bilberries covering the lower slopes with a grey-blue carpet and for raspberry-canes in the strips of forest descending to the junction.

To get to the Dolina Vodopadnv Valley cross the Kizgych-bash by a makeshift foot-bridge, or, should it be missing, use an avalanche snowbridge, 300-350m higher up. Once on the right bank do not try to make your way down through exhausting thicket. Instead, use the dry stream bed for climbing up to a strip of fir-trees which is a much easier way to the junction. From the latter walk up along the left bank to a step of glacial slabs at the head, 100m high. The river has cut a deep gully in it and falls from the step into a chaos of broken rocks and avalanche snow. Leave it to your left and climb the steep grass through rhododendrons to a flat floor strewn with stones. Camp there. 4-5 hours from the Bugoychat mouth.

Stage 3. On the south, right ahead, the fang of Chiganak Peak sticks up with the Salyngan glacier to its left. The Kongur Pass, invisible yet, is to the left of a high brown rock (under its abrupt eastern wall) seen to the south-west. Walk there along a hollow filled with snow. There is a small glacier under the saddle and the final ascent is either steep snow (200m, 30°) or loose scree. The alternative to that is the wide ledge, covered with rock rubble, along the base of the brown rock wall. Climb to it from the left-side moraine. Note that the wall above the ledge is prone to stone falls. The views from the rocky saddle are limited, unless you scramble up the ridge - either left or right. 2-2½ hours from the campsite.

Descend to a small, easily inclined glacier which ends with a cross band of glacial slabs. The way down is at its left edge. Scramble down over broken rocks, find a gully fitted with small scree and descend to the river. Follow its right bank through the wide upper valley of Pardgali studded with blocks. At the tree-line find a path and come through the forest down to the Bzyb. 2^1/2-3 hours from the pass, 5-6 hours total time.

ROUTE 56: From the Head of the Kizgych Valley to the Geological Base in the Shkhabztsa (see Route 44) the Right Tributary-Valley of the Bzyb Valley, via the Kizgych Pass (1B, 2,980m, at the Head of the Kizgych-bash Valley). *(See map 6)*

A route known for almost a century and one of the most popular in the area, without being a true caravan way. From the campsite at the mouth of the Salyngan River to the base the walk takes 8-9 hours: from the Arkhyz Village - 3 days, the last stage being 4-5 hours. For the way from down-valley and its attractions (in the Kizgych) see Route 53. Full set of equipment and a permit needed.

Stage 1. From the delightful campsite at the confluence of Salyngan and Kizgych-bash Rivers take a clear path on the left bank of the latter. It crosses a patch of packed avalanche snow and in 30-40 minutes comes to a left side-stream, Chuchkhur, with a breathtaking waterfall upstream. (The way to it is not obvious. Go 300m up on the path, reach a dry stream bed, turn to the right and follow it to the fall. The sight is well worth a 1 hour's deviation.) The path runs in the wide valley through an awkward terrain of high grass, holes and boulders. Eventually a stream flowing out of a dark, narrow slit in the mountainside on the right has to be jumped over, which, after rains, may be not easy. Should the crossing be found too dangerous, try the Kizgych-bash a little downstream (it is wetter but less tricky) and go up along the right bank.

Having passed over, ascend about 300m along another stream, coming from the right, turn to the left and traverse to the western side of the usual step of glacial slabs in the head of the valley. 1^1/2 hours from the campsite. The white pyramid of Kizgych Peak (3,420m) can be seen over that side and to the left is the Djal Glacier. Climb the broken rocks, interspersed with rhododendrons, of the western side (to the right of the cascading river) to a vast uneven plateau above. Walk south-west along the left-side moraine of the Djal Glacier (divided into two halves by a low snow ridge), rounding the spur of Kizgych Peak and gradually turning to the right. The pass opens out on the west. The snow under it grows steeper (80-100m, 30°). A war memorial stands on the rocky saddle. About 6 hours from the campsite.

Descend a steep, short, loose scree slope to a small glacier. Below the glacier find a poor path running down over a succession of terraces. On coming to a grassy one, with two streams winding among big blocks, go west along the edge of the drop, bordering the terrace on the south and find the clear path to the right of the falling river. Under the drop the path forks. Take the right branch which leads straight to the cottages of the base. 2$^{1}/_{2}$-3 hours from the pass, 8-9 hours total time.

ROUTE 57: From the Village of Arkhyz to the Bzyb Valley via the Naur Pass (1A, 2,840m, at the Head of the Psysh Valley). *(See map 6)*

A caravan way over the Main Range (not overcrowded though) through a rich northern valley, less wild than the Kizgych, the Reserve's territory, but no less scenic. No technical difficulties, no need for special equipment, except rope for river crossing, just to be on the safe side. The route takes 3 days.

Stage 1. 5km along the road, upstream from the village the bridge to the right bank of the Arkhyz River is reached. The road goes on the left bank of the Psysh River through the forest and clearings for 6km, to end up at a farm. First a forest track, then a good path take over, the valley narrows and the forest gets denser and darker. The twin rock summit of Tokmak Peak (3,400m) and the heavy ice mass of Pshysh Peak (3,780m) open out ahead.

The path climbs over the gravel floor to avoid steep sections of the bank, descends to the river and comes to a small rough hut made of tree trunks, under some tall trees. Camp there. 1,700m. About 5 hours from the village.

Stage 2. At the mouth of the Amanauz River the path disappears (there is a very poor one rising up on the right). Cross the Amanauz by a foot-bridge or wade it in the absence of the latter. It is not too serious an operation at the wide level mouth, but choosing the right place can take time. Use a rope for safety. After crossing find a path on the other side and continue on the same left bank of the Psysh. It runs over delightful sunny glades and through park-like birch and fir-tree groves.

At the tree-line a rough terrain begins: barricades of tree trunks brought down by avalanches, low, distorted, bent birches, steep eroded river banks, and a vague, disappearing path. But the sight of the soaring rock walls, hanging glaciers and waterfalls of Pshysh Peak is a good award for this.

151

Soon a meadow is reached, stretching along the river, with big boulders on it: a good place for camping. It has a name - the Psysh Glade (1,900m). $2^{1}/_{2}$-3 hours from the hut. On the other side, right opposite, the Sekirtme Valley, leading to the Chuchkhur Pass (Route 60) can be seen.

Walk on the path south through bushes and boulders. Soon it brings you to the levelled upper valley with the Main Range in view. The ice wall of the Psysh Glacier is seen high above a rock wall, and its three tongues descend much lower into the valley. Continue over screes, along the left bank, making for the farthest, southernmost ice tongue. Beyond it, a rock spur of the Main Range and a large snowfield behind it are seen. The Naur Pass is not visible yet, hidden by the spur. Go past a waterfall on the right, come to a second waterfall, opposite the tongue, and climb along it to a shelf on the mountainside. Camp there on the grassy shore of a tarn, encircled by glacial slabs (2,600m).

Stage 3. From the tarn traverse south-west, in the direction of the Naur Glacier, which lies west of the Psysh Glacier. Go on to the glacier and along the moraine (on the left), hugging it. Its curving line brings you to the pass, a small uneven plateau. In 1942 the pass was the scene of a fight between German and Soviet troops. The evidence of that is numerous dug-outs and pieces of rusty iron. An excellent view of the huge massif of Pshysh Peak is afforded by looking back north. On the east the abrupt western face of Pshysh Peak towers over the pass. From the narrow strip of the South-Pshysh Glacier along the base of the peak a stream falls into the deep upper cirque of the southern side. $1^{1}/_{2}$-2 hours from the tarn.

Go down a steep scree slope with sparse grass to a flat ledge above a steep drop. Turn to the left and skirt the step, making a slanting traverse of the left mountainside over scree and snow patches. There appears a more or less discernible path. On reaching a small tarn the path bears to the left and rises to a grassy depression on a spur of the southern ridge of Pshysh Peak. The name of this intermediate pass is Shtab ("Headquarters" - the War's legacy). $1^{1}/_{2}$-2 hours from the pass. A green pastureland stretches below, on the other side, and the deep Bzyb Valley is beyond it, with the rocky Bzyb range as a background. The path runs east along the ridge, then traverses, past a tarn, the upper slopes of the plateau, making a loop above it. In the end it descends west and comes to a kosh ($3^{1}/_{2}$-4 hours from the pass), from which a wide path goes down to the south through the forest. The beaten path in the Bzyb Valley is attained in 5-$5^{1}/_{2}$ hours. For details about the valley see Route 44.

ROUTE 58: From the Village of Arkhyz to the Head of the Bolshaya Laba Valley via the Dukka Pass (0 Grade, 2,570m, on the Arkasara Range), to the Head of the Amanauz Valley via the Brakonyerov Pass (1A, 2,950m, on the Arkasara Range) and through the Psysh Valley back to Arkhyz. *(See maps 6 & 8)*

A 4 days' circuit through wild valleys over easy passes which are by no means simple caravan ways, however, especially the second one. Its name means "the Pass of Poachers". The route skirts the last stronghold, steep, high and glaciated, of the Greater Caucasus - the Amanauz Massif.

Stage 1. At the southern edge of the village take the road on the left bank of the Bolshoy Zelenchuk River. Soon the deep Kizgych Valley opens out on the south, but the road goes further along the Psysh River (5km from the village the name will change again for the Arkhyz River). Two summer camps are passed (11km from Arkhyz), one is on the right bank, with a bridge to it, the other one is in the forest, $^1/2$km or so away from the road: a track leads there. A farm is reached in $2^1/2$ hours after setting out. The valley broadens and levels out, clusters of trees and groves are scattered along its floor. $1^1/2$ hours walk brings you to the mouth of the Dukka River, joining the Rechepsta and forming the Arkhyz. The road goes on to the west to the head of the valley and a forest track branches off over a bridge into the Dukka Valley, along the left bank. $4^1/2$-5 hours from the village. (This road part in the Arkhyz Valley can sometimes be made in a chance or chartered truck, then it will take only half an hour.). The Dukka track ends by another farm at the junction of Bolshaya and Malaya Dukka, where a path takes over, crosses the latter by a bridge and goes on the former's left bank, hugging the river. In $2^1/2$-3 hours time the tree-line is reached. Ahead (south) a high rock step is seen with the river cascading down, barring the way to the upper cirque. Camp on a convenient site under the step. 7-8 hours from Arkhyz.

Stage 2. Walk south over grass and moraine rubble on the left bank and find a vague path which runs up the step and to the right. Follow it over meadows, screes and snow patches to the broad, flat, grassy saddle of the Dukka Pass. $1^1/2$ hours from the campsite. The wide deep valley of Bolshaya Laba is on the south-west.
    The path does not come down to its floor. It descends steeply 250-300m, rounds a small tarn under the pass, turns south and traverses the western side of the Arkasara Range over a distance of 3km until the

153

Burnaya Valley is reached (its river falls into the Bolshaya Laba). The next pass, Brakonyerov, is in view at its head. The path descends to the river and follows its treeless right bank, past a kosh, up to a high old moraine across the valley. To the south a rare geological phenomenon can be seen in the cirque of the Ashirkhumara Peak - a steep "stone glacier", that is, a thick covering moraine, keeping the shape of a dead glacier. Climb to a flat meadow with the winding arms of the river and camp there. About 3 hours from the Dukka Pass, $4^1/_2$-5 hours total time.

Stage 3. South-east the head of the valley is divided by a rock wall into two sources. Skirt the meadow to its left, walking to the right-hand source, climb a rock step, overgrown with rhododendrons and the upper cirque brings into view the Brakonyerov Pass, south-west to west, on a high rock ridge. There are two depressions, separated by a minor peak; choose the left one. The steep ascent leading to it is an unstable scree slope which early in the season is covered with snow. The southern upper cirque with a glacier is left to your right. $2^1/_2$-3 hours from the campsite.

The pass is an excellent vantage point. The main feature immediately catching one's eye is towering Pshysh Peak (3,780m), its rock face almost 2km high. And on the south opens the austere icy head-wall of the Amanauz Valley. Descend into the upper cirque, with a snow patch and a frozen tarn, then skirt to its left the rock step at the cirque's eastern edge and go down to the second vast cirque with the snout of the Amanauz Glacier falling steeply through a narrow gorge from under the dramatic rock spire of Amanauz Peak (3,530m).

There are two ways down from the second cirque into the valley. One is to follow the steep canyon-like bed of the stream outflowing from the glacier, with many acrobatic crossings. In addition, once down, you will have to cross the Amanauz to its right bank because the left one is impracticable for 2km, and lower down to cross the river again by a snow bridge (if there is any) to the path on the left bank.

The other option is to climb to the crest of the rock spur bordering the second cirque on the north. From there (a good view point again) descend to a tiny tarn and follow the left bank of a stream to the forest lower down, through brushwood, and round a band of rocks, leaving it to your left. On reaching the left bank of the Amanauz, make your way through low birches distorted by avalanches. Find the path at the first stretch of fir-trees (4-5 hours from the pass) and in 1 hour it brings you to an old hut under tall pine-trees near the river. Total time is 8-9 hours.

Stage 4. It takes 6-7 hours to walk from the hut to Arkhyz, all the way on the left bank and with many charming views back south. With luck, the last 11km from the farm at the mouth of the Gabulu-Chat River can be made in a chance vehicle.

ROUTE 59: From the Arkhyz Village through the Bolshaya Dukka Valley via the Ayulyu Pass (1A, 2,890m, on the Gabulu Range) to the Psysh Valley and back to Arkhyz. *(See maps 6 & 8)*

An enjoyable 3 days' circuit, free of technical difficulties (no ice and snow) but not without some interesting navigation problems in the Belaya Valley, wild and unfrequented, populated only by bears. The route is rich in exquisite scenery, with many beautiful tarns in the broad, dry upper valleys.

For **Stage 1** see Route 58 Stage 1.

Stage 2. Under the high forbidding rock step in the head of the valley the vague path divides. The right branch rises west to the Dukka Pass, the left one crosses the river and climbs the step closer to the right mountainside through big blocks piled up there. At the top of the rise the rocky stark, majestic upper cirque opens out, enlivened by a large tarn. The way to the Ayulyu Pass is a succession of cirques divided by steps. To get to the first one follow a stream running down a grass slope on the left (looking up). It leads to another two tarns. The general direction is east. By the farthest tarn turn again to the left and rise to the second cirque. Its edge is the edge of a vast terrace overspread with chaotic moraine debris. An old flattened moraine leads to the third step, leaving the debris, gigantic blocks among them, to the left. The uppermost rocky plateau has many tarns - a world of calm and solitude. The low, flat saddle opens out on the north-east. $3^{1}/_{2}$-4 hours from the campsite.

The view east is admirable - of the Main and Sofiya Ranges, and again mighty Pshysh Peak catches one's eye irresistibly. To have an even better view walk to the summit north of the pass. It will take about 2 hours, thus prolonging the stage to 9-10 hours. (In this case the walk may be broken into three stages to make it less strenuous.) From the saddle descend to a tarn, almost black, in the cirque below. Leave it to your left, traverse grassy hills to the steep left side of the valley and descend into another large flat cirque. A low hill divides it into two parallel hollows. A stretch of poor path leading into the left hollow can be noticed on the hillside. Descend into the left hollow and follow the thin discontinuous path on the left bank of a stream.

Traverse with a slight descent the left mountainside of the side-valley. When the main valley, Belaya, opens out below descend into it. There is a swampy meadow with big boulders and sites for tents near the river. $1^{1}/_{2}$-2 hours from the pass.

Further on the way is no better, traversing the left side of the valley through birch brushwood. On nearing the forest, keep a good look-out for the path's turns - it must rise there instead of going down to the canyon. It is discernible in the forest but vanishes again at its edge, right where you need it most. Make your way over a steep slope through beech thicket into a side-valley with a stream. Beyond that in the forest the path springs up again, goes above the canyon and in the end zig-zags down to the river. It crosses it by a footbridge to a comfortable campsite on the right bank. 2 hours, 7-8 hours total time.

Stage 3. In 15-20 minutes the path brings you to a bridge again and to the track in the Psysh Valley. It is still $3^{1}/_{2}$-4 hours to the village, on the track, then, from the farm, on the road. All the way along the left bank. For details see Route 57.

ROUTE 60: From the Village of Arkhyz through the Kizgych Valley via the Chuchkhur Pass (1A-1B, 3,050m, between Chuchkhur and Sofiya Peaks) and back to Arkhyz through the Psysh Valley. *(See map 6)*

A 4-5 days' walk through the two longest valleys of the area, over a pass with a short snow ascent (30°) as the only difficulty. But the route is pretty strenuous, without good paths in the upper valleys, often overgrown with tenacious vegetation. The easy climb of an excellent view point, Chuchkhur Peak (3,500m), south of the pass, is an exciting option. Full set of equipment and a permit required.

Stage 1. For Stage 1 see Route 53, Stage 1. Camp in the upper part of the Kizgych Valley, somewhere near the mouth of the Bugoychat. 7-7$^{1}/_{2}$ hours from the village.

Stage 2. For the section from the mouth to Chuchkhur waterfall see Route

Mt Elbrus from the south-east
Refuge of 11, with Donguzorun and Nakra peaks across the Baksan valley

Baduk valley

Mt Elbrus from the south

56, Stage 2. The dry stream bed brings you in 30 minutes to an old scree slope above the brushwood. The upper part of Chuchkhur cascade is on the right. A step of yellow rocks is rounded by a grass gully not far from the river. Then climb by the last steep stretch of the river to the hill of an old moraine. The upper Chuchkhur Valley opens from there, encircled by abrupt dark rock faces, with the river flowing quietly through screes and meadows. Higher up the river is formed by three sources, the northern, western and southern ones. Walk up along the central source, leave to your right its short canyon and come to the upper cirque with a couple of turquoise tarns connected by a stream (Zelyoniye Ozyora - "Green Lakes"), 2,700m. Camp among the moraine hills near the tarns (there are sites there). $4^{1}/_{2}$-5 hours from the mouth of the Bugoychat.

Stage 3. The Chuchkhur Pass is seen to the west over the glacier, on the rock ridge linking the abrupt, 500m high, wall of Sofiya (3,640m, north of the tarns) with Chuchkhur Peak on the south. The tarns and the snout of the glacier can be passed to their left, over easy glacial slabs, or to the right, by screes. Go on the glacier (no crevasses) and climb the snow ascent leading to the pass (70-80m, 30°). About 1 hour from the tarns.

To start the optional climb of Chuchkhur Peak turn to the left and walk along the gentle ridge to the right of the pinnacles. Soon an eroded rock knoll is attained. Beyond that the ridge grows steeper and narrower, with many loose stones. The final pitch under the summit may prove to be too much for the modest walker. The scrambling is not technically difficult but rather exposed. The ascent and return takes $2^{1}/_{2}$-3 hours. The views encompass almost all the West Caucasus from Mt Elbrus to the Black Sea. Descend to the pass by the same way.

Go down to the west over a snowfield, keeping to the right-side rocks and come to the Ogary Glacier. It brings you to the edge of the rock step on which the glacier lies, 150m above (and to the right of) the other one, Bush. For descent take a steep gully to the right of the stream cascading from under the glacier and then continue to follow this line, choosing suitable grass ledges and rounding minor rock steps. In 1-$1^{1}/_{2}$ hours a flat meadow and a birch grove in the Sekirtme upper valley are reached. It is 40-50 minutes walk to the Psysh Glade (see Route 57 Stage 2) but two river crossings have to be made on the way there: over the Sekirtme and Psysh. The best time for the second one is in the morning, and even so a rope may be needed. If you have planned a five days' walk, the logical thing to do is to camp here, cross the Psysh in the morning and stop for the next camp at the hut. Total time with the ridge climb is 5-$5^{1}/_{2}$ hours. Without it and with an early start it is quite possible to be at the crossings about 9.00-10.00am and walk to the hut the same day.

Stage 4. Go along the right bank of the Sekirtme River, cross it where it turns north, come to the Psysh River and find a ford. Once on the left bank take a path there, rather awkward at places, and walk 7km to the hut (see Route 57, 58). 17km remain to Arkhyz Village.

ROUTE 61: From the Village of Arkhyz through the Sofiya Valley, via the Sofiyskoye Sedlo Pass (0 Grade, 2,600m, on the Cheget-Chat Range) and back to the Village through the Kizgych Valley. *(See map 6)*

Easy and scenic, like all the other routes in the area, this walk has an easy pass and a path all the way. But the path is not foolproof; it may be lost in places. In the Kizgych Valley the river has to be crossed (a rope should be at hand). For details about the valley see Routes 53, 56. The road in the Sofiya Valley reaches as far as the Lednikovaya Ferma ("Ice Farm") at the foot of the pass, 16km from the village. At the head of the valley stands the second highest peak of the area, Sofiya (3,640m) and its glacier, hanging over a rock wall 100m high, sends down numerous waterfalls. The route may be done in 2 days, but then the second day would be rather hard: 4-5 hours to cross the pass and 5-6 hours to return to the village. It may be broken with a night in the Kizgych Valley, in the hut (19km from the village). In that case a part of the third day could be spent in walking to Chortova Melnitsa waterfall, 3km upstream.

Stage 1. The road going into the Sofiya Valley breaks away 7km from the village, crosses the Psysh River by a bridge, runs through groves and glades and climbs a rise. Distant Sofiya Peak and its glaciers come into sight, and an impressive glittering war memorial is on the right. The road leads past two tourist camps, farms and koshes to the Lednikovaya Ferma, the uppermost farm sitting under a high old moraine at 1,900m. (At the mouth of the Kashkha-Etchki stream, the left tributary. 7km from the Sofiya's mouth, there is a cheese dairy offering a good chance to buy fresh cheese.) Find a place among birches higher up and camp. 6-7 hours from the village.

Stage 2. The low saddle of the pass, the steep rock of Gopal-Kaya Peak (2,916m) above it to the right, and the deep rocky hollow leading there are in full view from the campsite. Go south-east on the right bank, cross a stream, turn east and walk on a path zig-zagging up the wide grassy ridge to the left of the hollow. In 2-2$\frac{1}{2}$ hours it brings you to a plateau, several hundred metres north of the saddle. To the south Sofiya Peak rises stately as you climb higher and a breathtaking sight of the Kizgych Valley, 1km beneath, awaits on the pass.

The path cuts down to the right, aiming at a big boulder and from there to the nearest patch of fir-trees. It then plunges into the forest and comes to a large clearing on the left bank of the Kizgych, with the hut on it. 1$\frac{1}{2}$ -2 hours, 4-4$\frac{1}{2}$ hours total time. To the village is a further 19km, 5-6 hours walk, with a ford to the right bank 4km downstream.

ROUTE 62: From the Village of Arkhyz through the Arkhyz Valley via the Chilik (3,000m, on the Abishira-Akhuba Range), Semnadtsati (2,800m), Mylgval (2,800m), Agur (2,700m) and Fedoseeva (2,900m) Passes (all 1A Grade) and back to the Village. *(See map 8)*

An unusual route differing sharply from all the other routes of the area. For 3 days (out of 4) its line does not go below 2,500m, hugging on the northern side the crest of the Abishira-Akhuba Range and crossing under the sheer rock walls the open spaces of the stark northern cirques, rich in flowers and bird life, with large lakes. The landscapes resemble those of the Far North or Scotland. And the relief map of the whole Arkhyz area, stretching beneath, is an unforgettable sight afforded from the Abishira-Akhuba's crest. There are no reliable paths on the grass and scree slopes of the northern side, but the passes are easy and the line is so close to the crest that it is almost impossible to get lost there, even in bad weather. Note that the range is the first high obstacle which stops cold, fog and rain coming from the north, usually in the afternoon.

Stage 1. For the way to the confluence of Rechepsta and Dukka Rivers see Route 58. Stage 1. Walk on the road, then on a path in the lower Rechepsta Valley on the river's left bank and camp at the tree-line. 6-7 hours from the village.

Stage 2. Two depressions are in sight to the north on the Abishira-Akhuba Range, to the right of its highest point, Rechepsta Peak (3,210m). Head for the left one, (the Chilik Pass) climbing steep grass slopes (40-45°), insecure when wet. The head of the left source of the Kyafar River opens out from the pass. Two tarns connected by a stream lie in the cirque. A cosy place for camping is beyond the stream, on the soft, dry moss. 4-5 hours.

Stage 3. An easy 30-40 minutes ascent leads to the saddle of the Semnadtsati Pass on the south-east, right under Peak 3,080m. The vast upper cirque of the right Kyafar's source, studded with snow patches and tarns of different contours and sizes, lies on the other side. The descent is steep but straightforward. The largest lake of the area, Chilik, in the lower cirque, is not visible from the upper one. (To have a look at it walk a little north to the step of some glacial slabs.)

The next pass, Mylgval, is seen a little south of west, on the ridge branching off north from the Abishira-Akhuba, again close to it. There are two terraces with tarns on the way to the pass. A steep grass slope leads to the first one. The second, deep, tarn is on a rocky terrace, and beyond it a snow slope rises to the saddle. 4$^{1}/_{2}$-5 hours from the previous pass. The upper cirque and the next pass, Agur (a little south of east) can be surveyed from there. A table-like plateau is seen to the left of the pass on the ridge. Descend into the cirque and camp by a tarn. The cirque is walled on the north by abrupt rocks. 5-6 hours total time.

Stage 4. Climb to the Agur Pass. 30-40 minutes. The next pass, Fedoseeva, on the Abishira-Akhuba Range, is due south and very near, 600-700m as the crow flies. Choose the shortest and easiest way to it. From the Agur Pass you can make your way on to the plateau mentioned above, north of the saddle, with fine views of almost all the northern side of the Abishira-Akhuba Range. The pinnacles barring the way along the ridge are passed to their right and the rock with a cave at its top, right under the plateau, is clambered up to the right of the cave. About one hour.

An exhilarating bird's eye view of the Arkhyz area opens out from the Fedoseeva Pass, but as you go down on quite a decent, steep and direct path, the mountains close in again. Below, the path comes to a summer camp and from that a track leads to the road in the Arkhyz Valley. About 4 hours. There remain 11km to the village. 2$^{1}/_{2}$-3 hours. Total time is 7-8 hours.

Mt Elbrus

(See maps 9 & 10)

The fact that this mountain is the highest in Europe suffices for many to go and see it, or climb it. But this obvious attraction is not the main one, for Elbrus belongs to a handful of mountains with a special kind of beauty, which lies in their shape and setting. Most of them are volcanoes such as Fujiyama, Ararat, and Kilimanjaro. Like all these this mountain is a world apart. It stands 11km north of the Main Range and exceeds its neighbours in height by 1,500-2,500m. And like all big and isolated mountains it has the bewitching features of being elusive and unexpected. Even if you see its details in clear-cut lines, you never realize all its vastness until you try to walk to some point on its slopes, and you never expect it to be so high and majestic until its shining snows at the top come out of the clouds.

Like all outstanding mountains Elbrus has more than one name. Its second Balkar name, Mingi-Tau, is strikingly exact - *Resembling a Thousand Mountains.*

It can be a sight of celestial beauty: a rosy-white seemingly weightless mass, floating in the morning sky, high above the green pastures of the northern foot-hills. The point from which photographers take this favourite picture is 20-25km north-west of the mountain. The views from the summits are breathtaking: to the north a rolling carpet of pastures veiled by the blue haze of distance and on all other sides a sea of snowy peaks, half of the Caucasus. It is said that through the clear air of autumn one can see both the Black and Caspian Seas.

As a gigantic frontier post between the Balkars and Karachais and an ever present guard of the rich pastureland of the upper reaches of the Kuban, Malka and Baksan Rivers, Mt Elbrus has been presiding over all their history. From time immemorial it plays the major role in their myths and legends. But people living in the mountains never climb them for the sake of climbing, so, over the course of the centuries no Karachai or Balkar tried to climb Mingi-Tau. At least there is no evidence of it. The first declared ascent (and well paid for - 400 roubles) took place in 1829 when the Russian scientific and Ordnance Survey expedition led by the Commander-in-Chief of the Caucasian Fortification Line, General Emmanuel, came to the head of the Malka River. The expedition numbered about 1,000 soldiers and Cossacks. There were two attempts. The first one,

Looking to north-east from the slopes of Mt Elbrus

by a party of 5 members and 20 Cossacks, left for the summit from a hopeless height of 2,600m, attained 4,300m and went down.

On the second attempt, 2 members and 2 locals, Sottaev and Khashirov, reached the saddle between the summits, from where Kilar Khashirov went up alone (he was watched closely from the base through a powerful telescope). His companion Sottaev, aged 41, also felt well enough to continue, but unfortunately had to accompany the two members down. On the 10th of July the East Summit was reached and Khashirov grew rich and (much later) famous.

The second ascent by the route from the south-east, now known as the voie normale, was made in 1868 by the British climbers D.W.Freshfield, A.W.Moore, C.C.Tucker, the French guide Devouassoud and two local hunters. One of them Sottaev, now aged 80!, and he reached the summit along with the others. The views from the summit were much admired by Freshfield who put them high above those from Mont Blanc. In 1874 there followed another British ascent, of West Summit this time, which is 21m higher than the East one. The team consisted of F.C.Grove, H.Walker, F.Gardiner and Swiss guide P.Knubel. When Grove asked the local Balkar prince Urusbiev (he ruled a large part of the Baksan Valley) to help them with a guide, the smiling prince suggested Sottaev, aged 86. This guide, well known by then at the Alpine Club in London, was taken without murmur. So, indefatigable Sottaev became the first person to climb both the summits.

A person who made a noticeable mark in the climbing history of Mt Elbrus was a military surveyor and scientist called Pastukhov. The only rocks sticking out of the ice at 4,800m on the voie normale to the East Summit bear his name. That was the place where his surveying party spent a night on their way to the highest triangulation point in Europe.

No wonder this unique mountain became an irresistible attraction for a lot of people: scientists, climbers and modest worshippers of Nature's beauty. Luckily for Soviet climbing, when the Bolsheviks came to power, influential figures made a point of quickly developing mountaineering in the Caucasus. Thus, in the thirties a number of climbing camps sprang up in the Baksan Valley, with Mt Elbrus the goal first and foremost in the minds of the young and enthusiastic campers. The highest hotel in the Caucasus, the Refuge of 11, at 4,200m, on the south-east slope of Mt Elbrus, was built at this time. And Soviet climbers were doubly lucky in that those high rank Communists who had promoted the Caucasus were done away with by Stalin only after the main bulk of the work they had started was completed.

Typical Soviet obsessions for height and number records, to which Mt Elbrus could not help but fall a victim, tended to run to extremes. Thus it was that, supervised by the Party, Soviet climbing produced a unique type of climbing event - a mass ascent of Mt Elbrus. With its spacious slopes the mountain was an obvious scene for this manifestation of the Soviet Spirit, involving hundreds and thousands of people. The biggest event of this kind, with 2,500 participants, came about in 1967. Since no one could muster up so many climbers, even by recruiting all the mountaineering camps in the Caucasus, they had to be chosen somewhere else. All the members of the team were chosen as the best in his or her walk of life: the best turners, milkmaids, shop assistants etc! Most of those people expected simply a three or four days' paid holiday in the mountains... The most surprising aspect of the whole story of the mass ascents of Mt Elbrus is the incredible fact that not a single shop assistant has perished there, despite the enormous chances of doing so on the slopes which are often referred to as the highest cemetery in Europe.

Though technically no more than a snow plod, this mountain is far from being easy. It is difficult for people who do not know from their own experience what mountain sickness feels like (and most would-be conquerors

The slopes of Mt Elbrus near the Refuge of 11

of Mt Elbrus are of this kind) to realize that it can stop you on a gentle slope, under a calm blue sky, just a hundred metres short of the summit. And it can kill you, should the weather change dramatically and you become lost on those immense snowfields. Every year Mt Elbrus is attempted by hundreds of climbers and every year the fatal accident toll is raised by a dozen lives or so. Three points to remember. It is a high mountain, even if climbed in one day, and if you want the summit to be a joy, not a splitting headache and sickness, you need proper acclimatization, which normally, if you are fresh from the sea level, takes a week at least. It is also a large mountain. The way from the Refuge of 11 to the East Summit is about 6km long and it is the only safe corridor between crevassed ice-fields. So if your mountaineering experience is limited to crag climbing and hill walking in Britain, you'd better take a guide. As a high mountain, Elbrus is subject to quick changes of weather. It means you have to be well prepared and equipped for this, especially with the right footwear. And it goes without saying, you should be fit enough to enjoy the long, 10-12 hours' ascent.

Even in July it may be bitterly cold and windy at the 3.00am start and the slow pace of the ascent dictates the choice of boots and clothing. The best footwear is normal climbing boots, but any pair of heavy duty walking boots, stiff enough for crampons and large enough for a pair of woollen socks will do. If they are protected by super gaiters covering the whole boot, so much the better. A light duvet jacket is welcome but not indispensable, unlike a pair of warm and windproof mittens. Crampons are a must and a pair of ski poles, helping to keep you in balance, will save a lot of energy. A head-torch will be useful and, last but not least, a compass can increase immensely the safety margin in case of bad weather. Ice-axe is optional.

The caravan way to the east Summit begins at 2,200m on the Azau Glade, at the lower station of the Elbrus car cableway, right where the metalled road along the Baksan Valley ends at the foot of the mountain. The cableway operates from 9.00am till 3.00pm. There are two flights with an intermediate station at 2,920m and it takes 40-50 minutes to get from the lower to the upper station at 3,470m. A chair-lift takes over and takes you to a height of 3,750m. From there follow a line of posts going a little west of north. Normally many tracks and traces in the snow lead in the same direction. The Refuge of 11, standing on a low black volcanic ridge is reached in 1 $\frac{1}{2}$-2 hours. The hotel sleeps 120 people in rooms for 2 and 4 and is quite comfortable. But there is no food obtainable there and all the cooking utensils (except for some large pans) have to be brought with you. The usual practice is to spend a day for an acclimatization outing to the Pastukhov Rocks which are right on the voie normale, at 4,800m. It takes 3-4 hours return. On the way there take the rough bearings of the East Summit and put them down or remember them. If you have a week of active acclimatization behind you, walking or climbing over 3,000m, then this outing will help. If not, the benefit gained is minimal, but still, it is better than nothing.

Leave the Refuge no later than 3.00am; it is going to be a long day. The way to the saddle is well traced with hundreds of footprints and the two parallel low rock ridges on both sides help to keep the right direction even in darkness. The first noticeable rise is the Pastukhov Rocks, frozen scree of about 25°. From there to the saddle the steepness of 20-25° does not diminish and the way is marked with wooden stakes 2m high, about 100m between them. The saddle is an immense concave snowfield which is skirted by a snow track traversing the western flank of the East Summit. The direction here is due north. Leave 200-250m after the ruins of a wooden cabin at the narrowest part of the saddle, and bearing slightly to the right, make an ascending traverse of the slope of the East Summit. Thus, its steeper part above the ruins is avoided. Then turn to the right and follow a traceable path in snow, broken rock and frozen scree. The summit is a vast scree field, the former crater: without snow, swept away by ferocious winds.

Quite a decent time for the climb is 7 hours; 6 hours is good whilst 5 hours means you are fit and probably acclimatized for something more than Mt Elbrus! But if after 8-9 hours of plodding you are still on the saddle, it means the ascent is beyond your powers, even though you are able to force yourself to move up. In such a case the descent may turn out to be a big problem. Here is a piece of useful advice. A big (1 litre) thermos with a hot sour or salty tasting drink and a supply of a mixture of ascorbic powder and lemon acids are much more preferable to any solid food, especially a fatty one. In most cases it is carried up and down the mountain untouched. Take the acids by teaspoonfuls when feeling nauseous. And lastly: do not indulge in long rest stops, particularly sitting in the snow; it does not help. Instead, calm your heart and breathing down with short standing stops for a minute or so (ski-poles are indispensable for this), and go on.

The West Summit
Needless to say, the voie normale has a big disadvantage - it is overcrowded, unless you choose winter for your climb. Being the easiest way to easier East Summit, the route not only displays a lot of litter strewn all along it, it is much less scenic than the routes from the south-west and north. Seen from the Refuge, the East Summit is just a snowy mound and you can hardly get the feeling of a high mountain until you get to the top. Climbing the West Summit from the south-west you have this huge, icy and steep mountain in full view, and the sheer red rock walls of Kyukyurtlyu Peak (4,634m), into the bargain, from the base camp under the route. Basically it is a similar snow climb but, firstly, without a hut to spend three nights comfortably; secondly, half of it is done roped up because of some crevasses on the lower slopes and, thirdly, there is a snow ridge at its very beginning, 60-70m long, gently inclined but narrow, with unpleasant drops on both sides. To get on this ridge you have to climb 15-20m of snow (35-40°) and scramble up 5-6m of easy rocks. The ascent takes 4 days (with one day of the acclimatization outing to West Shoulder of West Summit, 4,900m).

Stage 1. In the Azau Glade take a car of the Elbrus cableway to the intermediate station Stary Krugozor and from there follow a dusty path on the crest of a ridge, running up parallel to the cables. After 250-300m on the crest the path turns to the left, goes over screes and broken volcanic rocks, falls, crosses a stream and comes to a rock step, 50-60m high. The step marks the lower end of the Maly Azau Glacier. The path climbs the step, veers to the left and rises to another crest on which it turns to the right.

Car cableway on Mt Elbrus, Stary Krugozor Station

It is clear enough but ramifies in places. The general direction is a little north of west, all the time keeping in view the edge of the glaciers. A large lake with a wall of ice as its northern shore is passed (1½ -2 hours from the station) and from there the path heads over screes and across a stream for the lower end of the high moraine between the Maly and Greater Azau Glaciers.

Cross to the west the awkward moraine hills and step on to the easier, but still rather rough part of the Greater Azau Glacier between two ice-falls. Go at right angles over half the width of that part, then turn to the right into the central lengthwise depression and walk 150-200m along it. Between two wide crevasses turn to the left and head for the long low medial moraine of the glacier. 1½ hours from the lake. Once there follow it in a north-west direction. Right ahead, across the vast snow fields the Khotyu-tau Pass is visible, between the rock pyramid of Ullukam Peak (3,736m) and a low embankment-like elevation on the ridge connecting the peak to Mt Elbrus. Follow the moraine along its right side. It leads to a large cauldron in the glacier, with a large moraine field north of it. Leave the cauldron to your right and make a wide loop, skirting the moraine and turning gradually to north. Walk to a low black ridge which opens out on the north-north-west. It stretches from the large moraine field to the north-west, at an acute (about 45°) angle to the connecting ridge. (The latter is purely a nominal, orographical affair, its two long sections obliterated by two straddling glaciers, overflowing into the Ullukam Valley.)

Head for the westernmost edge of the low black ridge (the steepness increases and now exceeds 20°) and from there walk due north, avoiding deviations to the left, on to the crevassed straddling glaciers. (NB: In poor visibility any descending, however slight, would mean you are on the way to the Ullukam Valley.) Beyond the second straddling glacier the connecting ridge appears, sticking out from the ice. Keep 200-250m east of it and walk north. The snowfields there are fairly level, with narrow crevasses easily avoided, but in bad or warm weather, rope up. Camp on the flat snow, under the rock buttress which marks the beginning of the rising south ridge of the West Shoulder. 4,000m, 3-3½ hours from the Greater Azau Glacier. Total time is 6-6½ hours. (If you do not like camping on snow, find some flat small scree at the upper end of the low black ridge - but the place is much more windy than that by the buttress, which is under protection of the rock wall of the connecting ridge. It is half an hour's walk between the spots.)

Stage 2. Go north and climb the snow slope (30°, 70-80m) to the right of the rock buttress. Turn to the left and traverse steep (35-40°, 15-20m) snow, to reach the top of the buttress. Because of the steepness and nasty looking gully lower down - a quick way to a huge drop - a fixed rope is necessary for a large party of inexperienced climbers or walkers or a simple shoulder belay for a small one. From the top climb a snow slope (20m, 30-35°) leading to a snow ridge, 60-70m long, gently inclined but narrow - the lower end of the south ridge of the West Shoulder. The walk along this 60-70m is not difficult but rather exposed, because of the drops on both sides, especially on the left one. Further up the ridge broadens to 100m and rises (15-20, up to 25°, four or five narrow crevasses) to the West Shoulder and the vast gently rolling snowfields of the western slopes of West Summit. 2½-3 hours from the base, 1-1½ hours descent.

Stage 3. Early start, 2.00-3.00am. From the West Shoulder the West

Mt Elbrus and the upper part of the Baksan Valley from helicopter

Summit, with its two rock towers separated by a saddle is in clear view to the north-east. The highest point is the left one. Walk there over moderate, undulating snowfields without crevasses. Strips of bare scree and eroded rocks descend from the left tower (there are two or three wide crevasses under them, $1^1/_2$ -2 hours from Shoulder). Unrope, put on crampons and climb towards the summit. The terrain is awkward, large scree with packed or soft snow among the rocks. The average steepness is 25°. $2^1/_2$ hours to the summit. Total time is $6^1/_2$-8 hours. Descent will take $3^1/_2$-5 hours.

Stage 4. Reverse the way to the intermediate cable car station at Stary Krugozor, $3^1/_2$-4 hours. For any needed details see the descent from the Khotyu-tau Pass, Route 17. Should you be late for the last run down, never mind - the descent on foot to the Azau Glade takes only half an hour.

The northern slopes of Mt Elbrus can offer good lines which are no more difficult than the voie normale (more crevassed though), but to get to the head of the Malka River from the Baksan Valley via a pass will take 3 days. It is quicker from the town of Kislovodsk (about 80km, mostly on a jeep road), even though there is no regular bus service. The question arises of where to build up the absolutely indispensable acclimatization. The place is of amazing beauty, but it does not have high enough acclimatizing climbs. Anyway, should you decide to go there, it will be a very interesting and highly self-sufficient expedition, Elbrus or not, to a remote and secluded part of the Caucasus.

There is no established, time-honoured route from the north. Climbers do not go there from the Baksan Valley because it is too far, and so it is usually trekkers who choose that side of the mountain. They do not leave much of a written record in the climbing press (the latter practically does not exist in the CIS anyway). It means your expedition will have a certain touch of discovery. For the way from the Baksan Valley to the Malka's head see Routes 13, 14, 15, 18 and to the Balkbashi Pass across the northern slopes - Route 16. For the way to the saddle you can choose either the Ullukol or Karachul Glaciers, but one would rather take the moraine between them and make a base at its upper edge.

KEY TO THE MAPS

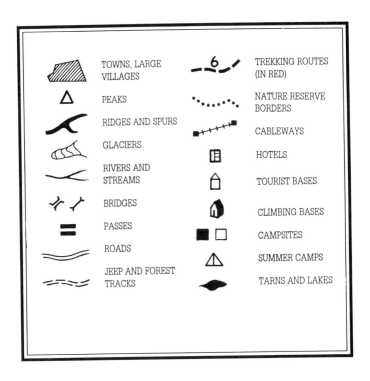

	TOWNS, LARGE VILLAGES	TREKKING ROUTES (IN RED)
	PEAKS	NATURE RESERVE BORDERS
	RIDGES AND SPURS	CABLEWAYS
	GLACIERS	HOTELS
	RIVERS AND STREAMS	TOURIST BASES
	BRIDGES	CLIMBING BASES
	PASSES	CAMPSITES
	ROADS	SUMMER CAMPS
	JEEP AND FOREST TRACKS	TARNS AND LAKES

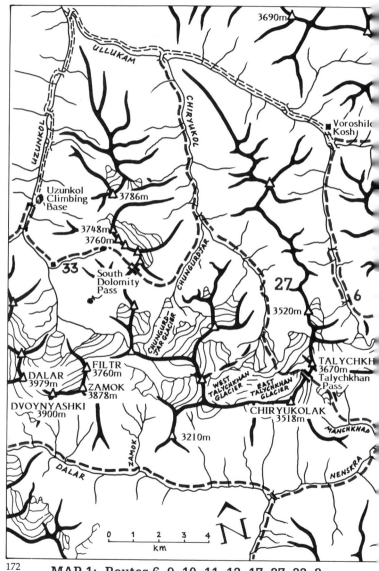

MAP 1: Routes 6, 9, 10, 11, 12, 17, 27, 33, 8

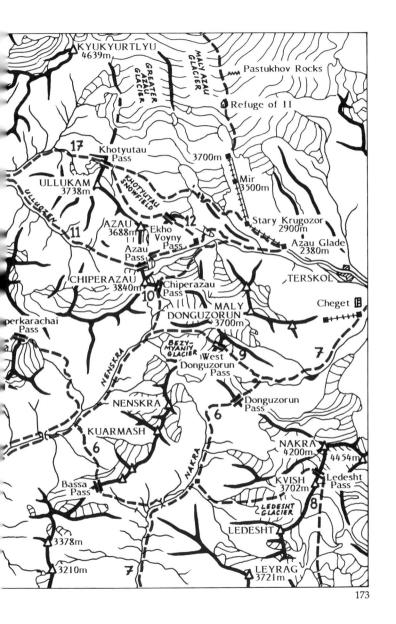

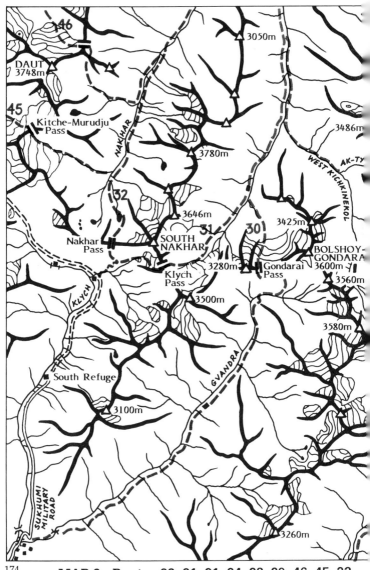

MAP 2: Routes 32, 31, 31, 34, 28, 29, 46, 45, 33

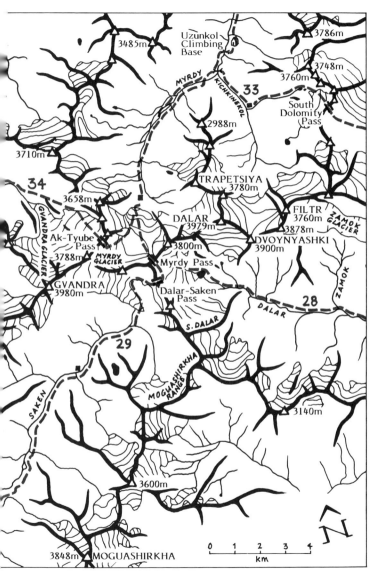

3786m

Uzunkol
Climbing
Base

3485m

MYRDY

KICHINEKOL

33

3748m

3760m

South
Dolomity
Pass

2988m

3710m

34

TRAPETSIYA
3780m

3658m

GVANDRA GLACIER

DALAR
3979m

FILTR
3760m

ZAMOK GLACIER

Ak-Tyube
Pass

3878m

3800m

DVOYNYASHKI
3900m

3788m

MYRDY GLACIER

Myrdy Pass

GVANDRA
3980m

Dalar-Saken
Pass

DALAR

28

ZAMOK

S. DALAR

SAKEN

29

MOGUASHIRKHA RANGE

3140m

3600m

0 1 2 3 4
km

N

3848m MOGUASHIRKHA

175

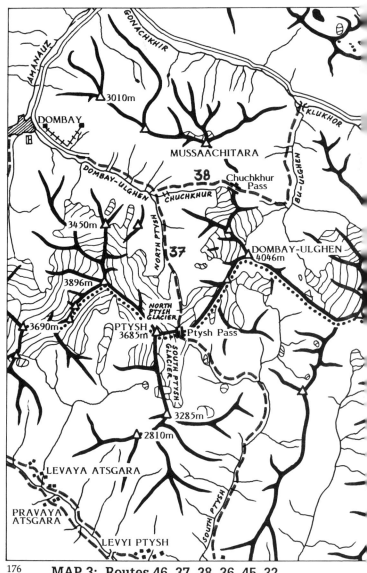

MAP 3: Routes 46, 37, 38, 36, 45, 32

DAUT
46
Uzlovoy Pass
DAUT GLACIER
S. DAUT GLACIER
DAUT 3748m
3185m
KITCHE-MURUDJU
45
Kitche-Murudju Pass
CHAULUCHAT GLACIER
KLUKHOR LAKE
CHAULUCHAT
NAKHAR
3780m
North Refuge
KLUKHOR
N. KLUKHOR
Klukhor Pass
32
36
31
SOUTH NAKHAR
GHEN
3630m
Nakhar Pass
3645m
KLYCH
Klych Pass
3410m
3440m
South Refuge
3100m
3515m

N

1 2 3 4
km

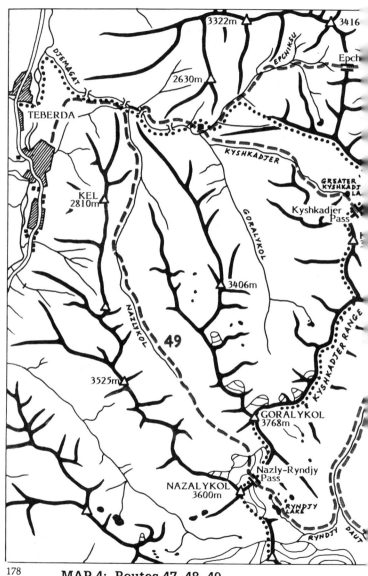

MAP 4: Routes 47, 48, 49

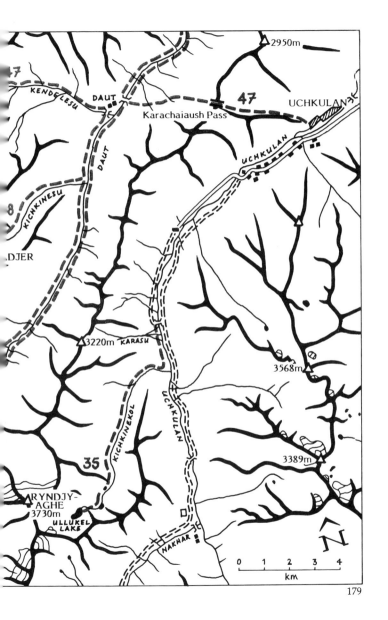

MAP 5: Routes 41, 42, 40, 43, 39, 50, 52, 53, 54

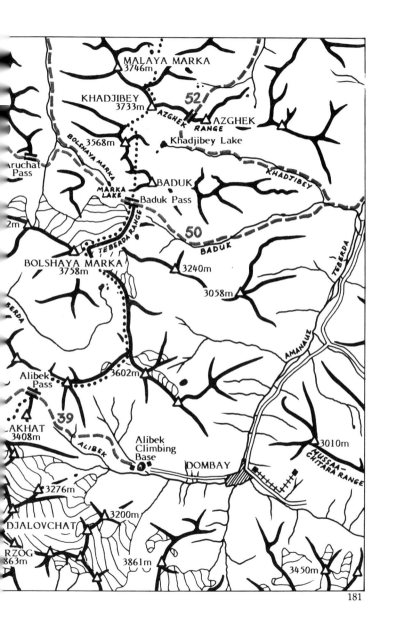

MALAYA MARKA
3746m

KHADJIBEY
3733m

AZGHEK
RANGE

52

AZGHEK

3568m

Khadjibey Lake

BOLSHAYA MARKA

aruchat
Pass

MARKA
LAKE

BADUK

KHADJIBEY

Baduk Pass

2m

TEBERDA RANGE

50

BADUK

BOLSHAYA MARKA
3758m

3240m

3058m

BERDA

TEBERDA

Alibek
Pass

3602m

AMANAUZ

AKHAT
3408m

39

ALIBEK

Alibek
Climbing
Base

DOMBAY

3010m

YUSSAA-
CHITARA RANGE

3276m

3200m

DJALOVCHAT

RZOG
863m

3861m

3450m

181

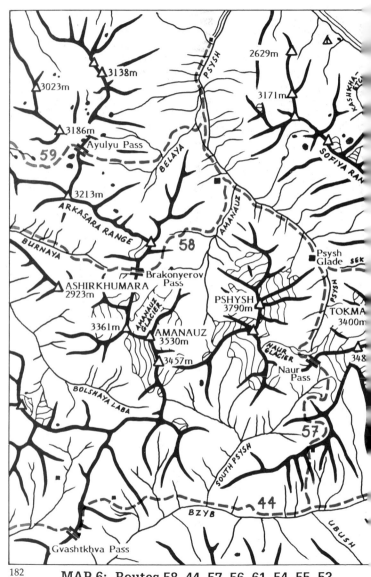

MAP 6: Routes 58, 44, 57, 56, 61, 54, 55, 53

EGET-CHAT RANGE
2963m
2988m
UJUM RANGE
Lednikovaya Ice Farm
2978m
MARUKH
Sofiyskoye Sedlo Pass
61
GOPAL-KAYA 2916m
SOFIYA 3640m
Bugoychat Pass
CHERTOVA MELNITSA WATERFALL
53
ZELYONIYE LAKES
khur ass
CHUCH RANGE
60
810th Regiment Pass
OGARY LACIER
KIZGYCH-BASH
SALYNGAN
54
3149m
CHUCHKHUR 3500m
55
BUGOYCHAT GLACIER
3434m
BELALAKAYA WATERFALL
ICIER
3443m
3420m
Kizgych Pass
Kongur Pass
CHIGANAK 3178m
SOUTH MARUKH
56
Geological Base
PARDGALI
3119m
SHKHAB-ETRA
SAKS
BZYB
Adanghe Pass
PSYKVA
N
0 1 2 3 4 5
km

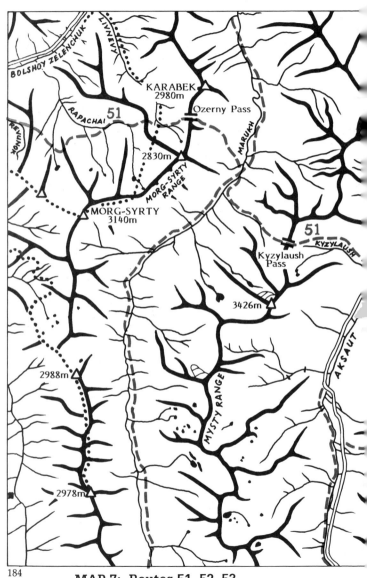

MAP 7: Routes 51, 52, 53

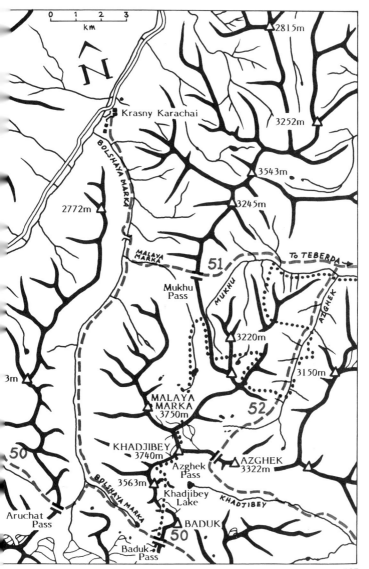

0   1   2   3
km

N

△2815m

· Krasny Karachai

BOLSHAYA MARKA

3252m △

△ 3543m ·

2772m △

△ 3245m ·

MALAYA MARKA

51

TO TEBERDA

Mukhu Pass

MUKHU

·

AZGHEK

△3220m

3m △

△

3150m △

MALAYA MARKA
△ 3750m

52

KHADJIBEY
△ 3740m

△ AZGHEK
3322m

△

Azghek Pass

50

3563m △

Khadjibey Lake

BOLSHAYA MARKA

KHADJIBEY

Aruchat Pass

△ BADUK

50

Baduk Pass

185

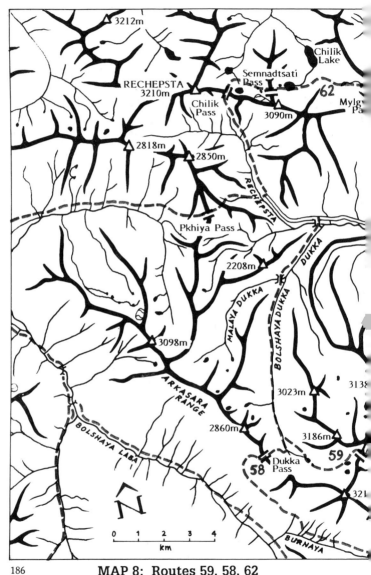

MAP 8: Routes 59, 58, 62

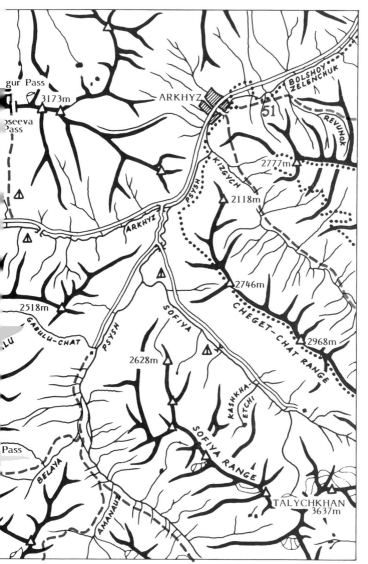

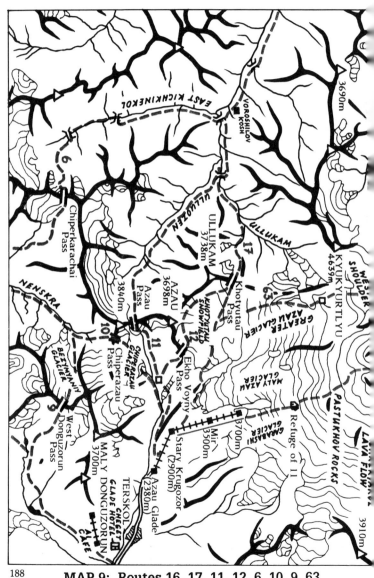

MAP 9: Routes 16, 17, 11, 12, 6, 10, 9, 63

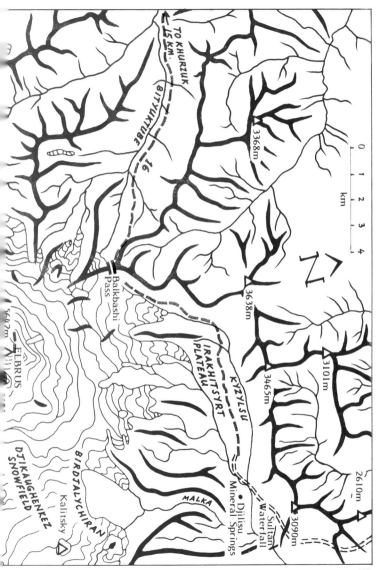

TO KHURZUK
15 km.

BITYIKTUBE

16

3368m

0
1
2
3
4
km

N

3638m

Balkbashi
Pass

ELBRUS
5642m

IRAKHITSYRT
PLATEAU

KYZYLSU

3465m

3101m

2610m

DJIKAUGHENKEZ
SNOWFIELD

BIRDJALYCHIRAN

Kalitsky

MALKA

Djilisu
Mineral Springs

Sultan
Waterfall

3090m

189

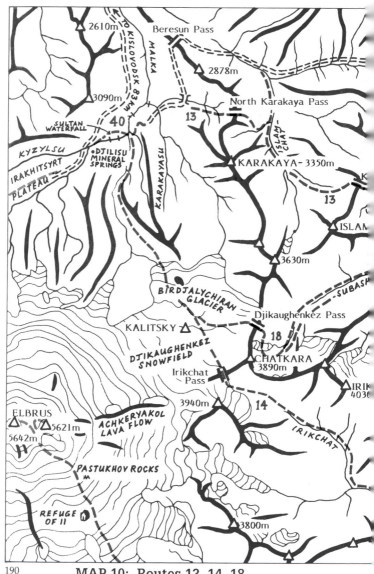

MAP 10: Routes 13, 14, 18

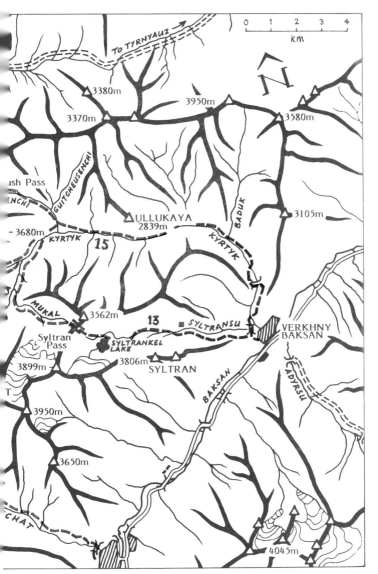

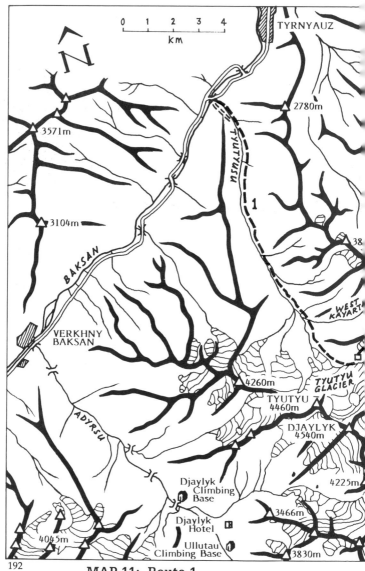

MAP 11: Route 1

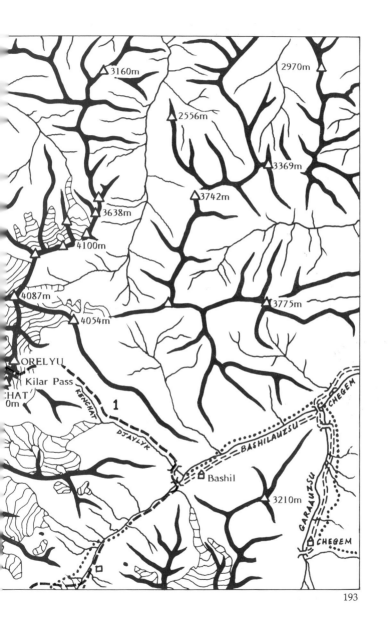

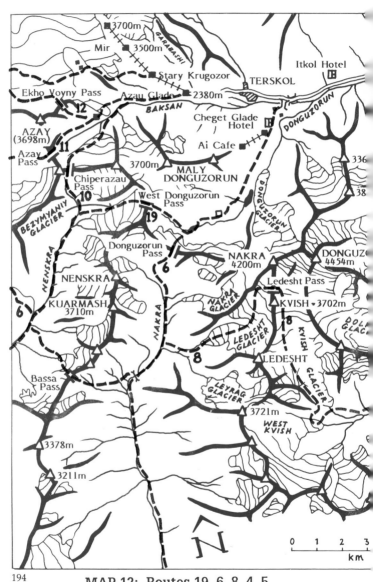

MAP 12: Routes 19, 6, 8, 4, 5

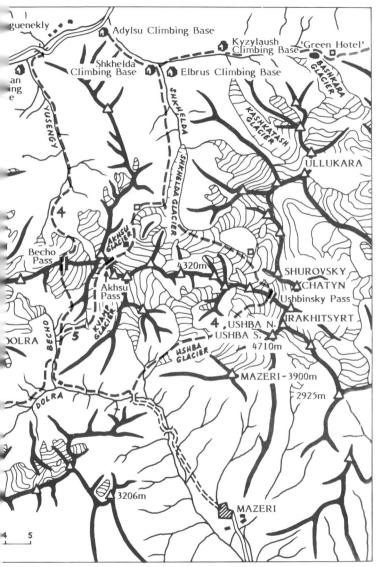

guenekly
Adylsu Climbing Base
Kyzylaush Climbing Base
'Green Hotel'
BASHKARA GLACIER
Shkhelda Climbing Base
Elbrus Climbing Base
an ing e
YUSENGY
SHKHELDA
SHKHELDA GLACIER
KASHKATASH GLACIER
ULLUKARA
4
AKHSU GLACIER
Becho Pass
Akhsu Pass
4320m
SHUROVSKY
CHATYN
Ushbinsky Pass
IRAKHITSYRT
BECHO
KVAN GLACIER
5
4
USHBA N.
USHBA S.
4710m
OLRA
USHBA GLACIER
MAZERI - 3900m
DOLRA
2925m
3206m
MAZERI

4 5

195

MAP 13: Routes 1, 2, 3, 19, 20, 21, 25

ORELYU
Kilar Pass
AT
m
KENCHAT
DJAYLYK
1
YK GLACIER
4360m
N
BASHILAUZSU
CHEGEM
Bashil
3210m
Chegem
TH
IL
BASHIL
3793m
KULAK
TYUTYURGU
SHAURTU
19
Upper
Bashil
22
KARAKAYA 21
Lychat
Pass
BODORKU
4180m
KARATYUBE
3000m
Bashilauz
Pass
LYCHAT
3900m
LYCHAT-
SKY
Tviber Pass
KULAK
GLACIER
TIKHTENGEN
4614m
BASHIL
4260m
LYCHAT
GLACIER
Bashil Pass
4060m
Semi Pass
25
Upper
Kitlod
T
m
DZYNAL GLACIER
NASHKODRA RANGE
TVIBER
GLACIER
KITLOD GLACIER
TSANNER GLACIER
TVIBER
KITLOD

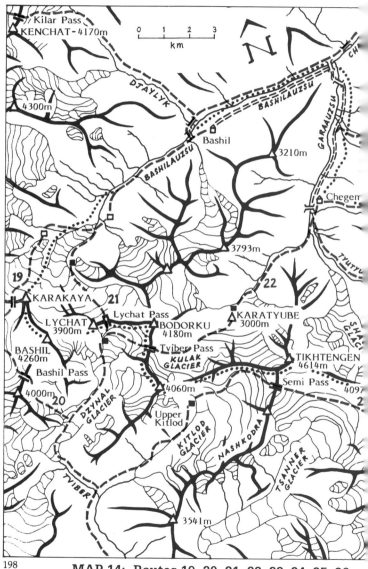

MAP 14: Routes 19, 20, 21, 22, 23, 24, 25, 26

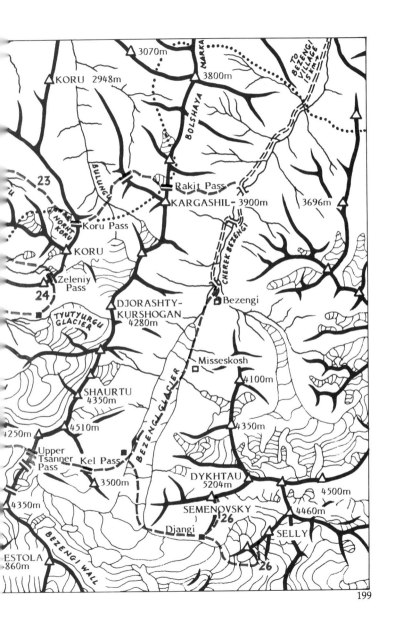

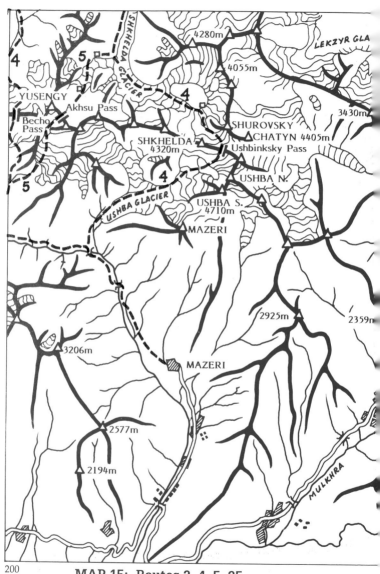

MAP 15: Routes 2, 4, 5, 25

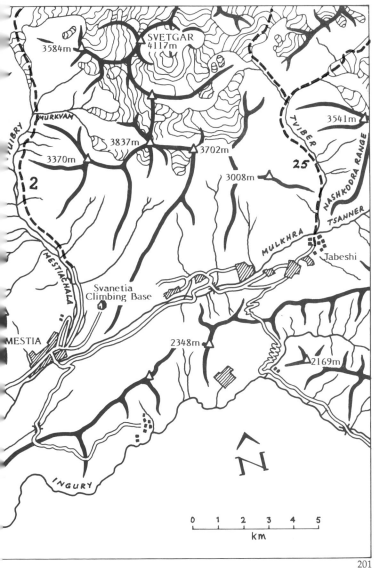

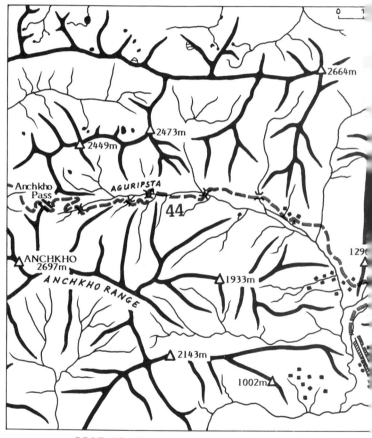

MAP 16: Route 44

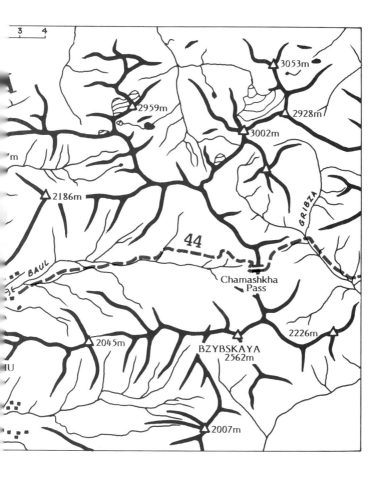

CICERONE GUIDES

Cicerone publish a wide range of reliable guides to walking and climbing in Britain, and other general interest books.

LAKE DISTRICT - General Books
A DREAM OF EDEN
LAKELAND VILLAGES
LAKELAND TOWNS
REFLECTIONS ON THE LAKES
OUR CUMBRIA
THE HIGH FELLS OF LAKELAND
CONISTON COPPER A History
LAKELAND - A taste to remember (Recipes)
THE LOST RESORT? (Morecambe)
CHRONICLES OF MILNTHORPE
LOST LANCASHIRE (Furness area)
THE PRIORY OF CARTMEL

LAKE DISTRICT - Guide Books
CASTLES IN CUMBRIA
THE CUMBRIA CYCLE WAY
WESTMORLAND HERITAGE WALK
IN SEARCH OF WESTMORLAND
CONISTON COPPER MINES Field Guide
SCRAMBLES IN THE LAKE DISTRICT
MORE SCRAMBLES IN THE LAKE DISTRICT
SHORT WALKS - SOUTH LAKELAND
WINTER CLIMBS IN THE LAKE DISTRICT
WALKS IN SILVERDALE/ARNSIDE
BIRDS OF MORECAMBE BAY
THE EDEN WAY
WALKING ROUND THE LAKES

NORTHERN ENGLAND (outside the Lakes
BIRDWATCHING ON MERSEYSIDE
CANAL WALKS Vol 1 North
CANOEISTS GUIDE TO THE NORTH EAST
THE CLEVELAND WAY & MISSING LINK
THE DALES WAY
DOUGLAS VALLEY WAY
HADRIANS WALL Vol 1 The Wall Walk
HERITAGE TRAILS IN NW ENGLAND
THE ISLE OF MAN COASTAL PATH
IVORY TOWERS & DRESSED STONES (Follies)
THE LANCASTER CANAL
LANCASTER CANAL WALKS
LAUGHS ALONG THE PENNINE WAY
A NORTHERN COAST-TO-COAST
NORTH YORK MOORS Walks
THE REIVERS WAY (Northumberland)
THE RIBBLE WAY
ROCK CLIMBS LANCASHIRE & NW
THE YORKSHIRE DALES A walker's guide
WALKING IN THE SOUTH PENNINES
WALKING IN THE NORTH PENNINES
WALKS IN THE YORKSHIRE DALES (3 VOL)
WALKS IN LANCASHIRE WITCH COUNTRY
WALKS IN THE NORTH YORK MOORS
WALKS TO YORKSHIRE WATERFALLS (2 vol)
WALKS ON THE WEST PENNINE MOORS
WALKING NORTHERN RAILWAYS (2 vol)
WALKING IN THE WOLDS

DERBYSHIRE & EAST MIDLANDS
WHITE PEAK WALKS - 2 Vols
HIGH PEAK WALKS
WHITE PEAK WAY
KINDER LOG
THE VIKING WAY
THE DEVIL'S MILL / WHISTLING CLOUGH (Novels)

WALES & WEST MIDLANDS
THE RIDGES OF SNOWDONIA
HILLWALKING IN SNOWDONIA
HILL WALKING IN WALES (2 Vols)
ASCENT OF SNOWDON
WELSH WINTER CLIMBS
SNOWDONIA WHITE WATER SEA & SURF
SCRAMBLES IN SNOWDONIA
SARN HELEN Walking Roman Road
ROCK CLIMBS IN WEST MIDLANDS
THE SHROPSHIRE HILLS A Walker's Guide
HEREFORD & THE WYE VALLEY A Walker's Guide
THE WYE VALLEY WALK

SOUTH & SOUTH WEST ENGLAND
COTSWOLD WAY
EXMOOR & THE QUANTOCKS
THE KENNET & AVON WALK
THE SOUTHERN-COAST-TO-COAST
SOUTH DOWNS WAY & DOWNS LINK
SOUTH WEST WAY - 2 Vol
WALKING IN THE CHILTERNS
WALKING ON DARTMOOR
WALKERS GUIDE TO DARTMOOR PUBS
WALKS IN KENT
THE WEALDWAY & VANGUARD WAY

SCOTLAND
THE BORDER COUNTRY - WALKERS GUIDE
SCRAMBLES IN LOCHABER
SCRAMBLES IN SKYE
THE ISLAND OF RHUM
CAIRNGORMS WINTER CLIMBS
THE CAIRNGORM GLENS (Mountainbike Guide)
THE ATHOLL GLENS (Mountainbike Guide)
WINTER CLIMBS BEN NEVIS & GLENCOE
SCOTTISH RAILWAY WALKS
TORRIDON A Walker's Guide
SKI TOURING IN SCOTLAND

REGIONAL BOOKS UK & IRELAND
THE MOUNTAINS OF ENGLAND & WALES
    VOL 1 WALES VOL 2 ENGLAND
THE MOUNTAINS OF IRELAND
THE ALTERNATIVE PENNINE WAY
THE PACKHORSE BRIDGES OF ENGLAND
THE RELATIVE HILLS OF BRITAIN
LIMESTONE - 100 BEST CLIMBS

Also a full range of EUROPEAN and OVERSEAS guidebooks - walking, long distance trails, scrambling, ice-climbing, rock climbing.

Other guides are constantly being added to the Cicerone List.
Available from bookshops, outdoor equipment shops or direct (send s.a.e. for price list) from
CICERONE, 2 POLICE SQUARE, MILNTHORPE, CUMBRIA, LA7 7PY

CICERONE GUIDES

Cicerone publish a wide range of reliable guides to walking and climbing abroad

FRANCE
TOUR OF MONT BLANC
CHAMONIX MONT BLANC - A Walking Guide
TOUR OF THE OISANS: GR54
WALKING THE FRENCH ALPS: GR5
THE CORSICAN HIGH LEVEL ROUTE: GR20
THE WAY OF ST JAMES: GR65
THE PYRENEAN TRAIL: GR10
THE RLS (Stevenson) TRAIL
TOUR OF THE QUEYRAS
ROCK CLIMBS IN THE VERDON
WALKS IN VOLCANO COUNTRY (Auvergne)
WALKING THE FRENCH GORGES (Provence)
FRENCH ROCK

FRANCE / SPAIN
WALKS AND CLIMBS IN THE PYRENEES
ROCK CLIMBS IN THE PYRENEES

SPAIN
WALKS & CLIMBS IN THE PICOS DE EUROPA
WALKING IN MALLORCA
BIRDWATCHING IN MALLORCA
COSTA BLANCA CLIMBS
ANDALUSIAN ROCK CLIMBS
THE WAY OF ST JAMES

FRANCE / SWITZERLAND
THE JURA - Walking the High Route and
    Winter Ski Traverses
CHAMONIX TO ZERMATT The Walker's
    Haute Route

SWITZERLAND
WALKING IN THE BERNESE ALPS
CENTRAL SWITZERLAND
WALKS IN THE ENGADINE
WALKING IN TICINO
THE VALAIS - A Walking Guide
THE ALPINE PASS ROUTE

GERMANY / AUSTRIA / EASTERN EUROPE
THE KALKALPEN TRAVERSE
KLETTERSTEIG - Scrambles
WALKING IN THE BLACK FOREST
MOUNTAIN WALKING IN AUSTRIA
WALKING IN THE HARZ MOUNTAINS
WALKING IN THE SALZKAMMERGUT
KING LUDWIG WAY
HUT-TO-HUT IN THE STUBAI ALPS
THE HIGH TATRAS

ITALY & SLOVENIA
ALTA VIA - High Level Walks in the Dolomites
VIA FERRATA - Scrambles in the Dolomites
ITALIAN ROCK - Rock Climbs in Northern Italy
CLASSIC CLIMBS IN THE DOLOMITES
WALKING IN THE DOLOMITES
THE JULIAN ALPS

MEDITERRANEAN COUNTRIES
THE MOUNTAINS OF GREECE
CRETE: Off the beaten track
TREKS & CLIMBS IN WADI RUM, JORDAN
THE ATLAS MOUNTAINS
WALKS & CLIMBS IN THE ALA DAG (Turkey)

OTHER COUNTRIES
ADVENTURE TREKS - W. N. AMERICA
ADVENTURE TREKS - NEPAL
ANNAPURNA TREKKERS GUIDE
CLASSIC TRAMPS IN NEW ZEALAND
TREKKING IN THE CAUCAUSUS

GENERAL OUTDOOR BOOKS
THE HILL WALKERS MANUAL
FIRST AID FOR HILLWALKERS
MOUNTAIN WEATHER
MOUNTAINEERING LITERATURE
THE ADVENTURE ALTERNATIVE
MODERN ALPINE CLIMBING
ROPE TECHNIQUES IN MOUNTAINEERING
MODERN SNOW & ICE TECHNIQUES
LIMESTONE -100 BEST CLIMBS IN BRITAIN

CANOEING
SNOWDONIA WILD WATER, SEA & SURF
WILDWATER CANOEING
CANOEIST'S GUIDE TO THE NORTH EAST

CARTOON BOOKS
ON FOOT & FINGER
ON MORE FEET & FINGERS
LAUGHS ALONG THE PENNINE WAY

*Also a full range of guidebooks
to walking, scrambling, ice-climbing,
rock climbing, and other adventurous
pursuits in Britain and abroad*

*Other guides are constantly being added to the Cicerone List.
Available from bookshops, outdoor equipment shops or direct (send for price list)
from CICERONE, 2 POLICE SQUARE, MILNTHORPE, CUMBRIA, LA7 7PY*

Printed by CARNMOR PRINT & DESIGN,
95-97 LONDON ROAD, PRESTON, LANCASHIRE, UK.

Zelenchukskaya

Marukh
Khasaut-Grechesky

Nijny Arkhyz

Arkhyz

Karachaevsk

K A R A C H A I - C I R C A S S I A

Teberda

Uchkulan
Khurzuk

Dombay

MAIN

RANGE

Kvemo-Aiara
Omarishara

SUKHUMI

A B K H A Z I A

Khaishy

BLACK

SEA

ZUGDIDI